Giorgio Morandi 1890-1964

Giorgio Morandi
1890-1964

Electa

*The following have
collaborated on this volume*

Photographies
Sergio Anelli

Graphics
Marcello Francone

Editing
Tiziana Quirico

Layout
Felice Bassi
Eliana Gelati

Technical coordination
Licio Beffagna
Mario Faré
Angelo Mombelli

on cover
Still life, 1948
(cat. no. 38)

Giorgio Morandi

London, Accademia Italiana
delle Arti e delle Arti Applicate
3 - 23 May 1989

Galleria Comunale d'Arte
Moderna "Giorgio Morandi"
Bologna

Civico Museo d'Arte
Contemporanea, Milano

*The exhibition is held
under the patronage of
the Ministero per gli Affari
Esteri and of the Ministero
per i Beni Culturali
e Ambientali of the Italian
Republic*

*The exhibition is organized
in collaboration with the
Pinacoteca Nazionale of
Bologna and the Fondazione
Magnani-Rocca of Parma*

Morandi Project for Europe

Tampere, Sara Hildénin
taidemuseo
4 November 1988 - 8 January
1989

Leningrad, Ermitage Museum
21 January - 19 February 1989

Moscow, A.S. Pushkin Museum,
Central Gallery of Artists
14 March - 16 April 1989

London, Accademia Italiana
delle Arti e delle Arti Applicate
3 - 23 May 1989

Locarno, Civici Musei,
Casa Rusca
3 June - 20 August 1989

Tübingen, Kunsthalle
23 September - 26 November
1989

Düsseldorf, Kunstsammlung
Nordrhein - Westfalen
19 January - 18 March 1990

Exhibition Organization
Galleria Comunale d'Arte
Moderna "Giorgio Morandi"
Bologna

Scientific Committee
Giuliano Briganti
Pier Giovanni Castagnoli
Fabrizio D'Amico
Andrea Emiliani
Mercedes Garberi
Flaminio Gualdoni
Marilena Pasquali
Eugenio Riccomini

Coordination
Marilena Pasquali,
Keeper of the Archivio
and Centro Studi "Giorgio
Morandi"

Administration Office
Patrizia Minghetti
(Archivio and Centro Studi
"Giorgio Morandi")
Daniela Semproli
Oriano Ricci

Administration
Angela Tosarelli Tassinari

Technical Assistance
Fabrizio Passarella

Official Sponsor

*Exhibition Organization
in Great Britain*
London, Accademia Italiana
delle Arti e delle Arti Applicate

Exhibition Committee
Rosa Maria Letts,
Director of the Accademia
Italiana delle Arti
Marilena Pasquali

Catalogue edited by
Marilena Pasquali

Translation/Administration
Adam Butler
G.G. Letts
Licia Bronzin
Joanna Simpson, *administration*

Photographies
Sergio Anelli, Milano
C.N.B, Bologna
Antonio Masotti, Bologna
Luciano Calzolari, Crevalcore
Alfio di Bella, Roma
Giuseppe Schiavinotto, Roma
Lasse Koivunen, Tampere

Installation
Exhibition Services, Oxford

Lighting
D.I.L. Illuminazione, Bergamo

Acclimatization
Jacorossi, Roma

Insurance
Assicurazioni Generali S.p.A.,
Central Office, Bologna

Transport
Rossi Art Brokers, Milano
Vigno Gnudi, Bologna
Windgade & Johnson, London

Acknowledgments
A very special thank goes
to Anna and Maria Teresa
Morandi, whose support
and contribution have been
essential to the realization
of the project.
A further thank is due
to Carlo Zucchini for is expert
cooperation.
And to all lenders and
collaborators our grateful
recognition:
Sara Hildénin taidemuseo,
Tampere
Angelo Tentorio, Bergamo
Carlo Traglio, Bergamo
Luciano Nicola, Biella
Direzione della Circoscrizione
Doganale, Bologna
Banca del Monte di Bologna
e Ravenna, Bologna
Elena Chiesa, Bologna
Sergio Conti, Bologna
Giorgio Galeati, Bologna
Oliviero Mazzoli, Bologna
Leone Pancaldi, Bologna
Efrem Tavoni e Ileana Guidi,
Bologna
Teresa Volpe, Bologna
Silvano Lodi, Campione d'Italia
Banca Toscana, Firenze
Maria Braghiroli, Milano
Maria De Luigi Casella,
Milano
Claudia Gian Ferrari, Milano
Giuseppe Domeniconi, Modena
Franco Fabbi, Modena
Enos Ferri, Medolla di Modena
Gianni Salvaterra, Modena
Alberto Galaverni, Padova
Simona Pizzetti, Parma
Augusta Monferini, Roma
Luisa Laureati, Roma
David Passini, Tolentino
Galleria Giraldi, Tolentino
Antonio e Marina Forchino,
Torino
Massimo Di Carlo, Verona

**Accademia Italiana delle Arti
e delle Arti Applicate**

Associates
Ferruzzi Montedison
Glaxo Holdings plc
Ditta DIL Srl Illuminazione
Ditta Domenica Neri Spa

Members
Arts Advisers
Bonifica Spa
Brenta AB Construction plc
British Italian Society
Bulgari Spa
Charles Letts & Co Ltd
Frette Spa
Gucci Ltd
Indesit UK Ltd
La Seta Mantero
Martini & Rossi Ltd
Barone Moncada lo Giudice
Snia (UK) Ltd
Gianni Versace Srl
Santo Versace

The Accademia Italiana in London has been described as "A Stage for the Genius of Italy". What better way then, than to open its doors with an exhibition on Giorgio Morandi, one of the geniuses among twentieth century painters.

Just one of his still lifes can summarize the heights to which this art-form has reached in the last ninety years. The new found freedom from the constraint of traditional perspective and spatial arrangements, the radical application of paint and colour in subtle but ever changing combinations derive from Cézanne and the Symbolists, Cubism and early Abstraction. Morandi has been able to appropriate these innovative styles and techniques to interpret with utter simplicity his inner vision, its pauses and silences. His language is serene and controlled, the result of profound meditation.

If only one visitor to this first exhibition will leave the halls of the Accademia enhanced by Morandi's message, enriched by his silences and strengthened to face the hustle outside, the Accademia will have fulfilled its role.

Together with the Trustees and Directors of the Accademia, the Associates and the Members, we are grateful to the Galleria Comunale d'Arte Moderna "Giorgio Morandi" of Bologna and in particular to Marilena Pasquali, Keeper of the Archivio and Centro Studi "Giorgio Morandi", to Pier Giovanni Castagnoli, Director of the Galleria d'Arte Moderna, to the Mayor of Bologna, Renzo Imbeni, and the Assessore alla Cultura, Nicola Sinisi, for allowing us to share with them one of the main public collections from their town.

To the Italian Authorities who have granted their patronage to the exhibition go our warmest thanks for endowing this event with the role of a major presentation of Italian Art to the British Public.

Rosa Maria Letts
Director of the Accademia Italiana delle Arti e delle Arti Applicate

*The guiding corporate policy of Bond Corporation is to develop as a major
Australian-owned public company with a strong cash flow base and an emphasis
on brewing, media and communications, and energy resources, supported
by property and industrial activities. In implementing this policy,
Bond Corporation will:*

*Apply entrepreneurial and managerial skills to develop existing activities and add
new wholly-owned and strategic investment interests.*

*Provide opportunities for people who work with the Bond Corporation Group
to develop skills and progress their careers to their personal satisfaction and
the benefit of the Company and communities in which they work and live.*

*Represent to international associations of Bond Corporation positive and
progressive view of Australia and encourage them to participate with Bond
Corporation and other Australian-owned groups in development of Australian
resources where appropriate.*

*Co-operate with Government at all levels and with communities in which Bond
Corporation operates to ensure that its activities reflect a proper concern
for environmental, social and cultural needs.*

*Promote and support the diffusion and exchange of cultural programs
by sponsoring the Accademia Italiana in London, an international organisation
fostering Italian artistic and cultural traditions around the world.*

Bond Corporation

Contents

Landscape, 1911
oil on canvas, 37.5 × 52 cm
Milan, private collection

Landscape, 1913
oil on canvas, 44.5 × 66 cm
Milan, private collection

It was only ten years after the time that Morandi, as a twenty year old student at the Accademia who had just embarked on his career as a painter, began to produce those characteristic, homely yet powerful still lifes. Just as the still life from Jesi collection was announcing the imminent demise of the vogue for "plastic values", and the end of the artist's interest in its programme of "style", a new chapter was opened in Morandi's work, the most important and mature. One of the main features of this was Morandi's discovery of a unique imaginative prospective, destined to be amongst the century's greatest.

And so the first period of Morandi's career ends in 1920 with the unsettling and dramatic appearance of those seven objects, placed as if seeking comfort from their combined solitude; this was a fertile ten years filled with ideas, statements and varied experiences during which Morandi was a conscious and active participant in the concerns and thoughts of modern contemporary culture and his study directly exposed to the reality of the period's artistic debates. To inaugurate this period are two paintings, the only ones to survive: two town landscapes painted in different seasons. Although similar, they differ in their final expression which is created from an inspiration to explore the possibilities and limits of image's ability to substitute reality. These are landscapes which appear to be sketched on an impulse, hastily scribbled down to evoke an experience without labouring the vitality of the movement. The composition of the paintings is simplified, their familiar domestic tone is arresting and yet there is no naivete in the assessment of spatial location and the correct equilibrium of tone.

There is undoubtedly a long way yet to progress from these paintings to the novel conception and absolute vision of that *Landscape* from the Vitali collection which in a year's time was to attain the critic's recognition as the most authoritative starting point of research on Morandi. We must neither ignore the fact that in his initial and still hesitant attempts, Morandi shows himself influenced by the ideas of French modernist naturalism rather than the secessionist nature of "Jugend" or the 'floral' attractions which had proved so popular in Bologna in 1900-1910.

As it is well known, Morandi in his first experiments did not have direct access to the Impressionists' work but had to make do with Pica's book on the movement published two years earlier. The volume was filled with reproductions, exceptionally well produced for that time, and which acted as a flare to Morandi's already acute sensitivity. He already knew how to select in his reading whatever best suited his character, even in the bare image offered by a black and white photograph. Even his knowledge of Cezanne's work, which was to play so dominant a role in Morandi's development to the extent that it provided an ideal model and perennial reference point, was gained from reproductions and favoured by influential comments which Ardengo Soffici wrote in *La Voce* on the works of Cezanne. *La Voce* was an art review which Morandi together with his generation read avidly. Soffici had recently returned to Italy after seven years in Paris where he had gained first hand information on the development of modern aesthetics and had contact with the literary contributors to the magazine *La Plume* – personalities like Max Jacob, Apollinaire and Picasso. Between 1909 and 1911, he prepared articles for *La Voce* on Impressionism, on Douanier Rousseau, on Braque's and Picasso's Cubism and on Cezanne: this last study was one which the young Florentine critic had already embarked on just after he returned to Italy in an 1908 article in the magazine *Vita d'Arte*. In the first draft, Soffici concentrates on re-emphasizing Cezanne's role in progressing beyond Impressionism and founding a new style in painting capable of fusing the modern with the classic, Impressionism with style. Soffici noted that Cezanne "had to perceive how the work of the impressionists was above all empirical and descriptive, and how it lacked that ideal which attracts the 9

Landscape, 1913
oil on canvas, 50 × 62 cm
Rome, private collection

Still life, 1912-1913
oil on canvas, 38.5 × 55 cm
Milan, private collection

shape of things, analyses, concentrates and returns them transformed to live forever in a universe called 'style''' and that "As a realist, [Cezanne's] ambition was always to prevent his dramatic vision of things in palpable, concrete shapes: not however without realising that the compactness of bodies is necessary to manifest the force of perception, things themselves would not appear to us if it were not for total contrasts. Contrasts from which the gigantic effort of synthesizing into one the sense of volume and light, the result of which was a work uniting the benefit of new research to experience gained from the past, a pictorial renaissance which would place the future generations on the road to a classicism which will prove the real eternal classicism: that of Tintoretto, Masaccio, Rembrandt and Goya".

These words would have found sympathy with Morandi and might have urged him to discern a line of study full of possibilities for the future as well as a call to blend the modern with the traditional – a call which would have appealed to the thoughtful character of the Bolognese Morandi. Just when it seems likely that Morandi would have read these words and thought about them, in 1910, he arrived for the first time in Florence to study the major works of Italy's most purist tradition; so it does not seem so far from the truth to imagine him seeing the frescoes of Giotto, Masaccio and Paolo Uccello and comparing them to the works of Cezanne and the interpretation of solidity and concreteness of his visual world which Soffici's words described and so authoritatively acclaimed.

It is a fact that the year after, when Morandi started work on the Vitali landscape he gives proof of having taken inspiration from both Cezanne's work and from a personal knowledge of the work of masters which the public at the time still referred to as "primitive". That mountain ridge, devoid of any pictorial feature gives no concession to description: the barren landscape, isolated and besieged which is set against a "vast sky of solitude

Still life, 1914
oil on canvas, 102 × 40 cm
Paris, Musée National d'Art Moderne,
Centre G. Pompidou

with no point of relief"; Brandi, in his incisive study of this landscape remains struck by the forceful influence of both Cezanne and Giotto"[1]. It is a surprising revelation that, when this is compared to Morandi's previous landscapes, as Arcangeli hypothesised, other attempts, later destroyed, must have been undertaken at the same time.

A powerful interlude came with his 1911 landscape: one of those which seems destined, from the confidence with which they define the artist's imagination, to trace a direct line to the artist's later work.

In fact, the painting establishes a point of no return in the development of Morandi's experience, being the culmination of a definitive move towards modernism which he expresses in the painting. But the outcome, even though consciously attained, cannot constitute a sufficient argument for the theory which is supported by exegesis on Morandi, of a coherent linear and consequential development which started from that incunabulum and by virtue of the conviction of its execution, would have characterised the future progress of the artist's study.

Arcangeli already warned, by explaining how the years up to 1915 had been in the artist's life "quite restless"[2], clarifying how the complexity of meetings, suggestions and different attempts, would affect the restless temperament, eager to learn, as was that of the twenty year old Morandi – of succumbing to a rigid interpretation of events, modelled on the belief of a flat, linear evolution in his studies. "It would be nice to read perhaps of a Morandi who was coherent from start to finish; but fortunately his work has developed differently to his legend", noted the critic while elucidating, a little later, how the artist worked "almost always within the arena of his personality, with its unique characteristics, probably so early a part of his character that they were never the subject of his scrutiny or concern". But the persistence of these objects which Arcangeli so acutely picks out in the "deep

understanding of tone which distances him from faith in the single chromatic tone" and in "the space through which the work abandones itself" did not conceal from the eyes of the observer the evidence that "in his ideals of a painting, the notions gained whilst young led him to many differing directions".

In fact, as is declared in 1913, the ideas which lead Morandi to his work, in the *Landscapes* of the Jucker and Rollino collections, form directly from ideas which produced and developed the Vitali *Landscape* – of a structural essentiality and of a vigorously disciplined constructive severity; if in the substance of these, the deepening of the lesson of Cezanne and his more personal appropriation reveal themselves fully coherent to his intention – already much expressed from the moment of his first contact with the Frenchman – of "creating figuratively" an order and measure which gives to every aspect and to every feeling an eternal value, a concealed harmony"[3]; if all this remains realised and with greater perfection in the works mentioned above, the appearance, in that same year of the *Still Life* with glasses from the Scheiwiller collection[4], with its crowding of objects into a delicate "excess" which takes over the vision as a witness of the entrance into Morandi's work of another type of reflection, unedited and not entirely similar to those thoughts which up till then had guided Morandi's inspiration.

The multiplication of spatial planes and of compositive directives, the tendency to punctuate the plastic surfaces, the dynamic force given to the shapes constitute other reports, clearly legible in the work; a shift in Morandi's attention towards the ideas being formulated by the Futurists which Morandi already knew, still before having a direct acquaintance with the paintings which were inspired by that movement, seen for the first time, in January 1914, at the collection presented by *Lacerba* in the "Exhibition of Free Futurist Painting" in Florence.

It is difficult to judge were previous indirect

experiences, gleaned from photographs, information in leaflets and catalogues. However, we can be sure that is not due to a scarcity of material that we must blame him for not being more rigorously up to date with modern movements before the completion of the Scheiwiller *Still Life*.

That this should mature in the year 1913 is motivated by the fact that he alters with the change in Soffici's attitude – who yet again seems to exercise his influence on the painter's output – towards the Futurist's thoughts between the end of 1912 and 1913. It is at this time that the writer-painter from Poggio a Caiano reviews his earlier thoughts of Futurism, changing from his initial stance of hostility which manifested itself in his critical review of the "Exhibition of Liberal Art" in Milan and which was published in the June 1911 edition of *La Voce*, to a position of gradual assent, even if tempered with a certain hesitancy that he valued the invitiation of the Futurists to share an exhibition with them at the Costanzi Theatre in Rome in February 1913; in that same month Papini wrote an article in *Lacerba* to emphasize the link between the Florentine avant garde and the Futurists entitled "The Meaning of Futurism" which announced the magazine and also Soffici's acceptance of the movement, credited as "the only Italian avant-garde".

It was in this time that Morandi's move towards Futurism matured, a brief period but sufficient to leave its mark in his studies at that time. Scheiwiller's *Still Life* remains the only example of that time; but other still lifes of glass objects, which seem stylistically similar, were painted at that time and certainly before March 1914, when some of them formed part of an exhibition of Morandi's work, together with that of Osvaldo Licini, Mario Bacchelli, Giacomo Vespignani and Severo Pozzati (all of whom were peers of Morandi, and with the exception of Bacchelli who was self-taught, were all friends at the Accademia in Bologna) which lasted for two days at the Hotel Baglioni in Bologna. This was a brief period because just as

Morandi formed a close link with the Futurist movement (1914 was the year in which Morandi took part in the "First Free Futurist Exhibition" organised in April-May at the Sprovieri gallery in Rome and which gave Morandi a real appreciation of Marinetti) he already seemed to be reassessing his judgement and the works of his colleagues. This can be seen in the change in his work in just a few months, as he moves towards the influence of Cubism which was to attract him during the next year.

The *Still Life* of 1914 of the Pompidou Museum, 'gothically' inserted into the accentuated verticality of the format, perhaps to compensate for the hesitancy of the composition, and the other of 1915 – compact, austere and implacable in the space occupied by its plastic planes belonging to the Mattioli collection; both affirm this latest Morandian experience and at the same time the extreme limits of this experience: from a declared interest in the dissaray of volumetric planes, to the individuation of a clearly supported geometrical construction and the intention of transferring the analytical Cubism into a new spatial synthesis, one could say motivated by a rising desire of "Style"[5].

It is not hard, bearing this in mind, to see the maturation of the Mattioli *Still Life* to that which Morandi executed the year after: to understand the implication, however far they seem at first sight, of the formal aspects and the colours. The same intellectual plan oversees the execution of the 1915 *Still Life* and that of the 1916 paintings – in contrast to his pioneering spirit, Morandi now brings in a more solid and confident tone with the appearance of effortlessness – maintaining his normal capacity for direction and selection, to the highest exercise of style which the artist can offer and approve in *Flowers* of the Jesi collection – now at Brera -, in the *Still Life* of the Museum of Modern Art in New York, and in the Mattioli *Still Life*; to that purist decantation of formal writing and to that miraculous distillation of colour which his most eloquent compositions portray.

Bathers, 1915
oil on canvas, 33 × 25 cm
Rome, Galleria Nazionale d'Arte Moderna
Donated by Riccardo Jucker

Still life, 1916
oil on canvas, 60 × 54 cm
Milan, private collection

Still life, 1916
oil on canvas, 82.5 × 57.5 cm
New York, Museum of Modern Art

Cactus, 1917
oil on canvas, 44 × 32.5 cm
Milan, private collection

Still life, 1918
oil on canvas, 54 × 38 cm
Mamiano di Parma,
Fondazione Magnani-Rocca

With these proofs which after the examples of Braque and Picasso (to whose names, in the catalogue of Morandi's influences, we must add that of Derain, repeatedly named by critics as a comparison to the *Nude* of 1914 and the *Bathers* of 1915) the work of the artist reflects the influence of Rousseau. He suggests by the stupified fixation of his still lifes and the sense of deep familiarity which pervades his objects, a model of 'internal style' and an example of sincerity of vision, which the thought of Morandi, inclined to recognize himself in the instance of 'origin' propagated at a particular time, could not but feel intimately solid in a co-ordination of intentions before that of methods.

This can result in contrast under this reading, the concurrence of a reading of the 15th century by Morandi, suggested by Brandi[6] and sustained by the explicit referral to the geometry of Paolo Uccello; especially when one is warned in taking this interpretation to consider how Morandi would have thought of the paintings of the ancient Tuscan artist in a way which is not too dissimilar to that which emerges from the interpretation given by Carrà in that same year 1916, in an article in *La Voce* at the point when, in conclusion, the painter declares: "From the twin bridge of our investigation, the silent music of the ancient mute poet conquers our soul, then we forget noble letters to modern pictorial vision which wants to be an external truth"[7]. The sincerity of the Douanier Rousseau could therefore find sympathy from Morandi's point of view, with that of Paolo Uccello, and together sound a median accent of modernity to the painter's sensibility.

1917 was a year in which Morandi painted little: a long illness prevented him from his work, but did not prevent him from thinking and realising the experiences surrounding him of the most advanced research in Italian painting. At that time, in those long months of forced inactivity, he nourished the convictions which motivated that change which pervades his painting from the fol-

lowing year, and maintains its effects for two years more.

The appearance of *Cactus*[8] from Mattioli's collection gives us the first direct introduction – with the precision of drawing, the meticulous modelling and chiaroscuro and the rendering of plastic form – to the series of still lifes in which the artist confronts 'metaphysical painting'. In this group of works, as Brandi wrote, "From a flat formulation he rises to a reconstruction of where these volumes appear in an impenetrable whole of celestial body, so glacial and exasperated, that one loses the abstract feel of archetypes like cylinders, cones, ovals; they are created, not reproduced: their existence is mental".

It is this mental evidence, revealing volumes and the measures which help create the spatial construction of a painting, the original text of Morandi's metaphysics. In this his metaphysics are completely foreign to literary suggestions and Weininger influences which give de Chirico's poetry its mystery and close to that intuition of the meaning of a feeling for time which surrounds the discovery of "ordinary objects" by Carrà when he wrote: "...it is the 'ordinary objects' which are such a benefit to our souls, giving us the supreme blessing, and those who abandon them will fall inevitably into an absurd void, both formally and spiritually [...] Ordinary objects reveal those forms of simplicity, suggesting the higher state of being which constitute all of the false secrets of art.... and since there is no form of communication other than with signs, we turn our minds to a sense of tranquil poetry, and we leave to vulgar beings the false dreaming of fantasy"[9].

De Chirico did not understand Morandi's works when, presenting an important selection of them in the catalogue of "La Fiorentina Primaverile" in 1922 he wrote: "He participated thus in the great lyricism of the last profound art of Europe: metaphysics of the most common objects. Of those objects which have become familiar to us, in as much as we are knowledgable of the mystery of

14

Still life, 1918
oil on canvas, 47 × 58 cm
Milan, private collection

Still life, 1918
oil on canvas, 80 × 65 cm
Milan, private collection

Still life, 1919
oil on canvas, 56.5 × 47 cm
Milan, Pinacoteca Nazionale di Brera
Donated by Emilio and Maria Jesi

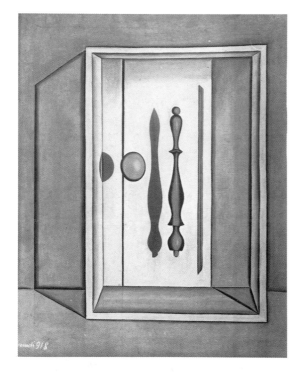

aspects, we now often regard them with the eye of the man who sees but does not know". At that date, 1922, Morandi's art had already taken a new direction, in respect to the research of the period of "plastic values" to which de Chirico refers; but the definition given by "Pictor optimus" embraced a deep strain of Morandi's art which was to unconsciously continue to have an effect, even in later times, in his creative process.

1. See E. Riccomini, "Morandi: memoria e presenza", in AA.VV., *Morandi e il suo tempo*, Mazzotta, Milano 1985.
2. The most important reconstruction of the beginnings of Morandi and his links with the contemporary artistic culture is by F. Arcangeli, *Giorgio Morandi*, Ed. del Milione, Milano 1964. More recently, a contribution has been given by Franco Solmi in "Dagli esordi alla metafisica", in AA. VV., *op. cit.*
3. C. Gnudi, *Morandi*, Ed. U., Firenze 1946.
4. This work, traditionally dated to 1912 after Morandi's own indications, has now been dated, more credibly, to 1913, after being included in the retrospective exhibition of the artist, organised at the National Gallery of Modern Art in Rome in May-June 1973 (see the exhibition catalogue, Editore De Luca, Roma 1973); more recently Solmi has even suggested that it may have been painted immediately after Morandi's visit to the "Exhibition of Free Futurist Painting" in Florence, in January 1914, after a direct contact with Boccioni's works which were shown there (see F. Solmi, *op. cit.*).
5. See F. Solmi, *op. cit.*
6. See C. Brandi, *Morandi*, Le Monnier, Firenze 1942.
7. C. Carrà, "Paolo Uccello's Constructions", in *La Voce*, Florence, 30 September 1916.
8. The painting, dated to 1917 in Vitali's general catalogue, seems to be very close to the watercolour of the same subject, dated on the sheet July 1918.
9. C. Carrà, *Pittura Metafisica*, Vallecchi, Firenze 1919.

Marilena Pasquali

The Emergence of an Inner Landscape

The development of Morandi's image between 1920 and 1943

Still life, 1920
oil on canvas, 60.5 × 66.5 cm
Milan, private collection

Giorgio Morandi belongs to the breed of men who seek, he is amongst those who are not willing to accept the existentiality which supports the daily struggle of existence. He searched into his own inner self to look for the very reasons of being, and the way in which to express the stoic suffering of this ceaseless research into the essence of the life of man.

Like other explorers of the mind, the artist followed his own idiosyncratic ways, guiding himself through the labyrinth of his inner self and overcoming his problems by virtue of a cold, controlled yet burning determination.

In research each one of us is alone – sometimes encountering similars in the outer regions of the imagination, in an undefinable place and time, radiating in the multifaceted universe of knowledge.

Morandi would probably not recognise himself in this fascinating Promethean interpretation, preferring to simply present himself as a "painter", a constructor of images, shunning the consideration of his daily work as a predetermined search to create that one painting – or watercolour, drawing or engraving – in a temporal environment, transcending words, contrasts or references. His companions in this – those with whom he conferred every day – were however Pascal and Leopardi, Rembrandt and Piero della Francesca, Cardarelli, Ungaretti and Montale, and possibly even Bach, Mozart and Petrarch.

We are in the realm of poetry, in a position to create new worlds and to bring them to life in the imagination. It is not important if the new dimension is comprised of few or many elements, nor if the interior reality is defined elaborately or just with the essentials of the expressive facilities; what counts is the wholeness of the invention and the autonomy – concrete yet elusive – of daily reality.

What every artist searches for is the "way" in which to answer the substance of a problem – an assumption which exists first and only in the mind – and to express itself through the most adherent and consubstantial form that can possibly exist in the fantasy of the mind.

There is an archetypal model with which the artist identifies, and to which he refers even when exploring the multiplicity of existence, reproducing it partially from time to time, and yet always betraying the intentions and the complex unity of the thought that determined it.

When a method is individuated and resolved, when form becomes one with inner desire, then a work of art is created. Cesare Brandi wrote in a brief article dedicated to Morandi after his death that he was, "if one wants, close to Picasso [...] the only artist whose paintings did not rely on the interpretation of the observer, and whose meaningful presence was wholly absolved. If not the message of no message, no other message can be deduced from this exemplary art, this in itself represents an absolute reality.

"Thus the real value to search for in the work of Morandi is certainly not that which is painted with brushes, but the faith in the auto efficiency of reality *sui generis*, distinct from existential reality, which for centuries has been known as art, even if many would like to put this notion in doubt, or to suppress it under the generic and undifferentiated cover of a message, or information. The acknowledgement of this intrinsic value in the works, and which is only deducible from the fruition of the paintings themselves, is that which continually renews the presence of Morandi as a fountain at which we can quench our thirst and which should not be searched for in fleeting time"[1].

The Roman scholar, with his profound knowledge of Morandi's work and perhaps today its most convincing interpreter, wrote these words at the time of the turbulent cultural period in the last months of 1968, which for better or worse would leave its mark on the following events. One can understand therefore his passionate defense of the autonomy of art against any symbolic interpretation; however this warning re- 17

Still life, 1921
oil on canvas, 44 × 52 cm
Cologne, Ludwig Museum

Flowers, 1920
oil on canvas, 46 × 39 cm
Milan, private collection

mains complete and valid, stressing the fact that Morandi belongs to that rare breed of authentic masters which have been able to bring together life and art to the point of living in and through their works, unconcerned with any existentialist distraction or disturbance.

This is the range of the human and artistic life of Morandi, the principal reason for his reclusiveness and apparent tranquillity, of his refusal to create controversy, and of his decision to see only few, chosen friends, and maintaining a close intellectual link with others, however far or near.

There are many who have interpreted in the "severity" of Morandi's life and work a probatory sympton of his beautiful, "classical" yet detached being; others have seen in it the suffering of his restless and troubled mind which only in his art comes to rest; another has seen, more superficially, a small bourgeois aspect, of which the artist himself is the first and most convincing interpreter. In my opinion, each of these interpretations are plausible in themselves – even the weakest one of the "singer of small things" – a further indication that Morandi's art defies definition and interpretations.

Personally finding myself close to the argument which sees in Morandi "someone who sets out anew" – to use once again the audacious words of Roberto Longhi[2] – that is, the heir to the most elevated classical tradition which infused the art of the Renaissance, I prefer to acknowledge in his work a "tendency" to classicism, a "desire" for harmony, in the ever more active argument between an increasing sensitivity and a sense of detachment, realising, however, its complete belonging to our time.

Beauty is the object, the aim of every "arti-fice", that unattainable goal which the artist pursues with determination, seeing it as the archetype of all his research, but knowing never to be able to reach it.

The beauty in his work is due to the co-existence of tension and sensitivity, with the doleful knowledge of never being able to "reach into the depths, into the essential of things" as he himself stated in the brief but comprehensive interview which he gave in 1937 to the director of *Frontespizio*[3]. The compilor of the article continues: "He says essence, yet it seems that he wants to say being. Not seeing, but being [...] on a trestle we see a collection of strange bottles". The bottles of Morandi. We are reminded how in Arezzo, Gianni Poggeschi[4], demonstrating the numerous composed limbs of Piero della Francesca, exclaimed, "See Morandi!".

To stress what I have tried to explain in words, despite being aware of their inadequacy in front of the complexity and richness of Morandi's art, it can be significant to re-examine his artistic career, across the long span of years from the warm volumetric "plastic values" of 1920, to the stark, transparent luminosity of the *Landscapes* of 1942-1943. In these very years, marked by cultural and social upheavals which embraced Europe and the rest of the world in one of its most profoundly tragic moments, Morandi continued the search within himself as far as his nature would allow, to later emerge again with a wealth of experience which would enable him in the years to come to master perfectly his image.

But it was in the melting pot of the 1920's and 1930's that his every impulse was destroyed by the old desire to "know oneself", in response to the exigences of that "study of man" which the artist, following the teachings of Pascal, considered to be his ethic and cultural goal.

After the "sidereal" metaphysical period which recalls the words with which Vincenzo Cardarelli reflects on his own poetry, in 1916, and which are well suited to Morandi's painting: "Light without colour, existence without attributes, hymns without interjections, impassability and distance, orders and non-figures"; following the "impenetrable integrity of the celestial body"[5] of the *Still Life* of 1918-1919, maintaining as a fundamental starting point for a study of Morandi between 1920 and 1943 the *Still Life with a Round Table and Jug*, of 1920.

The work is well known, and it is perhaps superfluous to stress, if not its seminal nature, it being a foundation for his artistic choice which was to place trust in nature – not to refute the diverse earlier paintings, but to capture the sense of bodily volume. Forms acquire again an aura of pure physical presence, and the value placed on the perspective laws of Piero della Francesca and Paolo Uccello returns to allow air to circulate again amongst the objects, caressing them with the luminosity of honey. The motif of the jug, of great interest to him and the most important link of his art to the contemporary classical – mediterranean ideals of Picasso and de Chirico, would return in the splendid *Still Lifes* of the Ludwig Museum of Cologne (1921) and in the Hermitage in Leningrad (1925) where the plastic solidity dissolves into the background, transforming the object into an apparition which slowly turns to face reality.

This effect was to be taken up again by the artist many years later in several disturbing *Still Lifes* of 1963, bringing to light unexpected portions of images as parts of a whole which for an instant manifest themselves according to that defined form which, seconds later, can assume an infinite number of others.

Even the *Flowers* of 1920 can be regarded as a poetical manifestation of "plastic values", the point of resolution of metaphysics after the frozen atmospheres and the secret fires of the magical scenes, manikins and prisms.

Even if purified, the space is no longer a virtuality and it has again the notion of heaviness and of material quality, whilst the forms are solidified and the barely defined shadows reconstruct the sense of depth. But if the vase reveals the attention to plasticity which is now being developed by the young artist (Morandi is just thirty year old), the foreground and background separated by just a subtle line and a lightening of tone, these paintings are linked uninterruptedly to the *Flowers* of 1917 and 1918 – with their crenellated rose buds, grouped together in a pyramidal form – naturalistic, organic.

Several "different" paintings of the same years, 1920-1921, apparently disassociated with the *Still Life with Round Table* or *Flowers*, allow us to glimpse the complex research of Morandi, and his refusal to follow the predictable paths. These are *Still Lifes* of deep tones, almost gloomy, with dramatic, crowded objects in a contracted space. If the *Still Life* of the Gallery of Modern Art in Bologna acts as a point of contact between the plasticity on the one hand and intensity on the other, the process is accentuated in the "nocturnal" picture from of a Bolognese collection, and in the *Dark Still Life* of a private Milanese collection, in which the objects, placed against the light are bound together by shadows on the frontal plane, from which they seem to be detached, fooling the eye. Francesco Arcangeli saw in these works an anticipation of the Roman School, recognising a model to which the vibrant works of Scipione and above all Mafai turned to form an intensity of expression (one can refer to the bare pulsating *Flowers* of 1924 in a Modenese collection). This is important in exploring the links between the Bolognese master and younger artists, above all to reflect on the surprising position taken by Morandi to bring close that reality chosen after close scrutiny.

Each object displays its undefined Saturnian face: sometimes appearing under the sun with the softness of its diurnal contours, sometimes it allows its hidden, lunar aspects to be seen – almost as if light, moving around, brings to the surface the hidden side of objects, that interior richness which renders them alive and vibrant. The Pirandello poetry of "one, no-one and a hundred thousand" comes to mind – the profound necessity to explore and not to stop at appearances to search into the most hidden folds of reality. It is an all-embracing European culture that is moving in this direction; and Morandi, knowledgeable of his role in it, uses his skill as an artist to bring to light the multiplicity of aspects of reality.

How far from all this is the poetry of the

Still life, 1920
oil on canvas, 33 × 38 cm
Milan, private collection

Flowers, 1924
oil on canvas, 38 × 42 cm
Modena, private collection

Still life, 1927
oil on canvas, 32 × 42.5 cm
Rome, private collection

Landscape, 1925
oil on canvas, 46 × 42 cm
Milan, private collection

"return to order" which was pervasive in those years in Europe, and how much closer was it to the contemporary, suffered experiences of Pirandello, of Lawrence, of Proust! If for the latter the task of poetry was to "liberate the essence of sensations, to compose them, to remove them from the contingency of time, in a metaphor", how well suited to Morandi are these other words: "It is our duty to break the spell which locks away objects, to bring them to us and to avoid them from falling for ever into the void!".

But the young Morandi accomplished all of this without any controversy, secluded in his provincial, reserved Bologna, becoming enlightened in front of a bunch of *Flowers*, just gathered and yet far away in an atmosphere suffused with memory, in front of the springtime image of a house in the fields, that lyrical *Landscape* of 1921 which reveals a purity of image and a poetic inspiration in the style of Leopardi.

In truth, Morandi slowly becomes more enlightened, and his expressive facilities, facing a reality which after the metaphysical flights of fancy revealed itself to him as startlingly richer and more surprising than dreams. He had no longer any need to remove objects to a supernatural dimension, because it was sufficient and more stimulating for him to delve into the reality of every day existence, and to gather and let flourish as in a mirror the plurality of his interests. He is like a musician who, faced with the vastness of the keyboard, tries all the notes to trace in each one the unity, the essence of pure sound, the contribution which all variations can bring to the substance of the imagination. In a kind of continuous counterpoint, the harmony of the whole is made richer, and the power of introspection of the artist is sharpened, knowing that he has chosen a difficult path, all along, and punctuated by setbacks and new attempts, but always inside a clearly defined spatial – temporal dimension.

Even that which in Morandi has been defined as the period of his greatest tangent to naturalism[6] can be reconsidered in this key.

It is well known today that the ties which brought close Morandi to the intellectuals who, on the pages of *Il Selvaggio* and *L'Italiano* fought for provinciality and who preached the necessity of an art linked to tradition, and the return to the good, simple things of life[7]. For several years Morandi was considered to be one of them, and articles on him and his pictures were published in the two magazines of Florence and Bologna. His approach to this is not at all forced, and sees his desire to engrave, which between 1927 and 1931 was to be the medium of his most tormented work (for example the large *Still Life with Lamp at Right* of 1928, reflecting how the most silent dance of everyday objects can rise to the blazing metaphor of nature). But even in those years, Morandi defies descriptions, distancing himself from the act of "painting done at home, like bread with oil"[8], with subtle works dense with references, contained within a singularly scrupulous image which makes them substantially unique.

One need only observe the *Still Life with Basket* of 1927 from a Roman collection and another of the same subject of 1928, like that with the *Copper Casserole* of the same year, to see that in each case there is nothing calm, and each time they become more agitated: those traditional academic "small lamps" of the former, liquid and transparent so as to hint an internal vibration; in the latter, the small bottle on the right, a piece of pure painting like the web of the background and the folds of the drapery; the secret shell – an unexplored cavity – in the last still life which seems rather like a painting done *en plein air* with the background of agitated air, the swaying geraniums and the Chardin-style casserole, synthesised in plastic forms, no longer naturalistic.

Morandi is at the threshold of what has been described as his "descent into hell"[9], that is his most turbulent years, expressively and formally, even if he never lost his carefully built images and that hint of control which kept the forms from collapsing into an abyss beyond return.

If in the preceeding years he alternated absolutely clear paintings like the *Landscape of Chiesanuova* of 1925 and the Piero della Francesca inspired *Still Life* now in the collection of Alberto della Ragione in Florence with works rich in pathos like the two *Still Lifes* of 1924 – the emaciated one from the Civic Museum of Contemporary Art of Milan, and that with the yellow drapery and the silhouette of the clock of the Fondazione Longhi, – from 1929 he began the "dissolving attack on the object", which Cesare Brandi mentions in his article of 1938-42[10], stressing how the "precise, reconstructed whole of the volumes yield their germinating force to the plastic inspiration of the broken, thickened colour, at once vibrating and soft like a skin". First shadows appear like the alter ego of objects, their projection given autonomous life, emerging from the background to affirm their own sensitive yet puzzling presence (see particularly the Brera *Still Life* of 1929); then the objects themselves become "corporeal metamorphoses of shadows"[11], taking on the appearance of larvae, transparent and like alabaster, yet sometimes burning and sulfurous like the *Dark Still Life* of a Roman private collection where – apart from every sensation of weight and mass – there remains only the cover of reality.

One can agree with Ragghianti when he mentions the "truly demonic sense of vitality in his painting ... sure of his passionate attractions to reality (in 1930, in 1934 and 1939), towards life in the act of its rising, vigorously entering into its soul and sensitivity"[12]. But even more must I stress the alchemy used in these years, between 1929 – 1930 and 1935 – 1936, in the making of a painting – the act of everything being put into the melting pot of artistic creation, just enough to leave on the bottom the superfluous, and to extract the *albedo*, the essence of matter, its decanted purity.

At the time of the "work in black", everything seems to boil, if not to dissolve, in magma embroidered with light, whilst sharp tentacles of matter lash the air and fragments of colour illuminate the closed space of the work.

Morandi is putting himself to the test, to reach into the centre of his essence to find the nucleus, that something more resistant and luminous than diamonds which alone can sustain the work of a whole life, giving strength to each act, to each image reflected in it.

In 1937 his paintings become appeased. Conscious of what he has found inside himself, the artist conducts his art with mastery over every conceptual and sensorial subtlety. In this his friendship with Roberto Longhi is certainly a great help, in the clearness and harmony of his teachings, first and foremost due to his love for art; in other words this is a right meeting at the right time between a fully mature intellectual and an artist who has found his path and who wants to follow it with the firm knowledge of his own capacities.

Morandi's research was never interrupted, in fact in these years, 1938 – 1943, he created certain of his most splendid works, creations of a positive vitality which affirms decisively his right to express himself.

The paintings of 1938, the incredible series of *Still Lifes* resplendent in red and ultramarine hues, laid out with crowded, proud and ardent objects, presented themselves to astonished observers at the third Roman Quadriennale at the beginning of 1939, surprising even those who knew well the artist. Arguments and controversies were raised, which were not to be attenuated until two years later, with the acknowledgement of Morandi having assimilated completely the whole spectrum of European art[13].

At the beginning of the 1940's, once the excitement of the Quadriennale had died down, Morandi's art increasingly was considered an *inner landscape*, persistent in its values and a sentiment of lasting time, the fruit of minimal variations, no longer of great changes.

The artist aspired to a new classicism; he

Still life, 1924
oil on canvas, 68 × 70 cm
Florence, Fondazione Longhi

Still life, 1929
oil on canvas, 53 × 48 cm
Rome, private collection

Still life, 1937
oil on canvas, 62 × 76 cm
Florence, Fondazione Longhi

Flowers, 1942
oil on canvas, 46 × 29.3 cm
Bologna, private collection

used an essential sense of structure in his *Landscapes,* often bringing to light the framework of the composition and initiating the subtle play of the interstitial spaces, which was to interest him greatly in his later period: see, amongst others, the *Landscape* of 1940 of the Civic Museum of Contemporary Art of Milan, with its white geometrical background defining pure, unnaturalistic space. In the *Still Lifes* air can again circulate more freely, light warms the objects, hinting at internal points of escape in the surrounding spaces, yet imprecise (examples are the Jucker *Still Life* of 1941, with those objects which seem to hint at something transcendental, or the Magnani *Still Life* of 1942 in which the background forces itself into the foremost plan of the picture, cutting up portions of space).

In *Flowers* the internal variations of the theme are even more accentuated, even in the affectionate touch of the artist who dresses them like fragments of life jealously guarded; the visual angle is often subdued, concentrating on the vase or on the single corollas; the silk of the musky rose alternates with the fragrance of fresh flowers. Along with oils which have the delicacy of watercolours are linked tense, projected images such as the *Flowers* of 1942 from Bolognese collection, significant in a period which saw the appearance, almost in unison, of Mafai's *Dried Flowers.*

Morandi had found his true self, although the world around him did not concede anything of certain, not even a sense of serenity. It was the war years, and everything seemed to dissolve in collective tragedy. Whilst aeroplanes passed over Grizzana and the front is pushed back, leaving a trail of pain and destruction, the artist confides his doleful reflections in small *Still Lifes with Shells,* cuttlefish bones abandoned on a coast alien to man, and in *Landscapes* of white light, where even the marks of trees seem to be bleached by dust and by the sun; landscapes devoid of man and nature, as if astonished of a life where sense is no longer comprehensible. Images of profound tran-

quillity, "glassy air" in the silence of day are these landscapes which represent the greatest achievement of Morandi.

Perhaps the poem by Eugenio Montale, when it is considered in a "painterly" manner, can serve to comment: "They were quiet, in the solitary lap / only Leno roco made a sound. / A ray of light blossomed, fire / crying in the air".

And also: "Do not take shelter in the shadows / of that thick shrubbery ... it is time to leave the cane thicket, / hardship which seems to sleep / and to look at the shapes / of life which crumbles ... our charred souls / in which the illusion burns / a fire full of ashes / are lost in the serenity / of a certainty: light".

The trials which Morandi will have to now affront will necessitate great concentration and wide knowledge of the many prismatic images of the One, but at the bottom of each invention will remain the serenity which Morandi has been able to achieve, at the price of the detachment due to raw sensitivity, in these years of adventure.

1. C. Brandi, "Then the painting disappears", in *La Fiera Letteraria,* Roma, 24 October 1968.
2. R. Longhi, "Moments of Bolognese painting", in *L'Archiginnasio,* a. XXX, nn. 1–3, Bologna 1935.
3. P. Bargellini (editor) "Italian Artists: Giorgio Morandi", in *Il Frontespizio,* Firenze, September 1937.
4. G. Poggeschi (1905-1972), Bolognese painter, is amongst the founders of the magazine *L'Orto.*
5. C. Brandi, *Morandi,* Le Monnier, Firenze 1942.
6. Cf. L. Vitali, 1957: "Scrupolo meramente oggettivo", F. Arcangeli, 1964: "Sentore d'Ottocento", F. Solmi, 1978: "Possibilità di caduta naturalistica".
7. Cf. my article "The transformation of Morandi's image between 1925 and 1939" in the catalogue of the exhibition "Morandi and his times", Bologna, Civic Gallery of Modern Art, November 1985-February 1986.
8. L. Longanesi, "Giorgio Morandi", in *L'Italiano,* Bologna, 31 December 1928.
9. F. Arcangeli, *Morandi,* Milano 1964.
10. C. Brandi, "Cammino di Morandi", in *Le Arti,* Roma, February-March 1939, an article later revised and expanded in the monograph published in 1942 by the publisher Le Monnier of Florence.
11. *Ibidem.*
12. C. L. Ragghianti, "Giorgio Morandi", in *Critica d'Arte,* Firenze, January 1954.
13. Cf. my article "Morandi and the artistic debate in the 1930's", in *Quaderni Morandiani 1. The international conference of Giorgio Morandi studies,* Mazzotta, Milano 1985.

Landscape, 1943
oil on canvas, 41.5 × 52 cm
Florence, Banca Toscana

Landscape, 1943
oil on canvas, 35 × 53 cm
Mestre, private collection

Still life, 1946
oil on canvas, 31 × 36.5 cm
Mestre, private collection

"In the overcrowded and often uncertain world of contemporary art Morandi appears as a fixed point".

Umbro Apollonio expresses with eloquence the change of interpretations and understanding before even the stylistic attitude itself, concerning the work of Morandi during the post Second World War period.

The amounting interpretative accounts, Brandi, Arcangeli, Raimondi, Gnudi and, in the lead, Longhi; the award at the Venice Biennale of 1948, the same that gives maximum recognition to Braque; the contemporary anthology held at the Calcografia Nazionale of Rome, followed by one held in Brussels in 1949, where they speak of the attention of a measured but precise popularity that sets up the artist as a model, a steady and definitively acquired reference during a time of the most complex and dubious, historical and cultural transition of the century.

There are too many needless prosecutions amongst the personalities active in the previous decades; the emerging generation too brusque and schematic, the gap between one 'engagement' that, measuring its own depth of conscience on the visible, it makes a mechanical derivation and a formalism that identified itself in an ideological non-objectivism, which is academically normative.

Morandi is for everyone a paradigm. Surrounded by unchecked respect, absent from the life of the debate as much as it is present in its fervidly expressive maturity; he is the object of extremes of adulation and repulsion as it happens with figures that are authentically founders.

The supreme estrangement, the severing of the mechanical reasonings of history present a figure that has come out of the political and cultural turbulences of the previous twenty years uncontaminated, morally exemplary. Conversely his embodiment of a value of modernity, qualitatively radicated, free of theorisms and experimentalisms of an avant-gardist approach, deeply rooted in an idea filtered through tradition, he creates a perfectly polemic edge.

Interpretations veined with a not always lucid idealism, establish stereotypes which run through the poetically pure painter alien to conceptual confrontations of an artistic attitude, naturally "classical", to more reductive though widespread image of the monotonous, orderly inventor of middle-class microcosms, meditative, intimist, incapable of adventure, indifferent to the reasoning of the modern.

From here the suspicion of the new standard-bearers of the renewed realism, that read inappropriately a base of ethical demobilization; give the rejections of the supporters of the modern, as language, as a declared style. In reality Morandi is not provincial, but rather the Italian cultural debate – and, at the moment, European – incapable, with the limited problematic instrumentation of the epoch, to overcome those stereotypes and press towards an understanding of Morandi's specific diversity, built and defended with decades of inflexible practise; diversity that induces him to a retracted, reticent position, not testimonial or exemplary, argumentative in declarations of intentions and demonstrations but such an incoercible tension and congruence to locate itself amongst the rare, not inauthentic adventures in thought and from of this century.

Morandi is a post-war 'case', and a case that is mainly Italian; this is the real limit, but of the world, not the artist Morandi in the 1940's is at the threshold of a maturity that proposes itself with an unusual fervour towards a continuity and intensity of achievements.

After the isolation of Grizzana for the events of the war (1943-1944), from which sprang a series of *paesaggi* (landscapes) in which the vision curdles and thins in greens veined with grey and lifted with whites toned in a clear, extended light, as though wrung with emotional song, the humble forms, here again series of flowers and still lifes.

The dramatic dissolving of forms into thick and tremoring substances, the thin, deaf vertigo of the object that grows in consistence with the light, the powerful advance of a vision that seems to impose itself on the eye, exciting the hand to brushstrokes that scrub, emphatic, marking the painting in caesura – shadow as body, toning that is soured with tone: the ultimate doubt, the question reiterated to existence, there for effect of figure of conscience in that measure which is at the same time monumental and precarious: all that which since the preceding years has passed.

Those that reasoned in the late 1940's have drawn Morandi to this. Things tidy themselves, they are articulated as complex on the plane of the horizon, still close and only just lowered, as though to guarantee an involving hold on the gaze, a penetrating mastery. They are stressed in apparent sobre paratax only just finding simple diagonals, or with a close-knit group, of objects to act as a closed scene to others more advanced. A full, high, often lateral light incises, almost saturating the objects with firm, unbroken tone.

The objects have, however, lost that spatial weight, that concreteness that is still corporeal, a strong correspondence to the gaze, although obvious, at the same time proud certitude of its existence within the world. Without the terse definition, volumetric and mentally stressed, of the accounts of 1920, it is to those transparencies that the images reach once again. A transparency that is now, for Morandi, absolute confidence in the object and at the same time, definitive devaluation.

The stride, brief and intensive, the long laboured intervals of the brushstrokes, that interlace not solid relationships of form but slow, relaxed tonal rhythms, minute and clearcut variations as for a luminous counterpoint – and shadow, the shadow itself is the tonal measure, a non diminishing modulation of the light, recovering objects in as much as they are accidents, irresponsible evidence in itself of a formation that is purified melodic cadenza of colour in light. There is a breadth, sober and meditated of a system that is born from Morandi's defini-

tive restraint or natural disinterest to understand things in terms of geometry – capable of a total and constricting space, and guaranteed by thought, as for a minimal but relentless cosmogony.

The object is no longer now the other, difference and distance have gained body, but an 'eventum' in itself insignificant, of the internal formation of the image primarily in the conscience and on the canvas through colour, an appearance that is luminous. It is not a monument nor a column of an architecture that can still signify an actual totality. it can be, for the eye, that impiously crosses the semblance, measure of a metrics that of the reality, it recounts the loss, without drama, without nostalgia. It is as though Morandi, having assayed to the point of paroxysm, the telluric tension of those forms until seeing the sublime possible, to perfection finally turning to the faculty – reticent of the new, secret to try painting as fullness avoiding the emotive strain, the 'pathos', the painting of the excavation.

It is not perhaps the Morandi, 'relieved' by some literary account of the moment, much less a 'gracious' Morandi. The value of perfection of sober withdrawal composed of form, of a correspondence distilled by tones, and tension ulterior to the plenitude of the sense of the image, but which trusts itself to a concentrated command, to an intensity of unemotive certainty, of irrevocable but already physiological, mental notomia.

"Pictor classicus" is sought after for good reasons and without proclamations from as many that follow his kind. This being also the reason.

Another confidence, relaxed and authoritative, Morandi displays on the other hand in this same passing of the years: with mastery, with a talent so possessed and unfolding to render him, without ever transcending the threshold of a natural severity, full and precious keyboard of poetic variations. The continual, subtle varying of certain whites, the saturating of the ochres haloed with pinks, the slow exhausting of the pale

Still life, 1949
oil on canvas, 30 × 40 cm
Bologna, Galleria Comunale
d'Arte Moderna "Giorgio Morandi"

Still life, 1953
oil on canvas, 35.5 × 45.5 cm
Mamiano di Parma,
Fondazione Magnani-Rocca

Still life with vases on a table, 1931
engraving on copper, 24.9 × 36.6 cm

Still life, 1960
oil on canvas, 30 × 35 cm
Rome, private collection

greys into yellow in a softened silver; just as the detail of certain strokes that carnally lift the colour or flake it in the indefinite pallor of the light; still the astuteness of certain minimal perspective rejections in reference to shapes and shadows, and the holding of the surface of things just this side of the luminous reflection, as for a subterranean irritation... without hair splitting, without extenuated torments.

Certainly Morandi concedes himself now, after decades of pictorial movements felt until the purely essential, unusual pleasures, unknown distensions; that are for him more conspicuous margins of variation and invention.

In 1949 and 1950 they do show, however, that Morandi is not yet prepared to limit himself within the terms of even a sublime and 'perfect' pictorial code of image.

Two *Still Lifes* of 1949 (both donated by the Morandi sisters to the Galleria d'Arte Moderna of Bologna), one is planned on a diagonal/horizontal plane, the other completely centripetal, axial, distanced – as is the *Flowers* of the same period, intransigent compositions at a metaphysical level, even in their exquisite execution, discrete forms in the light disclosing the artist's new problematic rejection.

Fallen every accidental reckoning, every residual descriptive accessory, in the newly moving and fluid brushwork soaked in thin luminous deflections, rendering the shapes evidenced from the intimidated edges – not for an anxiety about existence, now, but for the growth in space in as-much-as it is an intrinsic, unrelated pictorial event – coloured geometries without solidity or preventative space. Morandi tests to the extremities of a painting of subjects that do not value a certification of reality of sensible contingency.

Even more than the "original value of their existence" (Haftmann) that is certainly not denied filigree, the artist discounts now, definitively, even the question of a possible existence separated from those things in distonia of temporal space in relation to the

conscience that acknowledges, rethinks, does in pure pictorial form, perfecting in tension towards an absolute endowed with its own completely founded poetic substance and sensitive objectivity.

This is perhaps, that which Morandi intends when he affirms that "nothing is more abstract than the visible world". It is not only an answer that is acute, veined with ironic coquetry and wise detachment directed towards however many tried in those years to write in a key corresponding to the 'figurative' of a Mondrian, a Rothko, or they indicate (Courthion) "Chardin d'aprés le Cubisme".

Indifferent to contingent stylistic strategies, avaricious with placings that sound perspective of autohistoricization, Morandi well knows which is the team that modernity, the adventurous avant-garde is playing with the reasons themselves, with necessity of painting, of the image of art.

But his extremely private and intimate game is not with these relativities, with discorsive postulations that cross his course. Points of triangulation, not in the least underestimated or misunderstood, they certainly are: although to verify, with the intransigent to which he alone answers, the lucidity without reserve of the journey exclusive in the profound vertigo of the senses, in historical time made transient existence drawn to reflower and to come to another purified sensoriality to a restoration of existence all taken back to a mental plane, in the scent of the absolute possible: that it is so, he is certain, the founding reason of the great pictorial civilization of the West.

This is the aim of the series from the 1950's, preannounced by the sound and, at the same time suspended, a little predicted, a little matured change of pace – *Still Life* of 1949. Still more closely textured and together dried out thematic primes – it is pure composing and executing, since the variation is considered to be greater value than the theme, they recover a sharpened firmness of gaze, an inexorable penetration of the evidence, a tension of pictorial objectiv-

Landscape, 1961
oil on canvas, 40.2 × 40.2 cm
Bologna, private collection

ism (in place of any debt to objectivity) that for height of formal sentiment and together wholeness and qualitative clarity – this is the only naturalness possible in art – attaining results, in effect absolute.

The series proceed like "days" from a formal reasoning so acertained and taught to consent to the stressing occasion upon occasion the beats of a flow of messages endowed with its own daily life that is not sentiment of time, of being in the world, but conscious of existing in as-much-as total identification in the thinking of painting in the making of form.

This is the sense of duration, of concrete institutionalization of the images, that passes through the laborious, crystalizing composing of the years that run until 1954.

The point of view is raised and drawn further away, intensified in the candor of calcinating luminous incidence, conducted always more frontally until eliding the shadow or reducing a mere chromatic frontier; left in arrears with volumetrics and the perspective relativity of objects intending pure values by now appearing to light that being tempted by a two-dimensional marquetry composition. Morandi concentrates everything in the internal chromatic measure of the image wringing the tonal agreements to a few extremely decadent chords. Between a crumpled brown, soberly irritated and a white continually gnawed by direct luminous reflections, differentials take place from which depends, almost exclusively in absence of effect and externalization, the complexive, passing of tone running through with an almost rude grey to a suspended pearlized amber.

Few and grouped with humble simplicities or else closed to make groups of clear vertical tensions, or yet even more frequently arranged in such a way that the rectangular motive of the boxes presents the horizon in resonance and together closes it with the profile of the bottles in a central aggregation of severe geometric rhythms, the objects find their place there with their "trembling outlines" (Brandi) acting as pro-

27

tagonists, irresponsible towards the ultimate scrutiny of the artist.

Shapes, imprints of dematerialized luminous texture are now the subject, abstract in their conceptual substance even before, and much more fundamentally, than in appearance.

Certainly this is what Magnani means when referring, in regard to supreme Morandian geometries, to the notion of "meditated detachment" of which Goethe speaks.

On the other hand it is precisely a *Still Life* of 1953 of the Magnani collection that can be taken as a vexillum in this course of experiences. Three white bottles stand out as though in negative, in perfect symmetry on the thickening surface of the trio of boxes postponed, the same that in their time, stress the simple, strong vigour, the concert of verticals and horizontals.

It is not a new motive in Morandi's work. Already in the 1930's, he announces the closed body to body with the apparent substance of things, with their spatial physiology, the artist offers, in an example of an extraordinary etching of 1931, the germ of a rethinking of form for the luminous scansion driven to the extreme positive/negative, of a type of a pure two-dimensional differentiation, even then not ideologized.

Now that the intuition has fully evolved. That the responsibility of the evidence of the image resides, without impediment, in the formative process of thought, it is said articulating and strengthening itself from other choices.

Not only the technique of the application of paint now as never before, grows with the imponderable weavings, stratifying veils that imprison a luminous quality, with the sober surety that belonged to the metaphysic years, in addition the relaxed fullness that is born from a mastery devoid of demonstrations: with a strength even for emanating fascination, infinite beauty, as though by a deeply rooted vocation.

The practice of the drawing together assumes through intensity and tone of frequentation a role that is well more than the compositional laboratory, the ordering studio. The lines run without defining, without closing, without instituting strong, structural ganglions. It is rather like a monodical line that flows and draws out a resonance of the spaces, indifferent to anything that isn't the varying – at this point mental – of the luminous possibility of white.

At the same time the watercolour finds an unusual necessity. And along the very same lines of tradition, atmospheric colouring, destitution of any residual heaviness of the chromatic matter, growth in the light on a non-preventative architectural form. It is in the watercolour that the course towards the most rarified, stupified epifany, that in which finally even the structural and symbolic phantom of things flakes off in the pure qualitative zoning of colour, in the free play – but as conscious as it is non-facultative – of the thickenings and the pauses, that it composes.

This is Morandi's abstraction in which the term can indicate, only with an extreme margin of impropriety, the substance and height of the results.

Still Lifes such as that, of flashing poetry, in 1960 show how the gaze, penetrating sensorial experience to the point of changing the colour of relative reasons can fix itself in a mere statistic of conscience that is informed transcending the world by way of absolute poetic concentration, peaks of pinpointed totality, rather than estrangement, or substitution or alienation in relation to the world.

Others that mark the artist's last years of activity in a spectrum of variations by then in full beam offer shapes even more synthetic with acuminating imperfections made of gestures that soak the pictorial substance in movements of full, shooting intensity.

Even the landscapes renew the lines of the highest intuitions, but still veined with a dark subterranean 'pathos' in those wars. The edge of the wall that measures space, still enclosed and deep, the *Landscape* of 1961, between that extraneous sky and the slowly steeping greens, rediscovers itself as a thin beam of a melted structural weave by now in the crepitating of the smouldering browns and greens, of an introverted consistence of the *Landscape* of 1962: it is finally pure detachment, accent, 'metron', in that real and personal testament that is the *Landscape* of 1963, painting definitively not embellished, not in debt to anyone other than his own internal tension to express.

Even the relationship with painting, finally transpires as the definitive identification in a linguistic reasoning, the historical substance of which problematic, not on the plane of specific modalities, instruments in their own time, relative to the mode of thought, but upon that of the founding faculty that is at the very origin of painting, to form a conscience of its own possibilities to know itself before externalizing.

Traditional, modern; figurative, abstract: these accidental reasons then are of no value to Morandi. It a thinking of painting; his is not philosophical projection, but without reserve and transpositions at the highest level actuated philosophy; and poetry.

"Le poète" wrote Ponge, "ne doit jamais proposer une pensée mais un objet, c'est-a-dire que même à la pensée il doit faire prendre une pose d'objet".

Landscape, 1911
oil on canvas, 37.5 × 52 cm
Milan, private collection

Landscape, 1942
oil on canvas, 49 × 54 cm
Caracas, José Luis and Beatriz
Plaza collection

It seems only yesterday that I was cycling through the sunfilled day from Florence station to our house below the Impruneta where I and my family stayed during the summer months. I was pedalling furiously along the white roads, gradually gaining height but dipping now and then, a painting by Morandi strapped to my handlebars. He himself had handed it to me a few hours earlier in his studio in the via Fondazza. For it I paid nine hundred lira – a good price even then. It was 1941, I was 23 years old, and the painting I was so triumphantly bearing home (no. 244 in Vitali's catalogue) was a still life. Morandi had invited me in his distinctively hesitant and monkish manner to choose between three canvases. They were placed in readiness on the easel before my punctual arrival on the determined day. All three, like mine, had been commissioned months in advance. Two stood on the little ledge of the easel, and one rested below. One of the three was a landscape – and it was into landscape that I put all my heart – and yet straightway I chose a still life. Up to that time, by virtue of a sort of mechanism of which no one really seemed aware, one sought only after his still lifes; as if still lifes were the definitive expression of Morandi, the emblematic form of his particular vision. And now for a long time this prejudice has prevailed amongst the type of collector who only possesses, or only wishes for, one or two paintings by Morandi. Even today this still holds true; in the art markets Morandi's still lifes are more prized than his landscapes, and are therefore worth more in terms of money.

I have to say, even in admitting the existence of such a prejudice (or, more precisely, a narrow outlook on the part of the public, and indeed on the part of certain collectors and art dealers) amongst those who are ignorant of one of the true delights of painting, that I cannot think of anything more ridiculous, or for which there is less foundation in fact. There can be few modern artists born, like Morandi, with the true sense of vocation. Throughout his career he has set his course

without digression, without diminishing the quality of his work. Few can have sustained such unremitting dedication to such intense labour, which absorbs every external sensation, including that inherent in the subject, in the exactitude of its standards.

This essay is dedicated to Morandi's landscapes. I am almost certain to recognise that quality which, as I have recounted, I did not perceive earlier. By highlighting this aspect of Morandi's art I intend to offer a limited, but specific, contribution reinforcing our recognition of his greatness, if indeed there remains a need to say so. My words will be especially pertinent to those who too young to have had much direct experience of his works – who therefore come up against these works' will to know and to experience; against the exigencies of their concreticity; against paintings which insist upon themselves as paintings. In other words, art which is the measure of itself, reflecting in upon itself. Morandi's way of making art unequivocally reveals the synthesis of meditation and immediacy (two elements which are so often disjointed today), and the ability to liberate even within the constraints of the ancient Italian desire for form, creating expressive values which are original, intense and profound.

Landscapes account for approximately one quarter of Giorgio Morandi's oeuvre. Prior to 1944 there is little disparity between the output of landscapes, and still lifes (including flower paintings) which alone constitute the remaining three quarters of the artist's work. Before 1944 the number of landscapes he painted is only slightly below that of the still lifes. Aside from the earliest paintings, when landscapes predominate (although many were later destroyed by the artist) 1940 to 1944 were the most productive years of this genre. The variations in numbers (indicated here only summarily) are due for the most part to external factors, easy to locate in the habits of an artist whose life was directly in contact – in the most concrete sense – with things, places, the seasons and the sense of time. Morandi

Landscape, 1943
oil on canvas, 49 × 52 cm
Bologna, private collection

painted the majority of his landscapes during the summer at Grizzana, a tiny village in the Bolognese Appenines. The only alternative location to Grizzana was the courtyard of Morandi's house in the via Fondazza in Bologna. Here from his studio window he would look down across the rooftops, or along the treelined streets below. It was, however, mostly from the windows of the house in Grizzana that Morandi discovered the distant views, and the meditative frame of mind in which he fixed the objects of his painted landscapes. During the war years, when he sought a better quality of life after fleeting the bombardments, he spent more time than usual at Grizzana. There he was attracted to the images that could be seen through the windows opening onto a broad horizon of hills, woods and clearings. Before him was a panorama of mute, white dairy sheds and thin lines of vines, their greenness almost spent, punctuating the golden-ochre bands of fields of reaped wheat (as if in a landscape of Piero della Francesca); of dense hedgerows bordering the smooth curves of the white roads; and of the tangled mass of trees' foliage jutting out against the pallid blue of the summer sky. When the war came nearer, and the front, moving nearer step by step, stretched across the Bolognese Appenines with the attendant horrors known to all, Morandi remained in Bologna, never to return to his countryside until long after the war. This explains the scarcity of landscapes in the years immediately after 1944. The scarcity then continued into the succeeding years, but for reasons no longer to be found in the force of circumstances. It was as if something hindered him from taking up again what had been brutally interrupted; as if in the slight, but slow and deliberate variations in his art – in the change to a more severe tonality and towards the essential structures that reduced chromatically to black and white – Morandi distanced himself from the light of that felicitous season, far from the light of Grizzana.

The first securely dated painting by Morandi is the landscape in the Vitali collection, signed and dated in July 1911. There is what I shall call a moral element in this solitary little landscape, compounding the volatile essence of its poetry. This element is apparent in the quest for concreteness, the austere simplicity, and the desire to free the way in which a painting communicates from the snares of time – to liberate it from the orgiastic vitalism which flowed through Italian culture during those years from sources both old and new (which were simultaneously similar, yet opposed). Then the nascent Morandian world manifested itself, as if it was to have been found more in the landscape than in any other artform, and tending towards Morandi's first artistic interests (Cezanne, Seurat, and whatever he may have assimilated from Pica's 1908 volume on the Impressionists), as if landscape painting was best adopted to conduct the artist along the hard route to his own identity.

Nobody to my knowledge has ever seen Morandi paint. He has never taken his easel into the streets or to the edge of a field to paint "en plein air" or as the Italians say, "sul motivo". This may not hold true for the early years (although there is nothing to support anything to the contrary). The motifs and composition were gradually born only in the artist's mind. If, as he once confessed to Lamberto Vitali, his paintings were almost always conceived and resolved faultlessly in a single sitting, with his assured mastery of tone and form, and often solely on the basis of a lightly worked rapid pencil sketch, then this process of 'seizing' on the composition is valid only after a long gestation, after a long, meditative assimilation of the subject after a series of sketches, when the painting had already reached fruition in his intellect. There is a magnificently eloquent photograph of Morandi (reproduced in the second volume of the general catalogue) which serves as the perfect complement to the confession made to Vitali. On the first floor, in the studio-cum-bedroom described so many times by his friends, some of the humble objects which can form the subject of many of the still lifes are arranged on a table; two upturned milk churns (constructed of two cylinders of unequal diameter joined by a short cone; a form worthy of Piero della Francesca in its simple geometric solidity) which perhaps he himself made; the little turquoise and white striped vase; and a roughly glazed white bottle. He pushed his glasses up onto his forehead with the hand that supports his head, tilted a little to one side, and stares, his bottom lip stuck out, with a penetrating intensity, as if wishing to draw out some unknown essence from their forms. Thus is the wearisome toil of the mind perceived – of what I should call an intellect built of images, if such a phrase is not too Homeric. How much there is to read into the glance of an artist! Morandi appears like a chess player in the photograph, meditating on the next move in the knowledge of the succeeding moves, or the entire game. I am sure that he rearranged these objects in the quiet light of his studio in utter silence and profound contemplation, thoughtfully moving them across the table covered with white card dotted with signs, marks and figures corresponding to the constantly varied compositions. The conception of his landscapes was no different. It is not difficult to imagine Morandi at the window of the house in Grizzana staring steadily into the distance, his eyes narrowed to perceive some detail, searching for the right light to amplify, simplify and transfigure it, to make it into a painting by the process of thoughtful elaboration; first in the mind and then on canvas. Perhaps he has seen a white house behind a line of trees, fantastic shadows (a patiently disordered reality taken to its ultimate conclusion and then remade). Or another house abutting the limit of a copse, set on the hill's ridge and cut diagonally by a hedge – pure, regular volumes suffused with the vital breath of nature: or, a group of little houses etched against the sky which lends them its radiance, between them running the sunlit white road's grassy bank. Other more distant details, isolated in the great amphitheatre of hills circling Grizzana, were sometimes perceived with the aid of binoculars through a veil of summer haze, the contours rendered imprecise, the contrast between light and shade simplified, the colours lightly misted. A friend, who owns many of Morandi's pictures tells of how one day at Grizzana, as he indicated a distant point from the window, Morandi said, "Can you see your picture up there? I painted it in this room. "And handing over the telescope he used to comtemplate the landscape, he revisited that view, showing him the view chosen for a landscape painted in 1942.

Sometimes, after the lengthy mental toil, the quest for form reaches a certain harmony. Images are reworked almost to the point of violence, a real violence even when controlled. At that moment in the interior world of Morandi, blurred and fitful shades which barely retain the stamp of the old geometries rise to a classical meter, as if in a poem by Leopardi. When this transformation occurs, the still lifes and landscapes appear confounded in a unity, as if united by a subterranean explosion of the earth. Thus in a 1928 woodcut shells appear like mountains against the sky, and in 1935 landscapes are like fluid tissue, almost without form. But in the landscapes executed between 1940 and 1944 in the clear summer light – blazing, or almost invisibly veiled – the painting sometimes appears insubstantial. A few lines denote trees, the gentle curve of the hills, the unadorned geometry of the houses; and recall the silence of a remote Italy, bringing to mind the pensive echo of a past moment in our world, never repeated and therefore unique, and yet eternal. "The light of an age which in truth had no need of man, but is yet in accord with his handiwork: early rustic traces of walls, the lowly trails of footpaths, the harmonious patchwork of fields". I take pleasure in concluding with these lines from *Morandi* by Francisco Arcangeli which although biassed, albeit favourably so, still remains one of the better works of modern Italian art criticism.

Landscape. Courtyard of via Fondazza, 1954
oil on canvas, 56 × 56 cm
Bologna, Galleria Comunale d'Arte
Moderna "Giorgio Morandi"

(G. Briganti, E. Coen, *I paesaggi di Morandi*, Torino, 1984, pp. 7-11; licensed by Società Ed. U. Allemandi & C.)

*Still life with boxes and bottles
in an oval*, 1921
engraving on copper, 10.9 × 16.5 cm

Still life with the bread basket
(large plate), 1921
engraving on zinc, 16.5 × 22 cm

This brief text which attempts to consider such a conspicuous part of Morandi's art – that represented by his drawings, watercolours and engravings – and the crucial year of his career, 1921, making a major turning point, must be regarded as purely arbitrary. This is justified not only by the fact that only from this point was engraving to assume an importance in his work; or even that it is beyond – much beyond – that point which working in watercolour would free his particular talent; but especially in the manner of this article, which obviously does not offer an exhaustive survey of every aspect of Morandi's more than fifty year long career. This, which could be considered from the very occasion of the exhibition, I wanted to stress; referring back especially to the article by Pier Giovanni Castagnoli on the youth of the artist where, during those fundamental formative years, drawing substantially paralleled his painting, even if his watercolours and engravings were still rare. During the course of 1921, Morandi completed more than twice the number of engravings that he had done in the ten years from *The Bridge over the River Savena* of 1912. In comparing them, especially the one which Vitali classifies as the first of that year[1] (no. 6, *Still Life with Boxes and Bottles on an Oval Background*) with the most complex and involved, even for it's size, *Still Life with the Bread Basket* (no. 15), one notices immediately a significant difference, in the purely technical side, apart from the expressive intentions. The former, compared to the latter, is still uncertain and almost naive in the use, although quite varied, of the crossing of lines and of the density of shadows and body due to the close hatching. The objects, detached from the background by an excessively wide white halo – which is muddled with the white used as highlighting the turgid volumes on the frontal plane – does not lead to any depth; whilst the focus of the density in the centre echoes the jamb of the table which supports the objects, blunting the spatial planes of the image, precluding any sense of perspective.

All these technical difficulties are entirely mastered in the large engraving no. 15; such a difference in quality in such a short time must be due to a great study and concentration on engraving by Morandi; so much as to bring forward the date of Morandi's period of engraving from generally-acknowledged years 1927-1934. Not only is, in the *Still Life with a Bread Basket*, the spatial positioning of the objects unexpected, not only is the shading infinitely gradual in defining the objects; but almost, for the manner in which the little light that there is, is picked up in the neck of the carafe, seems to fall into the basket, to reflect itself more strongly in the bottles, one can physically touch the diverse textures of which the basket, the box, the jug and the bottles are constituted.

But this means nothing – that is all – just nothing this already masterly technique, matured in this magical year 1921, if one forgets to state that Morandi was discovering himself, having just completed his brief flirt with metaphysics. "This period of time is one of the greatest moments in all his career", stated Brandi; along with these "dark, secret, trembling years, amongst the greatest and most profound of [his] art" (Arcangeli).

The frozen isolation of the bottles and the manikins which animate, however distanced, the still lifes of 1918 and 1919 (in their turn far from the foreign mystery of de Chirico and from the detailed certainties of Carrà; and also alien from the normal habits which upheld the experiments of his occasional colleagues), after having spent a transitory moment in literary materialism, and in the full light of 1920, was all dissolved. From this point on, Morandi fearlessly was at one with things.

Engraving was to be a continued part of his work – especially from 1927 to 1933-34 (to those years more than eighty engraving have been attributed, in other words three quarters of his complete output in this technique); maintaining always autonomous from his painting, as has been stated many times. Just before that period extraordinarily rich in work, in the years which Arcangeli (and more subtlely Vitali) saw a preoccupation with "Strapaese", Morandi's graphic work was distanced from itself, as if it was timid of its magisterial formality. Sometimes there appears an almost simplified review of his work, sometimes a less essential style of landscape, embracing a still vibrant nature, not selected by that scrutiny which was "necessary to serve as a pretext to a painting"; sometimes again, a composition on the table of crowded objects with no hint of who composed them.

But apart from these very rare instances (from which I would subtract, however, certain works traditionally attributed to this group: for example the *Landscape* of 1927, Vitali no. 32, and the *Still Life* of the following year, no. 47) in which Morandi's soul tended "towards Strapaese", his engravings follow a path drastically independent from his painting, an intimate monitor of his intimate evolution, and which I seem to see developing in two directions. The first, represented by the *Large, Dark Still Life* of 1934, "baptized 'nocturnal' but which could better be called 'tragic'". (Vitali, whose interpretation was taken up and expanded by Arcangeli), is that which characterizes the engravings in which Morandi takes up and gives a last, strenuous formulation, to the "antique style" of etchings, making for himself the extreme point of a paradigmatic axis which begins, according to him, at least from Rembrandt.

In the work of 1934, the dense penumbra which covers and saturates the condensed space, tightly occupied by objects, moves apparently towards a single, pathetic protagonist of the large sheet; but this in reality depends upon the compression of shadow over shadow, body over body, leaving to each one, after having eroded their plasticity, their essential volumetrical consistency: thus, like the peaceful "rilievo schiacciato" of Donatello, from that space is diffused a living, externally active energy. In this way, certainly "nocturnal", and even "tragic" can

be seen in the *Large, Dark Still Life*, but this to the detriment of that sense of separateness, its immediate appearance, to the superb talent which created it; and also of the emerging melancholy under the aegis of the luminosity of the form which is interwoven into it.

On the other hand, the *Still Life* no. 107, being an image in some ways conclusive and liminal of a vast experience, of a great research, cannot and must not reorganise its formation solely, or prevalently, in that sense of melancholy which embraces it, it is indirectly acknowledged by the long and precious series of analogous compositions which precede it (and, to limit ourselves to the most important, we can point out the Vitali no.s 46, of 1928; 75, of 1930; 99, of 1933; 128 of the same 1934) and which are opposed to sentimental "tragic" of "nocturnal" interpretations, revealing a progressive approaching of the artist to the full knowledge of those forms which are broken up and perfectly achieved in the *Large, Dark Still Life*. One can refer to, in particular, the *Large Still Life with Coffee-Pot* of 1933, clear and luminous, where the composition is almost exactly identical to that of the *Still Life* of 1934, and also identical, even if less strongly expressed, that method of bringing the objects close to the viewer, shutting out and negating to the eye places of rest or escape; that way of placing close together the volumes in a minimal depth, all measured on the interweaving of objects, of which the closest projects beyond its resting place, towards us, whilst just a little further back the furthest away objects are cut out from the background into which they dissolve; a method of compressing space, rendering vague the outlines of the objects, and making them osmotic, intimately interchanging and gathered amongst themselves.

Morandi had gone far in 1934, from that first peak of technical perfection represented by the *Still Life with Bread Basket* of 1921. He had not changed his few tools, nor the sharpening stone; nor his bottles, jars, baskets, boxes; neither his closeness to life, nor

Large still life with the coffee-pot, 1933
engraving on copper, 29.6 × 39 cm

Landscape on the River Savena, 1929
engraving on copper, 25.3 × 24.8 cm

Still life, 1930
engraving on copper, 22.8 × 29 cm

Still life with vases on a table, 1931
engraving on copper, 24.9 × 33.6 cm

– apart from fleeting moments – the guarded melancholy from which they derived. He had, however, sharpened his reasons of form: all that could make the *Dark Still Life* different from and greater than the other, older engravings.

Another path Morandi had taken in the meantime was one in complete solitude, gathering and tasting the fruits in etchings. The first example is perhaps the *Landscape over the River Savena*, no. 57 of Vitali's catalogue, of 1929. There he represents, amongst fields and vegetation and beneath the distant profile of walls, the meandering course of the river, not touched at all by his tools: a totally white area surrounded by the close, and wider, criss-cross hatching. This is the first sign that Morandi has powers of evocation which this blank, silent area assumes with the economy within the image. Morandi realised that all the sheet can be made vibrant with this: reflected in that portion of blank space, all the rest of the image is rendered more natural, in its juxtaposition. The gentle graduation of chiaroscuro, elsewhere so tenaciously controlled, yields to the sudden contrast of areas of shadow and light: and more importantly than the progressive change in hatching is the perspective depth, infused with essential spatial directives.

This did not lead Morandi to use absolute white, with such breadth and rigor, in many of his engravings: but each time that he did, or more often when large light areas, just indicated by light stokes appeared in his compositions – he retains this sense of essentialism of the image, almost a studied impoverishment of his powers of subduing the evocation of nature, first and foremost of the density of air and atmosphere elsewhere so extraordinarily rendered by engraving. A precise index of this knowledge is, in 1930, the *Still Life* no. 74, whose composition repeats precisely that of the preceding *Still Life* no. 73: in the first, the blinding whiteness of the bottle on the left and the shell on the right causes the whole composition to "correct" in a sense the

accentuated plasticity of the objects, detracting them from that orchestrated symphony of penumbras and highlights that determines the warm apparition of the second (and chronologically antecedent) etching. Elsewhere, for example in the *Still Life* no. 84, of 1931, the important almost shocking, use of absolute white, with the five objects in the foreground contrasting with the dark silhouettes of the objects behind, reaches an almost heraldic effect; but, I repeat, rather than have these objects suggest a liminal radicality, in a certain experimental way, I would like to stress the manner in which the discovery of the "white area" determines in Morandi (who continued at the same time his "first path" in his engravings) a prolonged interest in engravings which, deduced from the more traditional values of this rich and illustrious technique, accepts consubstantially a similar "effraction" of an evidently antinaturalistic intention.

"There is nothing more abstract than the visible world". Famous in their apparent simplicity and mysteriousness, these words of Morandi do not support any of the two fundamental interpretations (which are fundamentally different) of his work. However uncertain and questioning they may be, I am inclined to repeat them since, due perhaps to their substantial ambiguity, they seem to offer a perfect introduction to that other creative method of Morandi which must be mentioned here: drawing. Nowhere else in such a way, apart from in drawing, can one see in Morandi – especially in his greatest years – the ineffability of the beginnings and achievement of his images whether they are to be found in a "necessary pretext" of nature, or in a path independent of ideas. "The relationship between drawings and paintings or engravings, even if often quite evident, is certainly not that between a project and the finished work"; in this way a few years ago Argan stated, in accordance with the others – not many – who had given to Morandi's drawings a more than generic attention, the great conceptual autonomy of

Still life, 1958
pencil on paper, 16.5 × 24 cm
Bologna, Galleria Comunale d'Arte
Moderna "Giorgio Morandi"

Still life, 1962
pencil on paper, 24 × 32.7 cm
Bologna, private collection

Landscape, 1962
pencil on paper, 24.2 × 33.3 cm
Modena, private collection

Still life, n.d. (1962)
watercolours on paper, 21 × 16 cm
Mamiano di Parma,
Fondazione Magnani-Rocca

his drawing technique. This, naturally, does not mean that in his vast corpus of drawings there is not a significant number of drawings to consider in direct relation to paintings and engravings; nor that there are only few cases in which drawings are true preparatory studies for a future work. It is therefore a completely finished drawing, extraordinarily able to prefigure, almost to "imitate" the expressive peculiarities of the preparatory technique (as an example of a pure, stringent rapport between drawings and engravings, can be suggested the sheets 29 and 32a of the catalogue edited by Efrem Tavoni[2], preparations for the engravings 74 and 34, as indicated by Vitali). Neither, to complete the exceptions to the sense of Argan's remark stated above, should one forget that in certain, brief periods (I would point out that which lies between the second half of 1943 to 1946, and, less continuously, certain moments of the latter part of the 1950's) his drawings seem to fulfill the role of preparatory studies.

But apart from these few examples, it is beyond doubt that for most of his mature years, Morandi's drawings were not just ancillary in respect to painting but served much more important functions. After 1910, in which certain of the rare drawings attest to tensions which were not expressed ultimately in painting – at least no longer documented today – it is at the beginning of the third decade that is determined, even for drawing, his first absolutely expressive maturity; from 1920 and 1921 are certain splendid sheets which, perhaps more than paintings and engravings, prolong into the new period the melancholy "plastic values" of Morandi.

One will have to wait to the end of the 1920's for the first definition of what will be regarded, in time, as the drawing of Morandi. It is then that he realised what was to be his dream: never again, at least in the happiest and fulfilled moments, a contour which encloses and determines space, defining volumes and plasticity, which leads the eye into an interpretation of solids and voids, of a clear syntax of objects advancing in a wholly stated space. Fully autonomous from engraving, those marks which Brandi saw as "chiselled, trembling" search for a poetry in the image, there where a profile joins another, where a shadow meets a highlight which will astonish it.

A great moment, in drawing, identifiable with landscapes and still lifes, is that at the beginning of the 1940's (hinted at by certain drawings of 1932, see for example, Tavoni's no.s 38, 39, 342): compositions of objects seen from below as if form a gorge, looking up with hope towards those visions which have become gigantic with their implausible being, like anxious shadows, at that height; landscapes constructed of a horizon of a single jagged line, ceasing for an instant and for ever by the rocky cube of a house; foliage of trees of which one cannot distinguish the trunks but only, now and again, the wind beating on the branches.

This process of a harsh reduction to the essentials of drawing is not, with Morandi, ceaseless and he did return to more traditional, normal practices, at least up to the mid 1950's. However, later than this date, up to his death, Morandi lets this progressively take over completely almost all of his drawings in his last decade. That stylistic trait which tends to focus in a small central area of the sheet that which has become the painful fragment of a vision, mentioned above, is stressed from 1956 onwards; to the right and to the left, above and below the white of the paper isolates and besieges the agitated, interrupted profile of the few objects which remain on their pedestal; often elementary hatching, forgetting the variations of intensity, frequency and direction of the criss-crossing lines gouges out small areas of shadow, designating minimal spatial caesura, veiling, this time, a last, shallow depth.

From this time begins also the last, intense and great period of watercolours. When, between 1956 and 1957, Morandi returns to this technique which he had embarked upon in the 1910's, and which he only briefly

experimented with later, his interest in organic constructions of form in the illusionary depth of the sheet had not waned. All that time his colours, already pallid and watery, consisted of extremely delicate, controlled overlappings of density and warmth which served to lineate an extreme, resistant spreading of space, and an exhaustive rapport between solids and voids, shadows and corporeal lights.

Soon after – from 1959 and eventually irreversibly from 1960 – drawings and watercolours together reached their ultimate destiny. No longer were the eroded skeletons of objects of still lifes reduced to trembling appearances; and the landscapes, only silhouettes in the wind, or bare topographical visions of these same domestic familiar places which Morandi once used to say that he brought close, and which, instead, he rendered untouchable and distant, with his telescope.

Now, in his drawing there remained only bare, insurmountable walls with no thickness, described by a lean, reticent line which extraordinarily resounds in the sheet which just barely touches, able to fill itself mysteriously of a power which is diffused over the whole page, in its brief inflexions and its syncopated step. Only in his watercolours are there juxtapositions of homogeneous quantities of single colours, in a reactive exchange between positive and negative, between solid and void, substance and dream.

Thus finishes, on a peak of Franciscan poverty, the slow and meditated path of Morandi.

Still life, 1962
watercolours on paper, 16 × 21 cm
Bologna, private collection

Still life, n.d. (1962-1963)
watercolours on paper, 21 × 31 cm

1. L. Vitali, *Giorgio Morandi, Opera grafica*, Einaudi, Torino 1957 (enlarged third edition, 1964).
2. AA.VV., *Morandi, Disegni*, 2 vols., edited by E. Tavoni, Sasso Marconi; vol. 1, 1981; vol. 2, 1984.

Paintings

1. *Landscape*, 1910
oil on cardboard on canvas,
37.7 × 48 cm
signed lower right:
Morandi
Bologna, private collection

2. *Landscape*, 1913
oil on cardboard, 41 × 55 cm
signed and dated on the back:
Morandi / luglio 1913
Bologna, Galleria Comunale
d'Arte Moderna "Giorgio
Morandi"
(donated by Morandi's sisters)

3. *Landscape*, 1913
oil on canvas, 62 × 43 cm
signed and dated lower right:
Morandi / 913
Bologna, Pinacoteca Nazionale

4. *Still life*, 1918
oil on canvas, 71.5 × 61.5 cm
signed and dated lower centre:
Morandi 918
Leningrad, Ermitage Museum

5. *Still life*, 1920
oil on wood, 30.5 × 44.5 cm
signed and dated lower right:
Morandi 920
Bologna, Galleria Comunale
d'Arte Moderna "Giorgio
Morandi"
(donated by Morandi's sisters)

6. *Still life*, 1921
oil on canvas, 38.2 × 55 cm
signed and dated lower right:
Morandi 921
Bologna, private collection

7. *Landscape,* 1921
oil on canvas, 33 × 29 cm
signed bottom centre: Morandi
Bologna, private collection

8. *Flowers*, 1923-1924
oil on canvas, 40 × 29 cm
signed top centre: Morandi
Bologna, Pinacoteca Nazionale

9. *Flowers*, 1924
oil on canvas, 58 × 48 cm
Bologna, Galleria Comunale
d'Arte Moderna "Giorgio
Morandi"
(donated by Morandi's sisters)

10. *Still life*, 1924
oil on canvas, 52.5 × 66 cm
signed and dated lower right:
Morandi 1924
Milan, Civico Museo
d'Arte Contemporanea
(donated by Boschi-Di Stefano)

11. *Self-Portrait*, 1925
oil on canvas, 63 × 48.5 cm
Mamiano di Parma,
Fondazione Magnani-Rocca

12. *Still life*, 1925
oil on canvas, 51 × 57.5 cm
signed upper centre: Morandi
Leningrad, Ermitage Museum

13. *Still life*, 1929
oil on canvas, 52 × 47 cm
signed on the back: Morandi
Modena, private collection

14. *Still life*, 1929
oil on canvas, 54 × 64 cm
signed lower left: Morandi
Milan, Civico Museo
d'Arte Contemporanea

15. *Still life*, 1932
oil on canvas, 62.2 × 72 cm
signed and dated upper left:
Morandi / 1932
Rome, Galleria Nazionale
d'Arte Moderna (deposited
by Galleria Comunale d'Arte
Moderna, Rome)

16. *Still life*, 1935
oil on canvas, 63.7 × 55 cm
signed and dated lower left:
Morandi 1935
Bologna, Pinacoteca Nazionale

17. *Landscape,* 1935
oil on canvas, 50 × 70 cm
signed and dated lower right:
Morandi 1935
Milan, Civico Museo
d'Arte Contemporanea
(donated by Boschi-Di Stefano)

18. *Landscape*, 1935
oil on canvas, 54 × 60 cm
signed lower right: Morandi
signed and dated on the back:
Morandi 1935
Modena, private collection

19. *Landscape*, 1935-1936
oil on canvas, 60.3 × 71 cm
Bologna, private collection

20. *Landscape*, 1936
oil on canvas, 46 × 61.5 cm
Bologna, private collection

21. *Landscape*, 1936
oil on canvas, 45.5 × 71 cm
signed lower left: Morandi
dated on the back: 1936
Bologna, Pinacoteca Nazionale

22. *Still life*, 1936
oil on canvas, 47.5 × 60 cm
Bologna, Galleria Comunale
d'Arte Moderna "Giorgio
Morandi"
(donated by Morandi's sisters)

23. *Still life*, 1940
oil on canvas, 42 × 53 cm
signed upper centre: Morandi
Milan, Civico Museo
d'Arte Contemporanea
(donated by Boschi-Di Stefano)

24. *Landscape*, 1940
oil on canvas, 35 × 50 cm
signed and dated lower left:
Morandi 1940
Milan, Civico Museo
d'Arte Contemporanea
(donated by Boschi-Di Stefano)

25. *Still life*, 1941
oil on canvas, 41 × 49.5 cm
signed and dated lower right:
Morandi / 1941
Campione d'Italia,
S. Lodi collection

26. *Still life,* 1941
oil on canvas, 27 × 52.5 cm
signed and dated lower centre:
Morandi 1941
Mamiano di Parma,
Fondazione Magnani-Rocca

27. *Still life*, 1942
oil on canvas, 47 × 40.5 cm
signed and dated lower centre:
Morandi 1942
Mamiano di Parma,
Fondazione Magnani-Rocca

28. *Flowers*, 1942
oil on canvas, 25 × 30 cm
signed and dated lower left:
Morandi / 1942
Modena, private collection

29. *Flowers*, 1942
oil on canvas, 30 × 26 cm
signed and dated lower right:
Morandi / 1942
Modena, private collection

30. *Landscape*, 1942
oil on canvas, 27.5 × 52 cm
signed on the back: Morandi
signed and dated on the
frame: Morandi 1942
Modena, G. Salvaterra
collection

31. *Landscape*, 1943
oil on canvas, 41.5 × 53 cm
Florence, Banca Toscana

32. *Still life*, 1943
oil on canvas, 28 × 38 cm
signed lower right: Morandi
Campione d'Italia,
S. Lodi collection

33. *Still life*, 1943
oil on canvas, 30 × 45 cm
signed lower right: Morandi
Modena, private collection

34. *Courtyard of via
Fondazza*, 1945-1947
oil on canvas, 56 × 58 cm
signed and dated on the back:
Morandi 1945/47
Bologna, private collection

35. *Flowers*, 1946
oil on canvas, 18 × 17 cm
signed lower right: Morandi
Tolentino, private collection

36. *Flowers*, 1948
oil on canvas, 45 × 35 cm
signed lower right: Morandi
dated on the back: 1948
Bologna, Conti collection

37. *Still life*, 1948
oil on canvas, 44 × 47.5 cm
signed on the back: Morandi
Mamiano di Parma,
Fondazione Magnani-Rocca

38. *Still life*, 1948
oil on canvas, 35.9 × 50 cm
signed lower right: Morandi
Bologna, private collection

39. *Still life*, 1949
oil on canvas, 25 × 35 cm
Bologna, Galleria Comunale
d'Arte Moderna "Giorgio
Morandi"
(donated by Morandi's sisters)

40. *Still life*, 1949
oil on canvas, 36 × 45.2 cm
signed lower centre: Morandi
Bologna, Galleria Comunale
d'Arte Moderna "Giorgio
Morandi"
(donated by Morandi's sisters)

41. *Still life*, 1949
oil on canvas, 32 × 50 cm
signed on the back: Morandi
Mamiano di Parma,
Fondazione Magnani-Rocca

42. *Still life* (1951)
oil on canvas, 28 × 52 cm
signed lower left: Morandi
Milan, private collection

43. *Still life* (1952)
oil on canvas, 35 × 40 cm
signed lower left: Morandi
Bologna, Conti collection

44. *Still life*, 1953
oil on canvas, 33 × 45.5 cm
signed lower centre: Morandi
Tampere, Sara Hildénin
taidemuseo

45. *Courtyard of via
Fondazza*, 1954
oil on canvas, 49 × 54 cm
signed lower left: Morandi
Mamiano di Parma,
Fondazione Magnani-Rocca

46. *Still life*, 1955
oil on canvas, 25.5 × 30.5 cm
signed lower left: Morandi
Winterthur, Kunstmuseum
(donated by Heinz Keller)

47. *Still life*, 1956
oil on canvas, 33 × 38 cm
signed and dated lower
centre: Morandi 56
Mamiano di Parma,
Fondazione Magnani-Rocca

48. *Still life*, 1957
oil on canvas, 27 × 40 cm
signed lower left: Morandi
Hamburg, Hamburger
Kunsthalle

49. *Courtyard of Via
Fondazza*, 1959
oil on canvas, 40.5 × 45.5 cm
Bologna, private collection

50. *Still life*, 1959
oil on canvas, 25 × 35 cm
signed lower left: Morandi
Modena, private collection

51. *Still life*, 1960
oil on canvas, 30 × 40 cm
signed lower left: Morandi
Modena, private collection

52. *Still life*, 1960
oil on canvas, 30.5 × 40.5 cm
dated on the back: 1960
Bologna, Galleria Comunale
d'Arte Moderna "Giorgio
Morandi"
(donated by the artist)

53. *Still life,* 1961
oil on canvas, 25 × 30 cm
signed lower left: Morandi
Winterthur, Kunstmuseum

54. *Landscape,* 1961
oil on canvas, 50.5 × 30.5 cm
Bologna, private collection

55. *Landscape*, 1962
oil on canvas, 30 × 35 cm
Bologna, private collection

56. *Landscape*, 1962
oil on canvas, 25.5 × 31 cm
signed lower right: Morandi
Bologna, Galleria Comunale
d'Arte Moderna "Giorgio
Morandi" (deposited by the
Banca del Monte di Bologna
e Ravenna)

57. *Still life*, 1963
oil on canvas, 20.5 × 35.5 cm
signed lower right: Morandi
Bologna, private collection

58. *Still life*, 1963
oil on canvas, 19.5 × 24.5 cm
signed lower right: Morandi
Mamiano di Parma,
Fondazione Magnani-Rocca

59. *Still life*, 1963
oil on canvas, 30 × 35 cm
signed lower left: Morandi
Bologna, private collection

60. *Landscape*, 1963
oil on canvas, 40 × 45 cm
signed lower centre: Morandi
Bologna, Galleria Comunale
d'Arte Moderna "Giorgio
Morandi"
(donated by Morandi's sisters)

61. *Still life*, 1964
oil on canvas, 25.5 × 30.5 cm
signed lower left: Morandi
Bologna, private collection

Watercolours

62. *Brown still life*, 1920
watercolours on paper,
17.5 × 23 cm
signed and dated lower right:
Morandi ottobre 920
Tolentino, private collection

63. *Landscape* (1956)
watercolours on paper,
16.1 × 20.6 cm
signed lower centre: Morandi
Bologna, private collection

64. *Landscape (Inside of Via Fondazza)*, c. 1956
watercolours on paper,
21.2 × 22.6 cm
signed lower centre: Morandi
Verona, private collection

103

65. *Landscape* (1957)
watercolours on paper,
16.5 × 23 cm
signed lower centre: Morandi
Bologna, private collection

66. *Landscape*, 1957
watercolours on paper,
21 × 31 cm
signed and dated lower
centre: Morandi 1957
Modena, private collection

67. *Landscape*, 1957
watercolours on paper,
34 × 25 cm
signed and dated lower
centre: Morandi / 1957
Venice, private collection

68. *Landscape*, 1957
watercolours on paper,
16 × 21 cm
signed and dated lower
centre: Morandi 1957
Biella, private collection

69. *Landscape* (1957-1958)
watercolours on paper,
29 × 24.5 cm
signed lower centre: Morandi
Bologna, private collection

70. *Landscape* (1958)
watercolours on paper,
15.5 × 23.5 cm
signed lower left: Morandi
Tolentino, private collection

71. *Landscape*, 1958
watercolours on paper,
31 × 21 cm
signed and dated lower
centre: Morandi / 1958
Modena, G. Salvaterra
collection

72. *Landscape* (1959)
watercolours on paper,
16 × 21 cm
Milan, private collection

73. *Landscape* (1958)
watercolours on paper,
33 × 25 cm
signed lower left: Morandi
Milan, private collection

74. *Still life* (1958)
watercolours on paper,
23.5 × 32 cm
signed lower centre: Morandi
Turin, A. and M. Forchino
collection

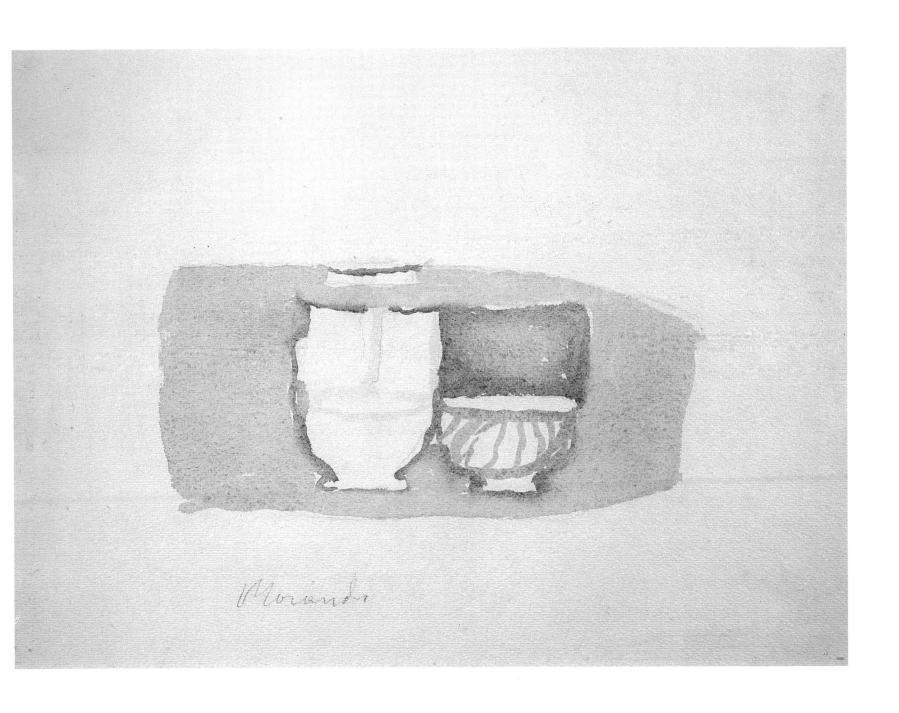

75. *Flowers* (1959)
watercolours on paper,
21.8 × 21.2 cm
signed lower centre: Morandi
Modena, private collection

76. *Landscape* (1959)
watercolours on paper,
21 × 16 cm
signed lower centre: Morandi
Bologna, private collection

77. *Landscape (House in ruins)* (1959)
watercolours on paper,
21 × 16 cm
signed lower centre: Morandi
Venice, private collection

78. *Still life* (1959)
watercolours on paper,
16 × 23.6 cm
signed lower centre: Morandi
on the back: A Ettore
Gian Ferrari, 8.4.1959
Milan, private collection

79. *Still life* (1959)
watercolours on paper,
22.5 × 30.5 cm
signed lower centre: Morandi
Biella, private collection
(certification by Maria Teresa
Morandi, 16.10.1986)

80. *Still life* (1959)
watercolours on paper,
27 × 37 cm
signed lower centre: Morandi
Bologna, private collection

81. *Still life* (1959-1960)
watercolours on paper,
27.7 × 15.8 cm
signed right: Morandi
Modena, private collection

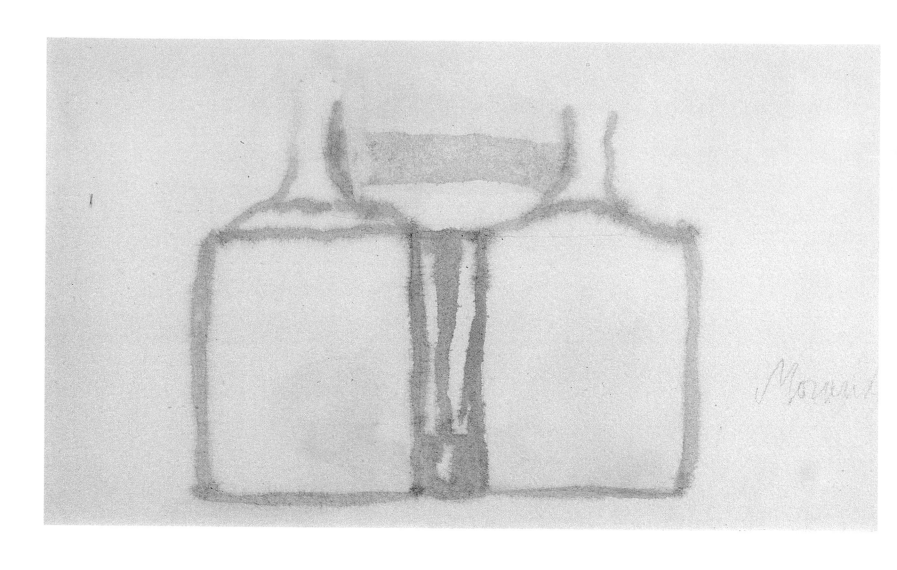

82. *Still life*, 1960 ca.
watercolours on paper,
21 × 27 cm
Verona, private collection

83. *Still life* (1962)
watercolours on paper,
21 × 30 cm
signed lower centre: Morandi
Venice, private collection

84. *Still life* (1962)
watercolours on paper,
15.8 × 20.9 cm
Bologna, private collection

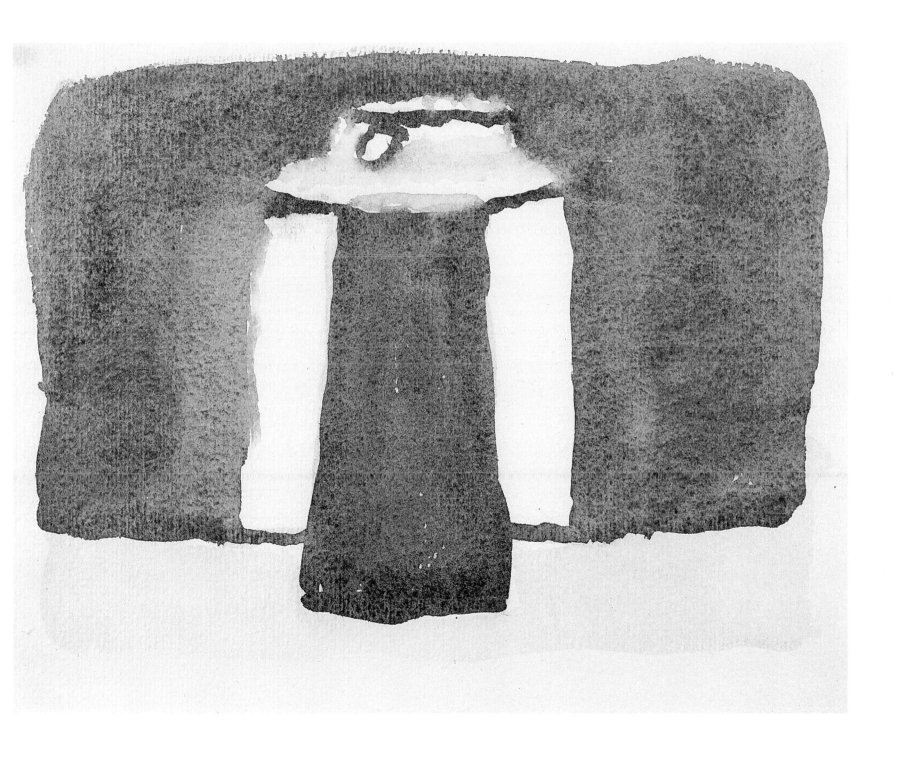

85. *Still life* (1962)
watercolours on paper,
16 × 21 cm
signed lower left: Morandi
Bologna, private collection

86. *Still life* (1962)
watercolours on paper,
14 × 21 cm
signed lower centre: Morandi
Bologna,private collection

Drawings

87. *Still life*, 1928
pencil on paper, 27 × 38 cm
signed and dated lower
centre: Morandi 1928
Bologna, private collection

88. *Still life*, 1930
thick pencil on paper,
29 × 23.2 cm
(irregularly shaped
and shredded on lower part)
signed and dated lower
left: Morandi / 930
Bologna, private collection

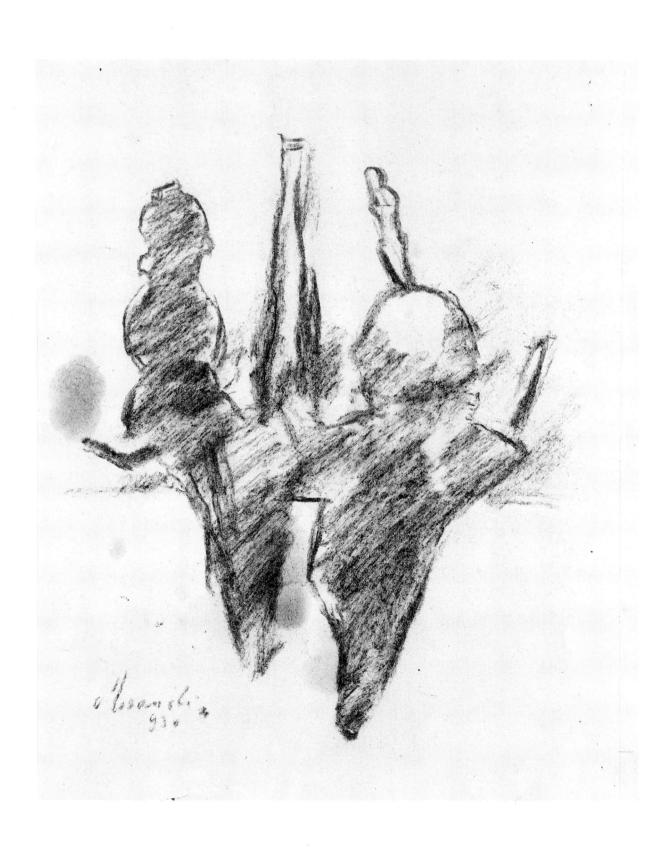

89. *Shells*, 1932
pencil on paper,
18.4 × 25.8 cm
signed and dated lower
right: Morandi 1932
Modena, G. Salvaterra
collection

90. *Bottles*, 1932
pencil on paper, 17 × 24.5 cm
signed and dated lower
centre: Morandi 1932
Modena, G. Salvaterra
collection

91. *Still life*, 1932
pencil on paper,
19.5 × 29.5 cm
signed and dated lower
right: Morandi 1932
Bologna, private collection

92. *Still life*, 1941
pencil on paper, 28.5 × 35 cm
signed and dated lower
centre: Morandi 1941
Bergamo, private collection

93. *Flowers*, 1946
pencil on paper, 31 × 22.5 cm
signed and dated lower
centre: Morandi 1946
Bologna, private collection

94. *Still life*, 1948
pencil on paper, 24 × 33 cm
Bologna, Galleria Comunale
d'Arte Moderna "Giorgio
Morandi"
(donated by Morandi's sisters)

95. *Still life*, 1948
pencil on paper, 21 × 29 cm
signed and dated lower
centre: Morandi 1948
Biella, private collection

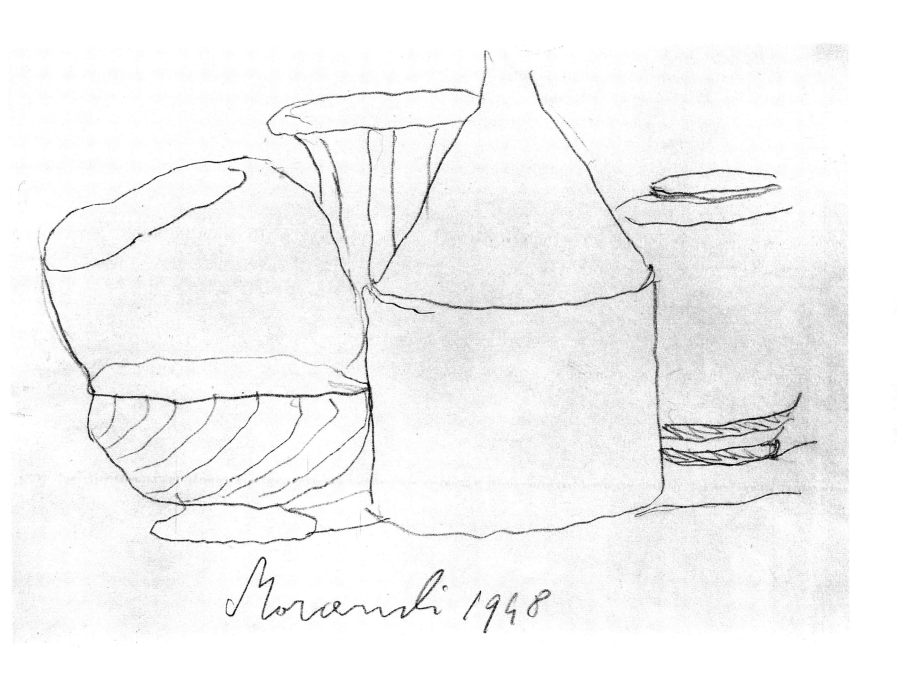

96. *Still life,* 1949
pencil on paper, 23 × 32 cm
signed and dated lower
centre: Morandi 1949
Bergamo, C. Traglio collection

97. *Still life*, 1949
pencil on paper, 34 × 25 cm
signed and dated lower
centre: Morandi 1949
Bologna, private collection

98. *Still life*, 1951
pencil on paper,
15.6 × 22.5 cm
initialed and dated
lower centre: M. 1951
Bologna, private collection

99. *Still life*, 1952
pencil on paper,
23.6 × 32.5 cm
signed and dated lower
centre: Morandi / 1952
Bologna, private collection

100. *Still life*, 1953
pencil on paper,
16.5 × 24.5 cm
signed and dated lower
centre: Morandi 53
Bologna, private collection

101. *Still life*, 1958
pencil on paper, 16.5 × 24 cm
signed and dated lower
left: Morandi 1958
Bologna, private collection

102. *Still life*, 1958
pencil on paper,
16.5 × 23.5 cm
signed and dated lower
right: Morandi / 1958
Bologna, private collection

103. *Still life*, 1959
pencil on paper, 24 × 32.9 cm
signed and dated lower
centre: Morandi / 1959
dedicated lower left:
a Leone Pancaldi / Morandi
Bologna, private collection

104. *Landscape* (1960)
pencil on paper,
21.3 × 27.6 cm
signed lower centre: Morandi
Bologna, private collection

105. *Landscape* (1961)
pencil on paper, 16.5 × 24 cm
signed lower centre: Morandi
Bologna, private collection

106. *Still life*, 1962
pencil on paper, 24 × 32.7 cm
signed and dated lower
centre: Morandi / 1962
Bologna, private collection

107. *Still life* (1962)
pencil on paper, 16.5 × 24 cm
signed lower left: Morandi
Bologna, private collection

108. *The clock*, 1962
pencil on paper, 16 × 23 cm
signed and dated lower
right: Morandi 1962
Bologna, private collection

109. *Landscape* (1962-1963)
pencil on paper,
32.5 × 23.5 cm
signed lower left: Morandi
Bologna, S. Conti collection

110. *Still life* (1963)
pencil on paper,
18.2 × 27.4 cm
signed lower right: Morandi
Bologna, private collection

111. *Still life*, 1963
pencil on paper, 13.9 × 22 cm
signed and dated lower
right: Morandi 1963
Bologna, private collection

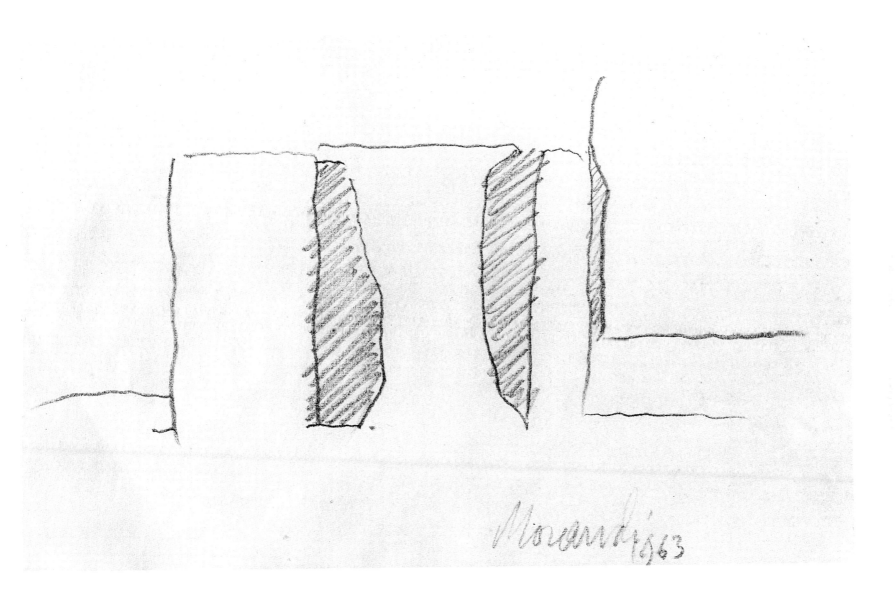

Engravings

112. *Grizzana landscape,*
1913
engraving on zinc,
16.2 × 23.4 cm
the plate is in Rome,
Calcografia Nazionale
not signed or dated
Bologna, Galleria Comunale
d'Arte Moderna "Giorgio
Morandi"

113. *Still life with bottle
and jug*, 1915
engraving on copper,
15.4 × 12.5 cm
the plate is in Rome,
Calcografia Nazionale
signed and dated lower
right: Morandi 1915
Modena, private collection

1915

Morandi

114. *Still life with sugar pot,*
lemon and bread, 1921
or 1922
engraving on copper,
8.4 × 10.1 cm
another ruined engraving is on
the back of the plate, which is
in Rome, Calcografia Nazionale
not signed or dated
Bologna, Galleria Comunale
d'Arte Moderna "Giorgio
Morandi"

115. *Still life with bread
basket* (small plate), 1921
engraving on copper,
11.8 × 15.4 cm
the plate is in Rome,
Calcografia Nazionale
signed lower centre: Morandi
Medolla, E. Ferri collection

116. *Bouquet of wild flowers*, 1924
engraving on zinc,
20.5 × 16.3 cm
the plate is the reverse of
no. 20 (Vitali), and is in Rome,
Calcografia Nazionale; the
composition is the counterpart
of painting no. 71 (Vitali)
not signed or dated
Bologna, Galleria Comunale
d'Arte Moderna "Giorgio
Morandi"

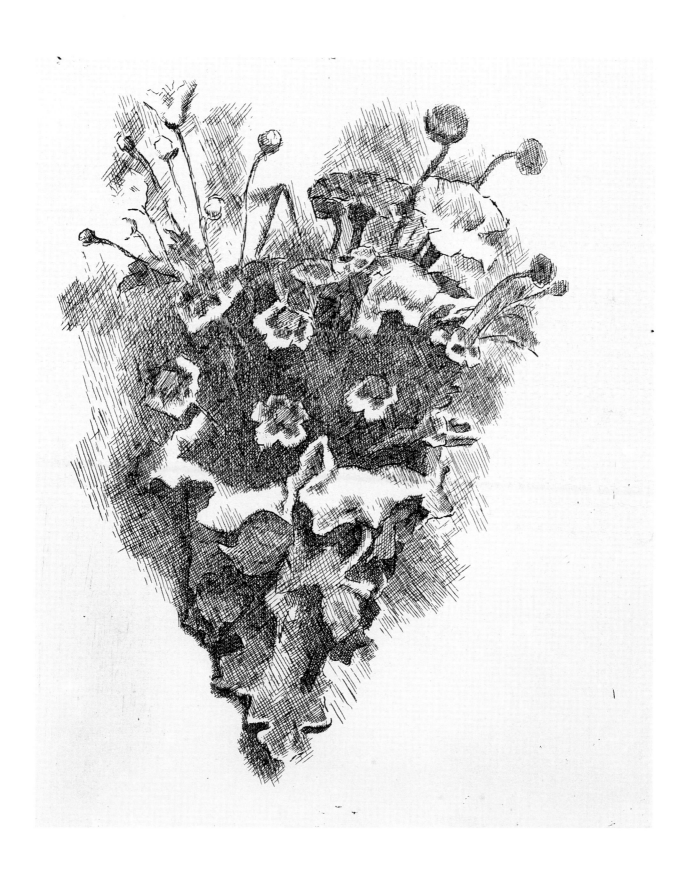

117. *Striped vase with flowers*, 1924
engraving on zinc,
23.5 × 20.1 cm
the plate is the reverse of
no. 21 (Vitali), and is in Rome,
Calcografia Nazionale
not signed or dated
Bologna, Galleria Comunale
d'Arte Moderna "Giorgio
Morandi"

118. *Landscape
(Chiesanuova)*, 1924
engraving on copper,
15.8 × 15.5 cm
the plate has on the back an
head not graved by Morandi,
and is in Rome, Calcografia
Nazionale; the composition
is the counterpart of painting
no. 110 (Vitali)
not signed or dated
Bologna, Galleria Comunale
d'Arte Moderna "Giorgio
Morandi"

119. *The garden in Via Fondazza*, 1924
engraving on zinc,
10.9 × 15.1 cm
the plate has on the back
a stroked out landscape,
and is in Rome, Calcografia
Nazionale; the composition
is the counterpart of painting
no. 102 (Vitali)
not signed or dated
Bologna, Galleria Comunale
d'Arte Moderna "Giorgio
Morandi"

120. *The road*, 1927
engraving on zinc,
19.5 × 26.1 cm
the plate is in Rome,
Calcografia Nazionale
signed and dated lower
right: Morandi 1927
Bologna, private collection

121. *Poggio landscape*, 1927
engraving on copper,
23.4 × 29 cm
the plate has on the back a
figure not graved by Morandi,
and is in Rome, Calcografia
Nazionale
not signed or dated
Bologna, Galleria Comunale
d'Arte Moderna "Giorgio
Morandi"

162

122. *Poggio in the morning,*
1928
engraving on zinc,
24.8 × 24.8 cm
the plate is in Rome,
Calcografia Nazionale
signed and dated lower left:
Morandi / 1928
Modena, private collection

123. *Large still life with
a lamp on the right,* 1928
engraving on copper,
25.2 × 34.9 cm
the plate, stroked out,
is in Milan, owned by
Lamberto Vitali
not signed or dated
Bologna, private collection

124. *Still life with fruit
bowl, long bottle and twisted
bottle*, 1928
engraving on zinc,
23.4 × 18.2 cm
the plate is in Rome,
Calcografia Nazionale; the
composition is the counterpart
of painting no. 28 (Vitali)
signed and dated lower
centre. 1917. Morandi
Bologna, private collection

125. *Still life*, 1930
engraving on copper, left side
23 cm, right side 22.7 × 29 cm
the plate is in Rome,
Calcografia Nazionale; the
composition is the counterpart
of painting no. 152 (Vitali)
signed and dated lower
centre: Morandi 1930
Medolla, E. Ferri collection

11/30

Morandi 1930

126. *Still life with six objects*, 1930
engraving on copper,
19.8 × 23.7 cm
the plate, stroked out, is in
Bologna, owned by Morandi
sisters signed and dated lower
centre (in reverse): Morandi
1930
Bologna, private collection

127. *Grizzana landscape*,
1932
engraving on copper,
29.9 × 23.9 cm
the plate is in Rome,
Calcografia Nazionale
not signed or dated
Medolla, E. Ferri collection

128. *Large dark still life,*
1934
engraving on copper,
29.6 × 38.4 cm
the plate, which is the
counter part of painting no. 99
(Vitali), is in Rome,
Calcografia Nazionale
not signed or dated
Bologna, Galleria Comunale
d'Arte Moderna "Giorgio
Morandi"

129. *Roffeno landscape*, 1936
engraving on copper,
15.8 × 19.9 cm
the plate is in Rome,
Calcografia Nazionale
not signed or dated
Bologna, private collection

130. *Still life with seven objects in a roundel*, 1945
engraving on copper
26.7 × 29.9 cm
the plate is in Rome,
Calcografia Nazionale; the
composition is the counterpart
of painting no. 425 (Vitali)
signed and dated lower
centre: Morandi 1945
Bologna, Galleria Comunale
d'Arte Moderna "Giorgio
Morandi"

131. *Large circular still life with a bottle and three objects*, 1946
engraving on copper,
25.8 × 32.5 cm
the plate, which has on the back a first version of *White road*, is in Rome, Calcografia Nazionale; the composition is the counterpart of painting no. 515 (Vitali)
signed and dated lower left: Morandi 1946
Bologna, Galleria Comunale d'Arte Moderna "Giorgio Morandi"

132. *Still life with four objects*, 1947
engraving on copper,
17.1 × 12.8 cm
the plate, once owned by
Cesare Brandi, is in Bologna,
owned by Morandi's sisters
signed lower centre: Morandi
Medolla, E. Ferri collection

133. *Still life with four objects and three bottles,* 1956
engraving on copper,
20.3 × 19.9 cm
the plate, stroked out, which
has on the back part of
no. 129 (Vitali), is in Rome,
Calcografia Nazionale; the
composition is the counterpart
of painting no. 989 (Vitali)
signed lower right: Morandi
Bologna, private collection

58/100   Morandi 1956

References

Edited by Marilena Pasquali

Giorgio Morandi was born in Bologna on the 20th July 1890, son of Andrea and Maria Maccaferri.

He is the first of five sons and daughters: apart from his brother Giuseppe who died when he was eleven, he had three younger sisters who, with their mother, were to help him all his life: Anna, Dina and Maria Teresa.

The boy showed an artistic talent whilst still young, as was seen for the first time at the international conference "Morandi and his time" held at the Galleria Comunale d'Arte Moderna of Bologna on the 16th and 17th of November 1984: amongst these were a small painting of *Flowers* and two terracotta figures made by Morandi whilst only thirteen and representing St. Joseph and the Virgin, made for the family nativity scene and still kept by the artist's sisters.

In 1907 the young man enroled in the Accademia di Belle Arti, attending the foundation course from 1908 to 1910, and the specialist Figure course from 1910 to 1913. Amongst his colleagues were Osvaldo Licini and Severo Pozzati, friends of Morandi from 1909-1910.

His studies up to 1911 were considered excellent, but the next two years were marked by disagreements with his professors, this was due to Morandi having developed his own, autonomous ideas as is seen in the Vitali *Landscape* of 1911, of which Cesare Brandi talked of the "vast, limitless sky of solitude", and in the *Portrait of the sister* of 1912, in which Giuseppe Raimondi saw similarities with certain severe traits which precluded the "gothic" period of André Derain.

Of importance to his formation were the artistic inspiration he sought from Cézanne, whose work he first saw in black and white in Vittorio Pica's *The French Impressionists*, published in Bergamo in 1908; from Henri Rousseau – to whom Ardengo Soffici dedicated an illustrated article in *La Voce* issue no. 40, of September 1910; from Picasso, to whom the same *La Voce* dedicated a study in November 1912, publishing a drawing with three female nudes from Soffici's collection, and

from André Derain, with whom Morandi had no direct contact, apart from through his friend Licini who lived in Paris from 1915.

Paralleled to this is the interest which Morandi showed for the great Italian artistic tradition: In 1910 he went to Florence to study the masterworks of Giotto, Masaccio and Paolo Uccello, in the churches and in the Uffizi. In 1912 produced an engraving *The Bridge over the River Savena*, in which Vitali stressed Cézanne's influence.

In the summer of 1913, the Morandi family went for the first time to Grizzana, it was during this holiday that the young Morandi produced his first *Landscapes*.

From 1913-1914 Morandi was drawn to Futurism, due to his contacts with Osvaldo Licini and with Giacomo Vespignani. Through them, Morandi met first Balilla Pratella and then Marinetti, Boccioni and Russolo. He was seen attending the futurist soirées at Modena (Spring 1913), at Florence (12th December 1913) and at Bologna (19th January 1914), and at the *Esposizione di Pittura Libera Futurista* organised in Florence by *Lacerba* from November 1913 to January 1914.

This year is widely recognised as a "key" year for Morandi who begins to exhibit: the 21st and 22nd of March was the date of the now famous *Exhibition of Five*, with Morandi, Osvaldo Licini, Mario Bacchelli, Giacomo Vespignani and Severo Pozzati, held at the Baglioni Hotel in Bologna. The event was much talked about because it was considered a "successionist" exhibition, meaning that it was as new and different as it could be in that era of turbulent cultural exchanges. Morandi presented 13 canvases and 4 pencil drawings: amongst the paintings there were the *Portrait of the Sister* of 1912, four Landscapes of 1913 and several still lifes of glass objects, described by Ascanio Forti in *Il Resto del Carlino* of the 22nd March as "interpenetrations of glass objects in half-shadow".

One of these Still Lifes and a drawing were a few days later included in the *Prima Esposizione Libera Futurista* which

opened on the 13th April at the Sprovieri Gallery of Rome. It is worth noting, however, that Morandi is invited to the *Second Roman Successionist exhibition*, where he showed a *Landscape with Snow* of 1913, whilst the Futurist group is excluded. Here, Morandi could see an entire wall of paintings by Matisse, and another of Cézanne's watercolours. Although Morandi was interested in the Futurist's activities he was independent from Marinetti's movement, and closer to the experiments of the Cubists north of the Alps, based upon Cézanne's work, as the Still Lifes of 1914 and 1915 testify.

He began to teach drawing in primary schools, this employment he kept until 1929. In 1915 he was called to arms and sent to the Second Regiment of Grenadiers at Parma: after a month and a half he became seriously ill and was put into the local military hospital, then he was sent home.

Even if this was a period of profound meditation there remain only very few works, because as Lamberto Vitali recalls – "many he destroyed". After the *Bathers*, the *Landscapes* and the *Still Lifes* of 1915-1916, during the winter of 1917 he became ill again. Of this year there remains with certainty only the *Flowers* of a private Milanese collection, and a relaxed summer *Landscape*.

A dozen of his works of 1918-1919 belong to the greatest period of Metaphysical painting; these reveal Morandi as playing a central and determined role in the movement. In 1919 de Chirico stressed in his autobiography, from the archives of Edita Broglio, that "along with Carlo Carrà, Ardengo Soffici and Giorgio Morandi, de Chirico always tended towards maintaining the sense of tradition, which had been so abused in Italy by the pseudo-academic official art and the clumsy brushwork of the successionists" (from Giorgio de Chirico, "The Mechanism of Thought" (now in *Criticism, Controversy, Autobiography 1911-1943*, Einaudi, Torino 1985, pp.74-76).

The first article dedicated to Morandi appeared on the 18th March 1918; written by Riccar-

The Morandi family in 1902. From left: Giorgio; his father Andrea with his sister Dina in his arms; his brother Giuseppe who died aged eleven; his mother Maria Maccaferri, and his sister Anna. Maria Teresa, the youngest sister, was to be born in 1906.

The Bridge over River Savena in Bologna, *1912 engraving on zinc, 16,4 × 22.1 cm*
The first engraving with this technique by the young artist.

Ink sketch from the letter of Giorgio Morandi
to his friend Giuseppe Raimondi, 23rd September
1919.
He wrote "This is the Still Life by which I took the
photograph. When I returned to Bologna I took
certain aspects of it, and now you will surely like
it". Morandi is referring to the Still Life, 1918
in a Milanese private collection (Vitali, no. 40).

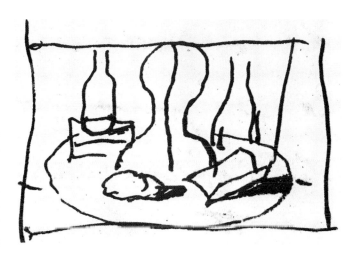

do Bacchelli, it appeared on the Roman newspaper *Il Tempo*. This interest in the young painter was continued by the Bolognese writer Giuseppe Raimondi, who completed part of the article in *La Raccolta* of the 15th April, illustrating the text with the etching *Still Life* of 1915. Through his friend Raimondi, Morandi met Carlo Carrà and Giorgio de Chirico in 1919, as well as the literary figures of *La Ronda*. At the end of 1918 he had already met Mario Broglio, who had launched the publication *Valori Plastici* on the 15th November. Broglio offered Morandi a contract for his works, stipulated on the 26th December 1919, and which, with successive reconfirmations, would be valid until 1924.

Whilst the paintings of the Bolognese artist were becoming more sculptural, reflecting the ideals of the group based around the Roman magazine (one must only refer to the seminal *Still Life with Jar* of 1920), Mario Broglio kept up his work and organised first in Berlin and in other German cities in 1921, and then at the *Fiorentina Primaverile* of 1922, group exhibitions with Morandi as the central figure. In the Florence exhibitions, his work was introduced in the catalogue by a brilliant text of di Chirico, from which comes the famous phrase: "he participated fully in the great lyricism created by the last profound European art: Metaphysics of the most common objects". From 1922-25 are a series of luminous landscapes which, wrote Vitali, "would not be comprehensible without Corot's example, and not only for the rigorous tonality".

Morandi was not excluded from the salient cultural exchanges: he was present at the two exhibitions of the Italian 20th century at the Permanente in Milan of 1926 and 1929, and even if he did not play an active role in the group of Margherita Sarfatti, he sent his works to various events. These included the exhibition at the Galerie Bonaparte in Paris (December 1929) in Basle (January-February 1930), Berne (March-May) and in Buenos Ayres and other Brazilian cities in 1930.

The artist had close links even with the intellectuals grouped around the magazine *Il Selvaggio*, established and edited by Mino Maccari from 1924: with them he participated in the "1st International Exhibition of Modern Engravings", held in Florence in 1927. Maccari wrote a long article on Morandi in *Il Resto del Carlino* on the 8th June 1927, stressing the *Italianate* quality and the "genuineness" of Morandi's art, just as Leo Longanesi was to do the following year in *L'Italiano*, defining Morandi as "the best example of 'Strapaese'". Four years later a complete edition of *L'Italiano*, dated 10th March 1932, was entirely dedicated to Morandi, with an article written by Ardengo Soffici.

The artist was invited to the Venice Biennale of 1928, where he showed four aquatints and a folder of engravings in the black and white hall; in 1930 he exhibited two aquatints and four paintings; in 1934 he again was present in Venice with two etching *Still Lifes*.

Morandi frequently exhibited abroad: apart from the already mentioned exhibitions of Italian 20th century art, in 1929 he was invited to the Carnegie Prize at Pittsburgh (to which he returned the next year, and again in 1933, in 1936 and three other times after the second world war); in 1931 he sent a *Still Life* to the Italian Week in Athens; in 1933 another *Still Life* is exhibited at the Kunstlerhaus of Vienna for the event *Moderne Italienische Kunst*; in 1934 his works were part of the exhibition of Italian art organised by the Biennale of Venice in the United States; in 1935 two recent *Still Lifes* were exhibited at the large exhibition of Italian contemporary art organised at the Jeu de Paume Museum of Paris; in 1937 his paintings were in the Universal Exhibition of Paris; in the same year the Biennale of Venice arranged a large exhibition in Berlin to which Morandi was invited. This was also the case in the exhibition in the Kunsthalle of Berne, where Morandi showed four works (1938).

It is worth noting that until 1956 Morandi never went abroad, however he was always alert for important international events:

in 1939 he sent a group of particularly important works to the *Golden Gate Exhibition* which opened in San Francisco; and the following year saw him at the exhibition of Italian art held in Zurich.

Equally important to understand the esteem in which he was held in intellectual and official circles was the progress of his teaching career: after having taught drawing for many years in state schools, from February 1930 he was "unanimously" chosen for the position of Engraver, "in acknowledgement of his fame" at the Academy of Fine Arts in Bologna, where he taught until the 1st October 1956 when he asked specifically to retire after more than twenty six years of teaching.

More important than his presence at the Venetian Biennals was his participation in 1931 and 1935 on the choosing committee at the Roman Quadriennali; at these he also exhibited few but significant works (*Still Life with Fruit Bowl* of 1931). But the real acknowledgement of his talent came at the third Roman event in 1939: an entire hall was dedicated to Morandi, where he exhibited 42 oils, 2 drawings and 12 engravings, and he was awarded the second prize for painting, behind the younger Bruno Saetti.

There was great controversy surrounding both the attribution of the first prize, and the intrinsic value of the Morandi hall. On his side the Bolognese artist could count important scholars such as Cesare Brandi, Giuseppe Marchiori and the young Duilio Morosini who stressed the poetic nature on the pages of *Corrente*. Apart from various articles on the same Milanese magazine, Arnaldo Beccaria published in this year the first, small monograph on Morandi.

Shrouded in these controversies but with the comforting and authoritative support of Longhi, Brandi, Vitali, Ragghianti and Gnudi amongst others, Morandi continued to work in his studio at via Fondazza, and during the summers at Grizzana. In June 1943 the artist was evacuated and went to this town in the Appennines, where he was to

Portrait of his sister, *1920*
Pencil on paper
Rome, private collection.

Harlequin *(1919-1920)*
Watercolour on paper
Bologna, private collection.
Morandi completed this watercolour for Giuseppe
Ramondi's book, Dialogo, *published in 1926.*

evolve the *Landscapes* and *Still Lifes* of 1942-1943.

In the Spring of 1945 Roberto Longhi organised a one-man show at the Galleria del Fiore in Florence of his distant friend, from whom he had still no news, and was only to see again several months later.

Whilst the controversy surrounding "engagement" in art started again, it is not by chance that at the renewed Biennale of 1948, where the Fronte Nuovo delle Arti took off, the first prize for painting was awarded to Morandi who exhibited eleven canvases of the years 1916-1920, in the halls dedicated to "Three Italian Painters from 1910-1920", featuring also the work of Carrà and de Chirico, and with an introductory presentation by Francesco Arcangeli. In the same year, to stress the importance of the graphic works of the artist, Carlo Alberto Petrucci set up at the Calcografia Nazionale in Rome an anthological exhibition of engravings, which renewed the interest of the public and the press in the great "isolated" Bolognese as he was now considered.

Morandi enjoyed the favour of the most exclusive international circles, and several of his works were included in prestigious exhibitions in northern Europe and in the United States.

In 1957 the first prize for painting was awarded to him at the fourth Biennale of São Paulo in Brazil (he was awarded the first prize for engraving in 1953 at this same event), as if to establish the esteem in which he held amongst critics. It is sufficient to list the exhibitions abroad to realise how highly his work was considered, these included one-man shows at the Palais des Beaux-Arts of Brussels in 1949 (engravings), at the Gemeentemuseum of Hague and at the New Burlington Galleries of London in 1954, at the Kunstmuseum of Winterthur of 1956, at the World House Gallery of New York in 1957 and 1960, at Siegen in 1962 where he was awarded the Rubens Prize and at the Badische Kunstverein of Karlsruhe in 1964.

After about a year's illness, Giorgio Morandi died in Bologna on the 18th of June 1964. In the same year there was held the first comprehensive critical and historical review of his work, by several well known scholars: the fundamental monograph by Lamberto Vitali, published by Milione of Milan, the gallery which for a decade followed the work of the master; and the long, passionate study of Francesco Arcangeli, edited by the same Milanese gallery.

Two years later, in October 1966, the great exhibition set up in the Archiginnasio of Bologna by Roberto Longhi, Gian Alberto dell'Acqua and Lamberto Vitali, was linked to the summer Biennale in Venice, where an important hall was dedicated to Morandi, representing the principle occasion to survey his inexhaustible career with works from 1911 to 1963 (108 oil paintings, 14 watercolours, 33 drawings and 131 engravings).

However, the general opinion of the last years of the master along with the following years of the sixties and seventies, was of an isolated, provincial figure, too modest, coherent and traditional compared with the turbulent controversies which lacerated the international artistic milieu. The work of Morandi, which had become the symbol of the highest formal and poetic nature, and of the moralistic stance against the excesses of the avant-garde, was for many years acknowledged but not discussed. One must wait for the great exhibitions and studies of the last ten years, in the subdued cultural climate which is again fascinated by painting, to witness his definitive recognition in the pantheon of 20th century masters.

A great contribution to research and spreading Morandi's popularity was given by the exhibition organised by the National Gallery of Modern Art of Rome in May 1973; by the City Council of Bologna in the same year; at the Ermitage Museum in Leningrad and at the Pushkin Museum of Moscow curated by Lamberto Vitali in collaboration with Franco Solmi; by the new Civic Gallery of Modern Art in Bologna, which was inaugurated in 1975 with an anthology of Morandi's work, again with the active and learned help of Vitali. In 1978 a new exhibition survey-ing his career from 1912 to 1964 opened in the Diamanti Palace in Ferrara, with the presentation by Franco Solmi. In 1981 a large exhibition took place in Munich, arranged by Franz A. Morat. In December of the same year was set up in San Francisco the exhibition organised by the Des Moines Art Center, later held in New York and at the De Moines Gallery in Iowa. In Italy the Milanese collections of the Pinacoteca di Brera – which houses the donations of Jesi and Jucker – and the Comune are reorganised. The De Fornariis Foundation allowed the civic authorities of Turin to acquire a corpus of 22 of Morandi's works including drawings, watercolours and oils from Pietro Rossini's collection.

In Bologna the study of Morandi and his diffusion of his work was helped by the opening of the "Giorgio Morandi" Centre of Studies. This centre co-ordinated by Marilena Pasquali with the collaboration of Morandi's sisters and major foreign and Italian Institutes, gathers got together and studies documents, reports and material relevant to the life and work of the Bolognese Master.

On the 11th December 1984 was opened in the Sala de Exposicciónes of the Caja de Pensiones of Madrid a major retrospective which presented to an international public the work of Morandi. This exhibition, arranged in collaboration with the Gallery of Modern Art in Bologna, was later held in Barcelona and at the Musée Cantini of Marseille. In November 1984 the "International Conference of Giorgio Morandi" was held at the Civic Gallery of Modern Art in Bologna, presenting the critical-historical themes to the major exhibition of the previous year, *Morandi and his times*. This examined the position of the artist in the culture of the 20th century, bringing to light the artistic and philosophical rapports which he had with the major exponents of this culture, first and foremost artists and literary figures. 116 works of Morandi were exhibited, in direct confrontation with those of other European and Italian masters, from Cézanne to Picasso, Derain to Braque, Rousseau to Modigliani and from de Chirico, Carrà and de Pisis.

In 1985 the Bolognese museum acquired the twenty two paintings from the Ingrao collection of Rome – a further sign of the Bolognese Civic Authority's profound interest for the image and work of Morandi – and organised with the Pinacoteca di Brera an exhibition dedicated to his work on paper (100 exhibits of watercolours, drawings and engravings).

Whilst various events dedicated to Morandi continued uninterrupted (notably the retrospective of the Hôtel de la Ville in Paris in the summer of 1987), his art was becoming increasingly more popular amongst critics and public alike; the Gallery of Modern Art of Bologna acquired other works, to make it the largest collection of Morandi in a public museum – totalling 85 works (42 paintings, 32 engravings and 11 drawings). It was to furthermore open a specific section reserved for the Morandi collection, and it also took on Morandi's name.

To present the *Year of Morandi* – commemorating his centenary – in 1990, the Bolognese museum is promoting a retrospective exhibition which will be shown between 1988 and 1990 in several prestigious European and Japanese museums, beginning with the Sara Hildénin taidemuseo of Tampere in Finland.

Bibliography

Works of a general nature have not been included in this bibliography, apart from those which give particular attention to Morandi. With regard to the exhibition catalogues, all the one man shows have been mentioned, and the important group exhibitions: this applies also to the articles published in periodicals and in newspapers. Apart from monographical volumes, a single chronological list has been drawn up. To render this section more homogeneous, the wording has been set out in the same manner throughout. (M.P.)

Monographies

Arnaldo Beccaria, *Giorgio Morandi*, Milano, Hoepli, 1939.
Cesare Brandi, *Morandi*, Firenze, Le Monnier, 1942; 2nd edition revised and enlarged, Firenze 1952; reprint in *Scritti sull'arte contemporanea*, Torino 1976.
Giovanni Scheiwiller, *Giorgio Morandi*, Torino, Chiantore, n.d. (1943).
Giuseppe Marchiori, *Giorgio Morandi*, Genova, Editrice Ligure Arte e Lettere, 1945.
Cesare Gnudi, *Morandi*, Firenze, Edizioni U, 1946.
Mario Ramous, *Giorgio Morandi - I disegni*, Bologna, Cappelli, 1949.
Francesco Arcangeli, *12 opere di Giorgio Morandi*, Milano, Edizioni del Milione, 1950.
Annamaria Nigro, *Giorgio Morandi incisore*, degree thesis, rapporteur Rodolfo Pallucchini, Università degli Studi di Bologna, academic year 1951-52.
Pier Maria Bardi, *16 dipinti di Giorgio Morandi*, Milano, Edizioni del Milione, 1957.
Lamberto Vitali, *Giorgio Morandi - Opera grafica*, Torino, Einaudi, 1957; 3rd edition revised and enlarged, Torino, Einaudi, 1964.
Cesare Brandi, *Ritratti di Morandi*, Milano, All'Insegna del Pesce d'Oro, 1960.
Lamberto Vitali, *Giorgio Morandi*, Ivrea, Olivetti, 1961.
Lamberto Vitali, *Giorgio Morandi pittore*, Milano, Edizioni del Milione 1964; 2nd edition, Milano 1965; 3rd edition enlarged, Milano 1970.
Marco Valsecchi, *Morandi*, Milano, Garzanti, 1964.

Francesco Arcangeli, *Giorgio Morandi*, Milano, Edizioni del Milione, 1964; 2nd edition, Torino, Einaudi, 1981.
Alberto Martini, *Giorgio Morandi*, in *I Maestri del Colore*, Milano, Fabbri, 1964.
Jiri Siblik, *Giorgio Morandi*, Praha 1965.
Jean Leymarie, *Acquarelli di Morandi*, Bologna, Edizioni de' Foscherari, 1968.
Giuseppe Marchiori, *Morandi - Le incisioni*, Roma, Ronzon, 1969.
Cesare Brandi, *Morandi lungo il cammino*, Milano, Rizzoli, 1970.
Giuseppe Raimondi, *Anni con Giorgio Morandi*, Milano, Mondadori, 1970.
Valerio Zurlini, *Cinquanta acquarelli di Morandi*, Torino, I.L.T.E., 1973.
Julianna P. Szucs, *Giorgio Morandi*, Budapest, Corvina Kiadò, 1974.
Valerio Zurlini, *Il tempo di Morandi*, Reggio Emilia, Prandi, 1975.
Neri Pozza, *Morandi... I disegni...*, Roma, Franca May, 1976.
Lamberto Vitali, *Morandi - Catalogo Generale*, 2 vols., Milano, Electa, 1977; 2nd edition enlarged, Milano 1983.
Guido Giuffré, *Giorgio Morandi*, in *I Maestri del Novecento*, Firenze, Sansoni, 1977.
Franco Solmi, *Morandi: storia e leggenda*, Bologna, Grafis, 1978.
Walter Hertzsch, *Giorgio Morandi*, Leipzig, E.A. Seeman, 1979.
L. Martì, *I geni della pittura: Giorgio Morandi*, Roma, Armando Curcio, 1979.
Marco Valsecchi, Giorgio Ruggeri, *Morandi - Disegni*, vol. I (edited by Efrem Tavoni), Sasso Marconi, La Casa dell'Arte, 1981.
Franco Basile, *Il laboratorio della solitudine*, Sasso Marconi, La Casa dell'Arte, 1982.
Jean Jouvet, Wieland Schmied, *Giorgio Morandi - Ölbider, Aquarelle, Zeichnungen, Radierungen*, Zürich, Diogenes, 1982.
Luigi Magnani, *Il mio Morandi*, Torino, Einaudi, 1982.
Giorgio Soavi, *La polvere di Morandi*, Milano, Officine Grafiche Elli & Pagani, 1982.
Carlo Ludovico Ragghianti, *Bologna cruciale 1914 e saggi su Morandi, Gorni, Saetti*, Bologna, Calderini, 1982; the essay

Bologna cruciale 1914 is taken from *Critica d'Arte*, no.s 106-107, Firenze 1969.
Giulio Carlo Argan, Franco Basile, *Morandi - Disegni*, vol. II (edited by Efrem Tavoni), Sasso Marconi, La Casa dell'Arte, 1984.
Cesare Brandi, *Giorgio Morandi - Seine Werke im Morat-Institut für Kunst und Kunstwissenschaft*, Freiburg, Morat-Institut, 1984.
Giuliano Briganti, Ester Coen, *I paesaggi di Morandi*, Torino, Umberto Allemandi, 1984.
Michele Prisco, *Morandi inedito*, in *Prova d'Autore*, monographical issue, I, no. 1, Roma, Antonio Rotundo, 1984.
Franco Basile, *Morandi incisore*, Bologna, La Loggia Edizioni, 1985.
Jean-Michel Folon, *Fiori di Giorgio Morandi* (with a poem by Giovanni Testori), Genève, Alice, Milano, Biti, 1985.
Franco Solmi, *Morandi alla Galleria Comunale d'Arte Moderna di Bologna* (scientific contribution by Marilena Pasquali), Bologna, Grafis, 1985.

Articles, essays and catalogues

1908
"I premiati all'Accademia di Belle Arti", in *L'Avvenire d'Italia*, Bologna, 30 June.

1914
Catalogue of the *II Esposizione internazionale d'arte della Secessione*, Roma, Palazzo delle Esposizioni, March-April.
"Un'esposizione di pittura e scultura - I 'secessionisti' del Baglioni", in *Il Resto del Carlino*, Bologna, 20 March.
"Due feste d'arte", in *Il Resto del Carlino*, Bologna, 21 March.
Ask. (Ascanio Forti), "La mostra dei 'secessionisti' al Baglioni", in *Il Resto del Carlino*, Bologna, 22 March.
Mazz. (Pietro Mazzuccato), "La mostra di pittura e scultura al Baglioni - Artisti d'avanguardia", in *Giornale del Mattino*, Bologna, 22 March.
Sebastiano Sani, "Pittori d'avanguardia", in *L'Avvenire d'Italia*, Bologna, 23 March.
"Caffè", in *Lacerba*, II, no. 11, Firenze, 1° June.

1917
Catalogue of the *Esposizione*

d'arte interregionale, Lugo, Scuole Comunali, September-November.
g.m., "Esposizione interregionale di arte a Lugo", in *Giornale del Mattino*, Bologna, 23 September.
b.p., "Cronaca cittadina - La nostra mostra d'arte", in *La Vedetta*, Lugo, 30 September.

1918
Riccardo Bacchelli, "Giorgio Morandi", in *Il Tempo*, Roma, 29 March.
"Terrazza", in *La Raccolta*, I, no. 2, Bologna, 15 April.
Raffaello Franchi, "Giorgio Morandi", in *La Raccolta*, I, no.s 9-10, Bologna, 15 November - 15 December.

1919
Raffaello Franchi, "Avvertimento critico", in *Valori Plastici*, I, no.s 4-5, Roma, April-May.

1921
Catalogue of the exhibition *Das Junge Italien*, Hannover, Kestner-Gesellschaft, May-June.

1922
Giorgio de Chirico, introduction to the catalogue of the exhibition *La Fiorentina primaverile*, Firenze, Palazzo delle Esposizioni, April-July.

1923
Giuseppe Raimondi, "Giorgio Morandi", in *Il Nuovo Paese*, March.

1925
Carlo Carrà, "Giorgio Morandi", in *L'Ambrosiano*, Milano, 25 June.

1926
Catalogue of the *I Mostra del Novecento italiano*, Milano, Palazzo della Permanente, February-March.
G.E. Mottini, "Novecento", in *Corriere Padano*, Ferrara, 9 May.

1927
Catalogue of the *II Esposizione internazionale dell'incisione moderna*, Firenze, April.
Achille Lega, "Giorgio Morandi", in *Il Selvaggio*, Firenze, 30 July.

1928
"Artisti emiliani e romagnoli alla Biennale di Venezia", in *Il Resto del Carlino*, Bologna, 13 May.
Corrado Pavolini, "Tosi, Carrà,

Morandi", in *Tevere*, Roma, 31 May.
Mino Maccari, "Giorgio Morandi", in *Il Resto del Carlino*, Bologna, 8 June.
Catalogue of the *XVI Esposizione Biennale Internazionale d'Arte della Città di Venezia*, Venezia, Giardini di Castello, Summe.
Leo Longanesi, "Morandi", in *L'Italiano*, III, no.s 16-17, Bologna, 31 December.

1929
Catalogue of the *II Mostra del Novecento italiano*, Milano, Palazzo della Permanente, March-April.
Carlo Carrà, "Alla mostra del Novecento", in *L'Ambrosiano*, Milano, 12 March.
Sandro Volta, "Il viaggiatore di pittura: Morandi", in *L'Italia Letteraria*, Roma, 29 September.
Mario Tinti, "La prima mostra d'arte del Sindacato emiliano-romagnolo", in *Il Resto del Carlino*, Bologna, 14 November.
"Artisti emiliani", in *Corriere Padano*, Ferrara, 16 November.
Cipriano E. Oppo, "Una mostra interessante", in *La Tribuna*, Roma, 16 November.
Nino Corrado Corazza, "La mostra degli artisti sindacati", in *L'Avvenire d'Italia*, Bologna, 27 November.
Nino Bertocchi, "La prima mostra del Sindacato emiliano-romagnolo", in *L'Italia Letteraria*, Roma, 1° December.
"La prima mostra a Bologna del Sindacato artisti emiliani-romagnoli", in *Arte Italica*, Roma, 1° December.
Catalogue of the *Twenty-eighth Annual Exhibition*, Pittsburgh, Carnegie Institute.

1930
Catalogue of the exhibition *Moderne Italiener*, Basel, Kunsthalle, January-February.
François Fosca, "Une exposition d'art italien moderne", in *L'Amour de l'Art*, Paris, 2 February.
Alberto Sartoris, text in the catalogue of the exhibition *Künstler des neuen Italien*, Bern, Kunsthalle, March-May.
"Artisti bolognesi a Venezia", in *L'Arca*, Milano, May-June.
Luigi Bartolini, "Morandi e altri giovani pittori alla XVII Biennale d'Arte a Venezia", in *Corriere Adriatico*, Ancona, 6 May

and in *Brennero*, Trento, 8 May.
Catalogue of the *XVII Esposizione Biennale Internazionale d'Arte di Venezia*, Venezia, Giardini di Castello, Summer.
Raffaello Franchi, "La XVII Biennale di Venezia: arcipelago, Guidi e Morandi...", in *Corriere Padano*, Ferrara, 26 July.
Lamberto Vitali, "L'incisione italiana del Novecento - I selvaggi: Giorgio Morandi", in *Domus*, Milano, December.
Gino Severini, "Da Parigi: qualche esposizione significativa", in *L'Ambrosiano*, Milano, 17 December.
Catalogue of the *Twenty-ninth Annual Exhibition*, Pittsburgh, Carnegie Institute.
Ugo Nebbia, *XVII Esposizione Internazionale d'Arte a Venezia* (with an introduction by Antonio Maraini), Milano.
Margherita Sarfatti, Catalogue of the *Mostra del Novecento italiano*, Buenos Aires (itinerant exhibition).
Margherita Sarfatti, *Storia della pittura moderna*, Roma, Paolo Cremonese.
Giovanni Scheiwiller, *Art italien moderne*, Paris.

1931
Guglielmo Usellini, "La I Quadriennale romana", in *L'Arca*, Milano, January-February.
Catalogue of the *I Quadriennale nazionale d'arte*, Roma, Palazzo delle Esposizioni, January-June.
Marziano Bernardi, "La Quadriennale d'arte nazionale - Le nuove vie della pittura italiana", in *La Stampa*, Torino, 6 January.
C. (Vincenzo Costantini), "La Quadriennale romana", in *Le Arti Plastiche*, Milano, 1° February.
Carlo Carrà, "La Quadriennale d'arte italiana: ultimo rapporto", in *L'Ambrosiano*, Milano, 4 February.
Nino Bertocchi, "Alla I Quadriennale - V: gli emiliani", in *L'Italia Letteraria*, Roma, 15 February.
Italo Cinti, "La cicuta a Carrà", in *Perseo*, Varese, 1° August.
Virgilio Guzzi, *Pittura italiana contemporanea - Origini e aspetti*, Milano.

1932
Luigi Bartolini, "Libelli - Visita a Morandi", in *L'Ambrosiano*, Milano, 28 January, and *Corrie-*

re Adriatico, Ancona, 9 February.
Ardengo Soffici, "Morandi", in *L'Italiano*, special issue, Bologna, March.
Catalogue of the exhibition *Artistes italiens modernes*, Paris, Galerie Georges Bernheim, March.
Antonio Aniante, "Nouvelles du Parnasse", in *La Liberté*, Paris, 5 April.
Cipriano E. Oppo, "La pittura di Morandi", in *L'Italia Letteraria*, Roma, 10 April.
Ardengo Soffici, "Morandi", in *Il Resto del Carlino*, Bologna, 16 April.
Benvenuto Disertori, *L'incisione italiana*, Firenze.

1933
Carlo Alberto Petrucci, *Dnesny stav italskei grafiky*, Praha.

1934
Catalogue of the *XIX Esposizione Biennale Internazionale d'Arte di Venezia*, Venezia, Giardini di Castello, Summer.
Gino Visentini, "Appunti per Morandi", in *Emporium*, Bergamo, October.
Vincenzo Costantini, "La peinture italienne après le futurisme", in *L'Amour de l'Art*, Paris, November.
Giovanni Scheiwiller, text in the catalogue of *Mostra di bianco e nero italiano in Svizzera*, St. Gallen, November; Bern, December 1934 - January 1935.
Vincenzo Costantini, *Pittura italiana contemporanea dalla fine dell'Ottocento ad oggi*, Milano.
"Morandi Giorgio", in *Enciclopedia italiana*, Roma, Istituto dell'Enciclopedia Italiana, vol. XXIII.
Dario Sabatello, text in the catalogue of the *Exhibition of Contemporary Italian Painting*, London, Western Art Museum Association; United States of America (itinerant exhibition in some California museums).
Lamberto Vitali, *L'incisione italiana moderna*, Milano, Ulrico Hoepli.

1935
Roberto Longhi, "Momenti della pittura bolognese - Prolusione al corso di Storia dell'arte dell'Università di Bologna", in *L'Archiginnasio*, XXX, no.s 1-3, Bologna.
Catalogue of the *Il Quadrien-*

nale d'arte nazionale, Roma, Palazzo delle Esposizioni, February-July.
Mario Tinti, "Panorama dell'arte italiana moderna", in *Giornale di Genova*, Genova, 2 February.
Carlo Carrà, "Giorgio Morandi", in *L'Ambrosiano*, Milano, 9 February.
Alberto Spaini, "La Quadriennale a Roma - Gli artisti emiliani", in *Il Resto del Carlino*, Bologna, 9 February.
Libero De Libero, "Stato dell'arte italiana contemporanea alla II Quadriennale", in *Broletto*, Como, March.
Paola Della Pergola, "Artisti bolognesi alla II Quadriennale", in *Il Comune di Bologna*, 3, Bologna, March.
Virgilio Guzzi, "Pittura alla II Quadriennale", in *Nuova Antologia*, Roma, 1° March.
Osvaldo Licini, "Correzioni a Carrà", in *Bollettino n. 41*, Galleria del Milione, Milano, 25 May.
Lionello Fiumi, "L'art italien du XIX et du XX siècle au Jeu de Paume", in *Dante*, Paris, June.
Nino Bertocchi, "La II Quadriennale romana", in *Il Frontespizio*, Firenze, July.
Catalogue of the *Exposition de l'art italien du XIX et du XX siècles*, Paris, Musée du Jeu de Paume, August.
Carlo Carrà, "Mostre milanesi: bianco e nero", in *L'Ambrosiano*, Milano, 9 November.
Antonio Maraini, *Wspòlczesna Sztuka Italska*, Warszawa, Styczen.
Carlo Alberto Petrucci, catalogue of the exhibition *Grafiska Maksla Musu Dienu Italija*, Rig.

1936
Alberto Sartoris, text in the catalogue of the *Mostra di pittura moderna italiana*, Como, Villa Olmo, September-October.

1937
Italo Cinti, "Pittori alla sbarra: Giorgio Morandi", in *Perseo*, Milano, 15 April.
Luigi Bartolini, "L'amatore d'arte", in *Quadrivio*, V, no. 32, Roma, 6 June.
(Piero Bargellini), "Artisti italiani: Giorgio Morandi", in *Il Frontespizio*, Firenze, September.

1938
Giuseppe Mesirca, "Venezia -

Giorgio Morandi", in *Emporium*, Bergamo, July.
Catalogue of the *Mostra d'arte italiana*, Bern, October-November.
Alberto Della Ragione, *Pittura italiana d'oggi*, text in the catalogue of the exhibition of Della Ragione collection, Torino, Galleria La Zecca.

1939
Giuseppe Marchiori, "Giorgio Morandi", in *Domus*, Milano, February.
Cesare Brandi, "Cammino di Morandi", in *Le Arti*, I, no. 3, Roma, February-March.
Catalogue of the *III Quadriennale d'arte nazionale*, Roma, Palazzo delle Esposizioni, February-July.
Giuseppe Marchiori, "La Quadriennale di Roma - Primi ragguagli... Morandi", in *Corriere Padano*, Ferrara, 5 February.
Ugo Ojetti, "La III Quadriennale d'arte: pittori e scultori... Morandi e la fantasia", in *Corriere della Sera*, Milano, 5 February.
"Le opere di pittura alla III Quadriennale", in *Corriere del Tirreno*, Livorno, 7 February.
Luigi Bartolini, "Un pittore fra i pittori della Quadriennale", in *Quadrivio*, Roma, 12 February.
Piero Torriano, "La III Quadriennale dell'arte italiana", in *L'Illustrazione Italiana*, no. 7, Milano, 12 February.
Virgilio Guzzi, "La III Quadriennale d'arte nazionale", in *La Nuova Antologia*, Roma, 16 February.
Piero Scarpa, "Alla III Quadriennale d'arte: mostre personali di alcuni pittori", in *Il Messaggero*, Roma, 17 February.
Giuseppe Marchiori, "Alla III Quadriennale: Giorgio Morandi", in *Corriere Padano*, Ferrara, 23 February.
Raffaele Calzini, "La III Quadriennale di Roma - Nature morte e bianco e nero: il caso Morandi...", in *Il Popolo d'Italia*, Milano, 25 February.
Raffaele De Grada, "La pittura italiana alla III Quadriennale romana", in *Corrente di Vita Giovanile*, Milano, 28 February.
Carlo Savoia, "Giorgio Morandi", in *Rivista del Comune*, Bologna, March-April.
Umbro Apollonio, "Morandi", in *Il Popolo di Trieste*, Trieste, 15 March.
Giuseppe Ardinghi, "Appunti

sulla Quadriennale - Morandi-Manzù", in *Il Bargello*, Firenze, 26 March.
Nino Bartoletti, "Viaggio attraverso la Quadriennale: ancora tra i pittori", in *Quadrivio*, Roma, 7 April.
Umberto Silva, "Giorgio Morandi", in *Corriere Padano*, Ferrara, 11 April.
Cesare Brandi, "L'Italia all'Esposizione di San Francesco: Morandi e Manzù", in *Panorama*, Roma, 27 April.
Duilio Morosini, "Giorgio Morandi", in *Corrente*, Milano, 30 April.
Luigi Bartolini, "Diario romano (dedicato ai superintelligenti)", in *Quadrivio*, Roma, 7 May.
Raffaele A. Oppo, "Sul caso Morandi: una lettera di R.A. Oppo", in *Quadrivio*, Roma, 21 May.
C.B. (Carlo Belli), "I premi alla Quadriennale", in *Corriere Padano*, Ferrara, 8 June.
Libero De Libero, "Bianco e nero alla Quadriennale: Maccari, Manzù, Morandi, Bartolini, Salvadori", in *Panorama*, Roma, 12 June.
Giorgio Casini, "Le bottiglie di Morandi" [non-identified daily], Pisa, July.
Attilio Podestà, "Giorgio Morandi", in *Arte Mediterranea*, no. 5, Firenze, September-October.
Carlo Savoia, "La pittura di Giorgio Morandi", in *Il Meridiano di Roma*, Roma, 1° October.
Libero De Libero, "Due monografie su Scipione e Morandi", in *Panorama*, Roma, 12 November.
Carlo Belli, "Morandi, o del pudore", in *Corriere Padano*, Ferrara.

1940
Umberto Silva, "D'una monografia su G. Morandi", in *Corriere Padano*, Ferrara, 3 January.
Arnaldo Beccaria, "A proposito di Morandi", in *Corrente*, Milano, 15 Juanuary.
Franco Catalano, "Artisti contemporanei: Giorgio Morandi", in *Eccoci*, Cremona, 1° February.
Carlo Belli, "Corrispondenza indiretta sul caso Giorgio Morandi", in *Corriere Padano*, Ferrara, 3 February.
Arnaldo Beccaria, "Ancora a proposito di Morandi", in *Cor-*

rente, Milano, 29 February.
Giuseppe Mesirca, "Giorgio Morandi", in *Il Meridiano di Roma*, Roma, 3 March.
Luigi Bartolini, "Artisti contemporanei: Morandi incisore", in *Emporium*, Bergamo, April.
A.T., "Cronache della critica figurativa", in *La Ruota*, Roma, April.
Raffaele Carrieri, "Giorgio Morandi", in *Tempo*, Milano, 16 May.
Mario Tobino, "Accenno a Morandi", in *Corrente*, Milano, 31 May.
Silvio Catalano, "Una natura morta del 1940 di Giorgio Morandi", in *Il Milione*, no. 47, Milano, 18 November.
Vincenzo Costantini, "Giorgio Morandi", in *Il Popolo d'Italia*, Milano, 21 November.
Raffaele Carrieri, *Otto pittori contemporanei: Campigli, Carrà, Cesetti, de Chirico, Morandi, Soffici, Tomea, Tosi*, Milano.

1941
Gino Visentini, "La pazienza di Morandi", in *Primato*, Roma, 1° January.
Umberto Silva, "Giorgio Morandi", in *Corriere Padano*, Ferrara, 5 January.
Giuseppe Bottai, "Giorgio Morandi", in *Le Arti*, no. 3, Firenze, February-March.
Giuseppe Raimondi, "Cartella di disegni: Giorgio Morandi", *ibidem*.
Michelangelo Masciotta, "Cronache d'arte: omaggio a Morandi", in *Letteratura*, Firenze, 8 April.
Natale Bencini, "Arte contemporanea di Giorgio Morandi", in *Popolo di Romagna*, Forlì, 26 April.
Massimo Bontempelli, "Giorgio Morandi", in *Corriere della Sera*, Milano, 20 August.
Luigi Serra, "Umanità di Morandi", in *Architrave*, Bologna, 31 December.
Giuseppe Lipparini, *La Reale Accademia di Belle Arti di Bologna*, Firenze, Le Monnier.
Ugo Nebbia, *La pittura del Novecento*, Milano, Società Editrice Libreria, 2nd edition, Milano 1946.

1942
Giuseppe Raimondi, "Armonia di Morandi", in *Primato*, Roma, 15 May.
Mario Escobar, "Testimonianza

a Giorgio Morandi", in *Festa*, Roma, 21 June.
Alessandro Parronchi, "Pittura di Morandi", in *Posizione*, Novara, 1° August.
Cesare Mercandino, "Cammino di Morandi", in *Rivoluzione*, Firenze, 16 September.
Arnaldo Beccaria, "Chiosa a un dipinto di Giorgio Morandi", in *Almanacco Beltempo*, Roma, Edizioni la Cometa.
Cesare Brandi, "Giorgo Morandi", *ibidem*.
Giampiero Giani, *Pittori italiani contemporanei*, Milano, Edizioni della Conchiglia.
Alessandro Parronchi, "Giorgio Morandi", in *Letteratura*, no. 23, Firenze.

1943
Mario Tozzi, "Evoluzione dell'Arte Moderna Italiana", in *Termini*, no.s 77-81, Rijeka January-February.
Alberto Sartoris, "Giorgio Morandi", in *Il Popolo di Brescia*, Brescia, 10 January.
Catalogue of the *IV Quadriennale nazionale d'arte*, Roma, Palazzo delle Esposizioni, May-July.
Bruno Romani, "Galleria dei pittori: Giorgio Morandi", in *Il Lavoro*, Genova, 9 May.
S.B. (Silvio Branzì), "Appunti per Morandi", in *Il Gazzettino*, Venezia, 1° August.
Alessandro Parronchi, *Nomi della pittura italiana contemporanea*, Firenze, Arnaud.

1945
Roberto Longhi, text in the catalogue of the one-man exhibition, Firenze, Galleria Il Fiore, April-May.
Roberto Longhi, "Giorgio Morandi", in *Il Mondo*, Firenze, 21 April.
Alessandro Parronchi, "La luce dipinta", *ibidem*.
Antonello Trombadori, "Serietà e limiti di Morandi", in *Rinascita*, Roma, May-June.
Raffaele De Grada, "Le Arti - Al Fronte della gioventù - Posizione di Morandi", in *L'Illustrazione Italiana*, Milano, 12-19 August.
Cesare Brandi, *Carmine o della pittura*, Roma; 2nd edition, Firenze 1947.
Raffaele Corrieri, *Disegno contemporaneo*, Milano, Damiani.

1946
Cesare Brandi, "Morandi", in

Comunità, no. 6, Milano, October.
Francesco Arcangeli, "Novità di Morandi", in *Il Mondo*, Firenze, 5 October.
Pippi Starace, "Guttuso e Morandi", in *Arte Contemporanea*, Roma, December.
Mario Lepore, "Triste non credo, ma claustrale, il modo di vivere di Morandi", in *Sabato del Lombardo*, Milano, 28 December.
Giulio Carlo Argan, "Giorgio Morandi", in *Prosa*, III, Roma.
Toti Scialoja, "Giorgio Morandi", in *Il Mondo*, no.s 33-35, Firenze.

1947
Corrado Corazza, "Artisti raccontati", in *Cronache*, Bologna, 17 May.
Cesare Brandi, "Europeismo e autonomia di cultura nella pittura italiana", in *L'Immagine*, no. 3, Roma, July-August.
Giuseppe Raimondi, "Presentazioni: Morandi dopo la Liberazione", *ibidem*.
Giorgio Roasio, "Una visita a Morandi", in *Gazzettino Sera*, Venezia, 2 August.
Aldo Borgonzoni, "Nello studio di Giorgio Morandi", in *Il Progresso d'Italia*, Bologna, 3 August.
Lionello Venturi, *Pittura contemporanea*, Milano, Ulrico Hoepli.

1948
Leone Minassian, "Giorgio Morandi - L'onestà di un maestro", in *Gazzetta di Modena*, Modena, 24 January.
Neri Pozza, "Morandi il pittore solitario sorpreso tra le sue bottiglie", in *Il Mattino del Popolo*, Venezia, 22 February.
Francesco Arcangeli, "Sulla pittura metafisica: Carrà, de Chirico, Morandi", in *La Vernice*, no.s 22-23, Venezia, April-May.
Catalogue of the *V Quadriennale nazionale d'arte - Rassegna nazionale di arti figurative*, Roma, Palazzo delle Esposizioni, April-June.
Albino Galvano, "La Quadriennale delle arti figurative: dalla grandezza di Modigliani al rigore di Casorati e Morandi...", in *Mondo Nuovo*, Torino, 10 April.
A.P. (Attilio Podestà), "La lezione di Morandi", in *Emporium*, Bergamo, May.
Francesco Arcangeli, *Tre pittori italiani dal 1910 al 1920*, text

in the catalogue of the *XXIV Biennale Internazionale d'Arte di Venezia*, Venezia, Giardini di Castello, May-September.
Ilario Rossi, "Lettere bolognesi: arte sotto le due torri", in *Mondo Futuro*, Roma, 3-9 May.
Antonello Trombadori, "Dalla Biennale di Venezia l'esigenza di un realismo nuovo - Morandi e Carrà", in *l'Unità*, Roma, 8 June.
Silvio Branzi, "Alla XXIV Biennale - I metafisici", in *Il Gazzettino*, Venezia, 22 June.
Raffaele De Grada, "Trinità metafisica - Perché de Chirico, Carrà, Morandi non hanno continuato nella pittura intellettuale?", in *Omnibus*, Milano, 22 June.
Umbro Apollonio, "La XXIV Biennale di Venezia", in *La Rassegna d'Italia*, Milano, July.
Attilio Podestà, "Il Padiglione italiano - La mostra della metafisica", in *Emporium*, Bergamo, July-August.
Mario Ramous, "Maestri alla Biennale - Picasso, Morandi e Braque", in *Corriere del Po*, Ferrara, 8 July.
Cesare Brandi, "La Mostra delle incisioni di Morandi", in *L'Immagine*, no.s 9-10, Roma, August-December.
Virgilio Guzzi, "Della pittura metafisica e di altri fatti italiani", in *Il Tempo*, Roma, 12 August.
Luigi Scarpa, "La XXIV Biennale - Il Padiglione italiano", in *Studium*, Roma, September.
Luigi Scarpa, "Artisti bolognesi alla Biennale veneziana - Giorgio Morandi", in *Pomeriggio*, Bologna, 2 September.
Franco Russoli, "Questo è il limite della pittura italiana del tempo nostro - Le voci di de Chirico, Morandi e Carrà non possono aprire un coro", in *La Gazzetta*, Livorno, 21 September.
Carlo Alberto Petrucci, *Le incisioni di Morandi*, text in the catalogue of the anthological exhibition of graphics, Roma, Calcografia Nazionale, Autumn.
Renato Giani, "Galleria - Morandi", in *Il Quotidiano*, Roma, 21 November.
Alfredo Petrucci, "Morandi incisore", in *La Fiera Letteraria*, Roma, 21 November.
Virgilio Guzzi, "Mostre romane - Le incisioni di Morandi", in *Il Tempo*, Roma, 23 November.
Ercole Maselli, "Mostra alla Cal-

cografia Nazionale - Bianco e nero di Morandi", in *Avanti!*, Roma, 10 December.
Benso Becca, "La mostra di Giorgio Morandi - Il successo delle nuove acqueforti del solitario maestro bolognese", in *Il Giornale dell'Emilia*, Bologna, 13 December.
Giuseppe Raimondi, "Le stampe di Giorgio Morandi", in *Paragone*, no. 2, Firenze.
Lucia Serra, "Significato di Giorgio Morandi", in *Convivium*, no. 6, Torino, SEI.
James Thrall Soby, *Contemporary Painters*, New York, The Museum of Modern Art.

1949
Virgilio Guzzi, "Incisioni di Morandi", in *Arte Mediterranea*, Firenze, January.
Giuseppe Raimondi, text in the catalogue of the one-man exhibition, at the Petite Galerie du Séminaire, Bruxelles, March.
Giuseppe Raimondi, "Giorgio Morandi", in *Les Arts Plastiques*, no.s 3-4, Bruxelles, March-April.
Corrado Sofia, "I pennelli di Morandi", in *Il Mondo*, Roma, 9 April.
Mario Puccini, "Un lirico della pittura: Morandi", in *Pagine Nuove*, Roma, May.
Cesare Brandi, "La mostra dell'arte moderna a New York", in *L'Immagine*, no. 13, Roma, May-June.
Giuseppe Raimondi, text in the catalogue of the one-man exhibition at the Palais des Beaux-Arts, Bruxelles, May-June.
Cesare Brandi, "Morandi incisore", in *L'Eco di Bergamo*, Bergamo, 8 June.
Roberto Rossi, "Fedeltà di Morandi", in *La Nuova Stampa*, Torino, 28 June.
Umbro Apollonio, "The Painting of Giorgio Morandi", in *Horizon*, no. 115, London, July.
Jean-Pierre, "Bologne: visite à Giorgio Morandi", in *Les Lettres Françaises*, Paris, 24 August.
Raffaele Carrieri, "Morandi ha smarrito il senso del tempo", in *Tempo*, Milano, 8-15 October.
Giuseppe Raimondi, "Le cose dell'uomo nell'opera di Morandi", in *La Fiera Letteraria*, Roma, 27 November.
Francesco Arcangeli, Cesare Gnudi, Roberto Longhi, Giuseppe Raimondi, "Arte di Giorgio

Morandi", in *Emilia*, Bologna, December.

Cipriani E. Oppo, "Album di Morandi", in *Giorni*, Roma, 2-25 December.

Cesare Brandi, "La fiera dell'avanguardia", in *L'Immagine*, no.s 14-15, Roma; reprinted in *Arte d'oggi*, Milano, Edizioni della Meridiana, 1952.

Giuseppe Raimondi, "Morandi", in *L'Immagine*, no.s 14-15, Roma.

Sergio Solmi, "Giorgio Morandi", in *Pittori di ieri e di oggi*, Milano, Edizioni Ferrania.

1950

Marco Valsecchi, "Morandi è maestro nell'arte di fare i pacchetti - In mostra a Milano le celebri bottiglie del pittore bolognese", in *Oggi*, Milano, 19 January.

Elena Salvaneschi, "Giorgio Morandi", in *Scena Illustra*, Firenze, February.

Vitale Bloch, "In casa di Giorgio Morandi", in *Maandbland Voor Beeldenden Kunsten*, Amsterdam, July.

Silvano Giannelli, "Bottiglie e umanità di Morandi", in *Le Caste Parlanti*, Firenze, July-September.

Guido Ballo, "Purezza di Morandi", in *Bellezza*, Milano, September.

Silvano Giannelli, "Solitudine di Morandi", in *Idea*, Roma, 10 September.

Cesare Brandi, "Morandi's Early Development", in *Mandrake*, no. 7, London, December 1950-April 1951.

Umbro Apollonio, *Pittura metafisica*, Venezia, Edizioni del Cavallino.

Gian Alberto Dell'Acqua, "La peinture metaphisique", in *Cahiers d'Art*, XXV, Paris.

Giuseppe Raimondi, *Giorgio Morandi*, in *Panorama dell'arte italiana*, edited by Marco Valsecchi and Umbro Apollonio, Torino, Lattes.

Ardengo Soffici, *Trenta artisti moderni italiani e stranieri*, Firenze, Vallecchi.

Lamberto Vitali, "Preferenze", in *Domus*, Milano.

1951

Diego Valeri, "Sironi, Morandi", in *La Biennale*, no. 3, Venezia, January.

Leone Minassian, "Giorgio Morandi incisore", in *Le Arti*, Roma, February.

Lamberto Priori, "Artisti italiani - Destino europeo di Giorgio Morandi", in *La Fiera Letteraria*, Roma, 1° April.

Giuseppe Raimondi, "La congiuntura metafisica Morandi-Carrà", in *Paragone*, no. 19, Firenze, July.

Leone Minassian, "Il più recente Morandi", in *Valori*, Bologna, July-October.

Giuseppe Raimondi, "Morandi", in *Il Mondo*, Roma, 22 September.

1952

Guido Ballo, "Le bottiglie di Morandi non sanno di cantina", in *Settimo Giorno*, Milano, 10 September.

Carlo Manfredi, "Incontro con il pittore Giorgio Morandi", in *Il Lavoro Nuovo*, Genova, 14 September.

Leone Minassian, "Artisti italiani: Giorgio Morandi", in *La Fiera Letteraria*, Roma, 19 October.

Marco Valsecchi, *24 dipinti in una raccolta d'arte moderna*, Milano, Edizioni del Milione.

1953

Orio Vergani, "Giorgio Morandi", in *L'Illustrazione Italiana*, Milano, March.

Mario Puccini, "Tra le sue bottiglie Morandi dipinge i sogni", in *La Settimana del Sud*, Salerno, 28 March - 4 April.

Tyra Lundgren, "Italienska Konstnärsprofiler: Giorgio Morandi", in *Svenska Dagbladet*, Stockholm, 31 March.

Angelo Del Boca, "Ha perdonato sette volte il pittore delle bottiglie", in *Gazzetta Sera*, Torino, 6 October; in *Il Mattino dell'Italia Centrale*, Firenze, 23 October.

1954

Carlo L. Ragghianti, "Giorgio Morandi", in *Critica d'Arte*, no. 1, Firenze, January.

Renzo Biasion, "Le bottiglie di Morandi sono celebri in tutto il mondo", in *Oggi*, Milano, 7 January.

Severo Boschi, Giorgio Fusi, "Parliamo di Giorgio Morandi", in *Nazione Sera*, Firenze, 22 March.

Vitale Bloch, text in the catalogue of the one-man exhibition, Den Haag, Gemeentemuseum, April.

"Kunst van Morandi in Den Haag", in *Het Binnenhof*, Den Haag, 2 April.

"Werk von Giorgio Morandi in Gemeentemuseum", in *Haagsche Courant*, Den Haag, 3 April.

Cornelis Basoski, "Giorgio Morandi", in *De Nieuwe Haagsche Courant*, Den Haag, 24 April.

"Giorgio Morandi: tovert met het doodgewone", in *Het Binnenhof*, Den Haag, 24 April.

"Morandi - Een schilder voor fijnproevers", in *Nieuwe Rotterdamse Courant*, Rotterdam, 24 April.

G.G. Lampe, "Giorgio Morandi vereld vol geheimzinnige Kracht", in *Vrij Nederland*, Amsterdam, 8 May.

J.M. Prange, "Morandi - Variates op de soberheid", in *Parool*, Amsterdam, 8 May.

"Giorgio Morandi, een verstildegeest", in *De Tigd*, Amsterdam, 18 May.

Dh., "Giorgio Morandi wird in Hamburg", in *Hamburger Anzeiger*, Hamburg, 20 May.

Hans Redeker, "De Zeer Eigen Wereld van Professor Giorgio Morandi", in *Haagsche Post*, Den Haag, 24 May.

Vitale Bloch, Lamberto Vitali, texts in the catalogue of the one-man exhibition, London, The Art Council of Great Britain, June.

Cornelis Veth, "Werk van Giorgio Morandi in Het Gemeentemuseum", in *Haagsche Courant*, Den Haag, 3 June.

"Modern Italian Painting", in *The Times*, London, 29 June.

Eric Newton, "Morandi and a New Mural", in *Time and Tide*, London, 3 July.

Vitale Bloch, *Morandi - Sei tavole a colori*, Milano.

Werner Haftmann, *Malerei im XX Jahrhundert*, München, Prestel.

Fernand Hanz, *Dictionnaire de la peinture moderne*, Paris, F. Hazan.

1955

Francesco Arcangeli, "Morandi on Guido Reni of Bologna", in *Arts News*, no. 10, New York, February.

John Berger, "Morandi the Metaphysician of Bologna", *ibidem*.

Francesco Arcangeli, "Ha scelto della città il volto più nascosto e profondo", in *Carlino Sera*, Bologna, 22 February.

Umbro Apollonio, "Giorgio Morandi - Pienezza del suo linguaggio", in *La Fiera Letteraria*, special issue dedicated to Giorgio Morandi, Roma, 25 September.

Francesco Arcangeli, "Giorgio Morandi - La più umile sincerità", *ibidem*.

Carlo Carrà, "Giorgio Morandi - Abbandono dei sentimenti", *ibidem*.

Libero De Libero, "Giorgio Morandi - Dalla luce aurorale alla dorata fermezza", *ibidem*.

Giuseppe Marchiori, "Morandi - Fogli di un vecchio diario", *ibidem*.

Michelangelo Masciotta, "Giorgio Morandi: davanti a un paesaggio", *ibidem*.

Vero Montebugnoli, "Giorgio Morandi - Un esempio di arte, di vita, di poesia", *ibidem*.

Milla Nigro, "Luce e volume nelle incisioni di Morandi: un'atmosfera che avvolge gli oggetti", *ibidem*.

Alessandro Parronchi, "Avevano un'anima tutti i suoi oggetti", *ibidem*.

Giuseppe Raimondi, "Giorgio Morandi - Pensosa armonia", *ibidem*.

Giuseppe Sciortino, "Giorgio Morandi a Bologna e a Roma: incontri con l'uomo e con l'artista", *ibidem*.

Giuseppe Raimondi, "Sensibilidad y metafisica en la pintura de Giorgio Morandi", in *Latina*, no. 4, Caracas, October.

Catalogue of the *VII Quadriennale d'arte*, Roma, Palazzo delle Esposizioni, November 1955 - April 1956.

Giuseppe Pensabene, "Mostre d'arte a Roma - Morandi in controluce alla Galleria della Medusa", in *Il Secolo*, Roma, 2 November.

Ennio Francia, "Mostre d'arte - Morandi alla Medusa", in *Il Popolo*, Roma, 8 November.

Mauro Innocenti, "Mostre romane - Morandi alla Medusa", in *La Fiera Letteraria*, Roma, 20 November.

Marco Valsecchi, "Una buona stagione della pittura italiana... miracolo di Morandi", in *L'Illustrazione Italiana*, Milano, December.

Giancarlo Cavalli, "Alla VII Quadriennale romana - In Italia la pittura del primo Novecento non fa parte della storia degli 'ismi'... L'opera di Morandi", in *Il Resto del Carlino*, Bologna, 22 December.

1956

Milla Nigro, "Appunti sul linguaggio di Morandi", in *La Biennale*, Venezia, March.

Heinz Keller, introduction to the Giorgio Morandi and Giacomo Manzù exhibition, Winterthur, Kunstverein, June-July.

Corrado Corazza, "Morandi ha fede nell'uomo", in *Colloqui*, Bologna, 28 October.

Lorenzo Montano, "Il silenzio di Morandi", in *Corriere della Sera*, Milano, 29 December.

Guido Ballo, *Pittori italiani dal futurismo a oggi*, Roma, Mediterranea.

André Chastel, "L'art italien", in *Larousse*, Paris.

1957

Luigi Carluccio, "Il professor Morandi", in *Gazzetta del Popolo*, Torino, 5 January.

Giuseppe Raimondi, "La valigia delle Indie - La carriera di Morandi", in *Il Mondo*, Roma, 8 January.

Cesare Brandi, "Saluto a Morandi", in *Il Punto*, Roma, 12 January.

Giovanni Carandente, *Giorgio Morandi*, conference text, Roma, Galleria Nazionale d'Arte Moderna, 17 February.

Francesco Arcangeli, "L'opera grafica di un grande pittore", in *L'Europeo*, Milano, 10 March.

Giuseppe Sciortino, "Morandi grafico", in *La Fiera Letteraria*, Roma, 17 March.

Marco Valsecchi, "Una rete d'oro l'incisione di Morandi", in *Tempo*, Milano, 11 April.

Lionello Venturi, "Acqueforti di Morandi", in *L'Espresso*, Roma, 21 April.

Luigi Carluccio, introduction to the one-man exhibition, Torino, Galleria Galatea.

Pier Maria Bardi, "IV Biennale italiana: sala Giorgio Morandi", in *Habitat*, no. 44, São Paulo do Brasil, 16 September.

Rodolfo Pallucchini, "Alla Biennale di San Paolo - Omaggio a Morandi", in *Il Resto del Carlino*, Bologna, 17 September.

Rodolfo Pallucchini, "A Giorgio Morandi il Gran Premio della IV Biennale di San Paolo - Personalità dell'artista", in *Fanfulla*, Sao Paulo do Brasil, 17 September.

"Art - Good Man with a Bottle", in *Time*, New York, 30 September.

Marco Valsecchi, "Gran Premio

a San Paolo - Il massimo premio è stato vinto da Morandi", in *Tempo*, Milano, 17 October.

Lionello Venturi, text in the catalogue of the one-man exhibition, New York, World House Gallery, November-December.

Virgilio Guzzi, "Italianità di Morandi", in *Il Tempo*, Roma, 15 November.

Silvano Giannelli, "Artisti di tutto il mondo alla IV Biennale di San Paolo - Morandi: un'isola di assorto silenzio", in *Il Popolo*, Roma, 29 November.

Roberto Tassi, "L'opera grafica di Morandi", in *Palatina*, no. 4, Parma, December.

Giuseppe Raimondi, "La pittura metafisica - De Chirico, Carrà, Morandi", in *Comunità*, Milano, December.

Dorothy Sandler, "Giorgio Morandi - Work Reflects His Life: 'So Simple, Clear' ", in *The Daily American*, Roma, December.

G.L. Verzellesi, "Pitture di Morandi", in *Gazzetta di Mantova*, Mantova, 17 December.

Carlo L. Ragghianti, *Diario critico - Estetica critica linguistica*, Vicenza, Neri Pozza.

Carlo Volpe, "L'arte del Novecento", in *Storia dell'arte italiana*, Milano-Messina, Principato.

1958

G.L. Verzellesi, "Un'antologia di Morandi", in *Nuova Rivista di Varia Umanità*, III, Verona, January.

Rodolfo Pallucchini, "Atualità di Morandi", in *Arte Antica e Moderna*, no. 1, Bologna, January-March.

Riccardo Bacchelli, "Maestri della pittura contemporanea - Giorgio Morandi a Bologna", in *Settimo Giorno*, Milano, 9 January.

L.C., "Reviews and Previews - Braque, Mirò, Morandi", in *Art News*, no. 56, New York, February.

Leonida Repaci, "Dio può essere chiuso in un tubetto di colori", in *Tempo*, Milano, 20 May.

Fritz Laufer, "Italiens Berühmtester - Maler Giorgio Morandi bekennt: 'Mein Ruhm kam zu spät' ", in *Die Woche*, Olten, 21 July.

Pierre Courthion, *Giorgio Morandi*, in *Art indépendent - Panorama international de 1900 à nos jours*, Paris, Albin Michel.

Waldemar George, Raymond Cogniat, Max Fourny, *Encyclopédie de l'art international contemporain*, Paris, Prisme des Arts.

Maurice Raynal, *Peinture moderne*, Genève, Skira.

1959

Raffaele Carrieri, "I maestri della pittura contemporanea in Italia - Giorgio Morandi", in *Epoca*, Milano, 24 May.

Cesare Brandi, "Un inatteso segreto nei paesaggi di Morandi", in *Corriere della Sera*, Milano, 21 August.

Marco Valsecchi, "Morandi l'inaccessibile infrange il voto del silenzio", in *Il Giorno*, Milano, 22 September.

Leone Minassian, "Una visita a Morandi", in *Il Taccuino delle Arti*, Roma, November.

G.M. (Garibaldo Marussi), "Una mostra di Giorgio Morandi", in *Le Arti*, Milano, November-December.

Silvio Branzi, "Assenza di Morandi", in *Il Gazzettino*, Venezia, 4 November.

Mario Fin, *Variazioni sul tema Morandi*, text in the catalogue of the one-man exhibition, Milano, Galleria Annunciata, December 1959 - January 1960.

Giorgio Mascherpa, "Un grande maestro al di fuori della mischia", in *L'Italia*, Milano, 27 December.

Georges Floersheim, *Ist die Malerei zu Ende?*, Zurich, Atlantis.

1960

Picus, "Giorgio Morandi", in *Candido*, Milano, 3 January.

Guido Ballo, "Chiarezza di Morandi", in *Ideal Standard Rivista*, Milano, April-June.

Duilio Courir, "Giorgio Morandi compie oggi settant'anni - Un classico", in *Il Resto del Carlino*, Bologna, 20 July.

Umbro Apollonio, "Morandi", in *Das Kunstwerke*, no. 3, Baden Baden, September.

Georges Floersheim, "Morandi", in *Preuves*, Paris, September.

Heinrich W. Petzet, "Von Morandi zu Romiti", in *Deutsche Zeitung*, Stuttgart-Köln, 1° September.

H.T., "Morandi", in *Art News*, New York, December.

Sidney Tillin, "Giorgio Morandi", in *Arts*, New York, December.

Cesare Brandi, "Appunti per un ritratto di Morandi", in *Palatina*, no. 13, Parma.

Giuseppe Marchiori, *Arte e artisti d'avanguardia in Italia (1910-1950)*, Milano, Comunità.

1961

Lamberto Vitali, "Giorgio Morandi", in *Notizie Olivetti*, no. 70, Ivrea, January.

E.G., "Giorgio Morandi", in *Herald Tribune*, New York, 1° January.

"Giorgio Morandi", in *New York Times*, New York, 1° January.

H.J. Barr, "Giorgio Morandi", in *Nation*, New York, 21 January.

H.J. Barr, "Giorgio Morandi", in *Du*, Zürich, March.

Marco Valsecchi, "La pittura metafisica", in *Art Club*, Milano, March-May.

Silvio Branzi, "Giorgio Morandi", in *L'Osservatore Politico Letterario*, Milano, 5 May.

Mino Borghi, "Galleria di artisti italiani, Giorgio Morandi", in *Rivista delle Provincie*, nos. 11-12, Roma, November-December.

Corrado Maltese, *Storia dell'arte in Italia 1785-1943*, Torino, Einaudi.

1962

Luigi Lambertini, "Morandi e la sua città", in *Segnacolo*, Roma, January-February.

Valerio Zurlini, "Peinture - Giorgio Morandi", in *L'Express*, Paris, 4 January.

Catalogue of *XXXI Biennale Internazionale d'Arte di Venezia*, Venezia, Giardini di Castello, Summer.

Lamberto Vitali, "Giorgio Morandi", in *Goya*, no. 49, Madrid, July-August.

Umbro Apollonio, text in the catalogue of the one-man exhibition, Siegen, Haus Seel-am-Markt, October-November.

Roberto Longhi, "Antologia di critici - Momenti della pittura bolognese - Da Carracci a Morandi", in *Paragone*, no. 155, Firenze, November.

Giorgio Mascherpa, "Usa come modello cento bottiglie polverose - A Giorgio Morandi, uno dei più grandi pittori italiani, è stato assegnato il Premio Rubens", in *Gente*, Milano, 16 November.

Marco Valsecchi, text in the catalogue of the exhibition *Magini-Morandi*, Milano, Galleria Lorenzelli, December.

Anna Maria Brizio, *Ottocento-Novecento*, Torino, UTET.

1963

Franco Russoli, "Pretesti e appunti... La mostra Magini-Morandi, o della polivalenza della natura morta", in *Pirelli*, Milano, January-February.

Giovanni Testori, "Un singolare confronto a Milano - Le meditazioni di Morandi e le 'cucine' del Magini", in *Settimo Giorno*, Milano, 8 January.

Arnaldo Beccaria, "Il pittore che detesta il denaro", in *Tempo*, Milano, 26 October.

Jean-Luc Duval, "Patient, solitaire, concentré - Giorgio Morandi", in *Journal de Genève*, Genève, 23-24 November.

Werner Helwig, "Morandi Maler des Schweigens", in *Die Tata*, Zürich, 27 November.

Pierre Rosemberg, *Chardin*, Genève, Skira.

1964

Paola della Pergola, "La pittura di Morandi", in *Paese Sera*, Roma, 17 April.

Sergio Maldini, "Vita e opere di Morandi", in *La Nazione*, Firenze, 17 April.

Marcello Venturoli, "Intervista con Morandi", in *Europa Letteraria*, Roma, 29 May.

Marcello Venturoli, "Morandi sta male", in *Le Ore*, Roma, 18 June.

Marziano Bernardi, "La morte di Giorgio Morandi. Il lirico più puro dell'arte moderna", in *La Stampa*, Torino, 19 June.

Leonardo Borgese, "È morto Giorgio Morandi. Un pittore che cercava l'innocenza del mondo", in *Corriere della Sera*, Milano, 19 June.

Corrado Corazza, "È morto Morandi", in *L'Avvenire d'Italia*, Bologna, 19 June.

Virgilio Guzzi, "Addio a Giorgio Morandi pittore classico moderno", in *Il Tempo*, Roma, 19 June.

G.M., "È morto Giorgio Morandi, francescano osservatore della verità", in *Il Piccolo*, Trieste, 19 June.

"Morandi, un ideale di perfezione", in *Il Resto del Carlino*, Bologna, 19 June (articles by: Giuseppe Raimondi, "La sua lezione"; Riccardo Bacchelli, "Gli insegnanti non credevano che sarebbe diventato un grande pittore"; Giorgio Ruggeri, "Una vita fra Bologna e Grizzana"; critical anthology).

Duilio Morosini, "L'arte solitaria del grande Morandi", in *Paese Sera*, Roma, 19 June.

Alessandro Parronchi, "È morto Giorgio Morandi", in *La Nazione*, Firenze, 19 June.

Nello Ponente, "Era il più grande pittore italiano del nostro secolo", in *Avanti!*, Milano, 19 June.

Paolo Rizzi, "È morto Giorgio Morandi, pittore delle forme pure", in *Il Gazzettino*, Venezia, 19 June.

Marco Valsecchi, "Ha dato agli oggetti sentimenti umani", in *Il Giorno*, Milano, 19 June.

Gino Visentini, "È morto Giorgio Morandi", in *Il Messaggero*, Roma, 19 June.

Catalogue of the *XXXII Biennale Internazionale d'Arte di Venezia*, Venezia, Giardini di Castello, Summer.

Cesare Brandi, "Il miracolo di Morandi", in *Il Punto*, Roma, 24 June.

Rodolfo Pallucchini, "Sono personaggi arcani le bottiglie di Morandi", in *Il Gazzettino*, Venezia, 24 June.

Raffaele Carrieri, "Ricordiamo il pittore del silenzio", in *Epoca*, Milano, 28 June.

Roberto Longhi, "Exit Morandi", in *Paragone*, no. 175, Firenze, July.

Luigi Magnani, *Ricordo di Morandi*, in RAI - III Programma, 18 July.

Giuseppe Raimondi, "Morandi 1916", in *Il Resto del Carlino*, Bologna, 15 August.

Mino Maccari, "Il mondo immobile di Giorgio Morandi", in *Panorama*, Milano, September.

Margit Staber, "Das stilleben bei Giorgio Morandi", in *Nachrichten Kunst*, Luzern, November.

Arnaldo Beccaria, "Visite a Morandi", in *La Botte e il Violino*, no. 2, Roma.

Giuseppe Marchiori, *Universalità di Morandi*, in *Studi in onore di Giusta Nicco Fasola*, Milano, La Rete.

Carlo L. Ragghianti, "Un'antologia di Morandi", in *Critica d'Arte*, no. 62, Firenze.

Roberto Tassi, "Giorgio Morandi", in *L'Approdo Letterario*, no. 26, Roma.

Marco Valsecchi, "Giorgio Morandi", in *Rivista Italsider*, no.s 3-4, Genova.

Carlo Volpe, "Morandi", in *La Biennale di Venezia*, no. 55, Venezia.

1965

Giuseppe Raimondi, "L'anima di Morandi", in *Il Resto del Carlino*, Bologna, 10 January.
Giovanni Scheiwiller, text in the catalogue of the one-man exhibition, Milano, Galleria Annunciata, April-May.
Giuseppe Raimondi, "Morandi -I camini e il dadaismo", in *Il Resto del Carlino*, Bologna, 3 April.
Lorenza Trucchi, "I silenzi di Morandi", in *La Fiera Letteraria*, Roma, 4 April.
Werner Haftmann, text in the catalogue of the one-man exhibition, Bern, Kunsthalle, October-December.
José Luis Plaza, text in the catalogue of the exhibition *Omaggio a Morandi*, Caracas, November.
Anne Marie Thormann, "Ein Master der Stille", in *National Zeitung*, Basel, 12 November.
Angelo Dragone, "Morandi a Bologna", in *Marcatre*, no.s 11-13, Milano.
Giuseppe Marchiori, "Universalità di Morandi", in *Arte Lombarda*, special volume, X, Milano.

1966

Giuseppe Marchiori, "Diario di un critico", in *La Voce Repubblicana*, Roma, 22 April.
Roberto Longhi, text in the catalogue of the *XXXIII Biennale Internazionale di Venezia*, Venezia, Giardini di Castello, Summer.
Giuseppe Raimondi, "Rivive il mondo di Morandi", in *Il Resto del Carlino*, Bologna, 26 June.
Giuseppe Raimondi, "Il mondo di Grizzana",in *Il Resto del Carlino*, Bologna, 26 July.
Guido Perocco, "Un'atmosfera di intimità nella poesia di Morandi", in *Il Gazzettino*, Venezia, 3 August.
Lamberto Vitali, *L'opera di Giorgio Morandi*, text in the catalogue of the anthological exhibition, Bologna, Archiginnasio, October-December.
Paolo Fossati, "Un omaggio a Morandi", in *l'Unità*, Milano, 27 October.
Mario De Micheli, "Morandi - Una sorgente profonda in un palmo di terra emiliana", in *l'Unità*, Milano, 30 October.
Giuseppe Raimondi, "Un grande del nostro secolo", in *Il Resto del Carlino*, Bologna, 30 October.

Tommaso Paloscia, "Berna - Venezia - Bologna - Un discorso sempre più limpido", in *La Nazione*, Firenze, 3 November.
Corrado Corazza, "Un Morandi più intimo", in *L'Avvenire d'Italia*, Bologna, 6 November.
Giuseppe Raimondi, "Cézanne e Morandi", in *Il Resto del Carlino*, Bologna, 11 November.
Giuseppe Raimondi, "Morandi e i cubisti", in *Il Resto del Carlino*, Bologna, 24 November.
Luigi Tallarico, "Giorgio Morandi", in *L'Orologio*, no.s 11-12, Roma, December.
Sandro Salvi (Luigi Lambertini), "Morandi spirito inquieto", in *L'Adige*, Trento, 14 December.
Guido Ballo, "Morandi", in *Domus*, no. 443, Milano.

1967

Virgilio Fagone, "Morandi e il problema dell'oggetto pittorico", in *La Civiltà Cattolica*, Roma, 7 January.
Carlo L. Ragghianti, text in the catalogue of the exhibition *Arte moderna in Italia 1915-35*, Firenze, Palazzo Strozzi, February-March.
Marco Valsecchi, text in the catalogue of the one-man exhibition, Ferrara, Galleria Duca d'Este, May.
Massimo Carrà, *Carrà e Morandi*, in *L'Arte Moderna*, IX, Milano, Fabbri.

1968

Enrico Paulucci, text in the catalogue of the exhibition *I pittori italiani dell'Associazione internazionale arti plastiche UNESCO*, Torino, Galleria Civica d'Arte Moderna, February-March.
Josip Kolar, text in the catalogue of the exhibition *Bolonjsko Slikartsvo XX Vijeka*, Zagreb, Galerija Moderne Umjetnosti, May.
Gertrud Kobke Sutton, introduction to the catalogue of the one-man exhibition, Copenhagen, Kunstforeningen, September.
Cesare Brandi, "Poi la pittura scompare", in *La Fiera Letteraria*, Roma, 24 October.
Zeno Birolli, "Pittura e intimità poetica", in *Nac*, no. 3, Milano.
Massimo Carrà, *Metafisica*, Milano, Mazzotta.
Carlo Zucchini, "Visita a Giorgio Morandi", in *Il Foglio di Crevalcore*, no. 3, Crevalcore.

1969

André Piejre de Mandiargues, text in the catalogue of the one-man exhibition, Paris, Galerie Villand et Galanis, January.
Marcello Azzolini, "Gli acquerelli di Morandi", in *Le Arti*, Milano, January-February.
Paolo Possenti, "Morandi, ovvero dell'invenzione", in *Gazzetta di Mantova*, Mantova, 22 January.
Dino Buzzati, "Solitudine di Morandi", in *Corriere della Sera*, Milano, 6 May.
Virgilio Guzzi, "Momenti e figure dell'arte italiana - Giorgio Morandi", in *Levante*, Roma, June.
Carlo L. Ragghianti, "Bologna cruciale 1914", in *Critica d'Arte*, Firenze.

1970

Giancarlo Cavalli, Franco Solmi, Carlo Volpe, texts in the catalogue of the exhibition *Due decenni di acquisizioni alle raccolte comunali d'arte*, Bologna, Museo Civico, April-May.
Francesco Arcangeli, text in the catalogue of the exhibition *Natura ed espressione nell'arte bolognese ed emiliana*, Bologna, Archiginnasio, September-October.
Maurizio Bernardi, "Da Wiligelmo a Morandi", in *La Stampa*, Torino, 12 September.
Luigi Carluccio, "Da Wiligelmo fino a Morandi: gli itinerari dell'arte emiliana", in *Gazzetta del Popolo*, Torino, 12 September.
Giorgio Fanti, "Raimondi - I miei anni con Morandi", in *Paese Sera*, Roma, 18 September.
Raffaele Carrieri, "Morandi rivive nelle pagine di Giuseppe Raimondi", in *Epoca*, Milano, 27 September.
Guido Giuffré, text in the catalogue of the exhibition *L'opera grafica di Giorgio Morandi*, Roma, Il Nuovo Torcoliere, December 1970 - January 1971.
Roberto Tassi, text in the catalogue of the exhibition *Morandi-Morlotti*, Milano, Galleria del Milione, December 1970 - January 1971.
James Thrall Soby, *A Visit to Morandi*, text in the catalogue of the anthological exhibition, London, Royal Academy of Arts, December 1970 - January 1971.
Raffaello Uboldi, "Più di cento-

mila inglesi alla mostra di Morandi", in *Il Giorno*, Milano, 21 December.
Marco Valsecchi, "Il diverso tormento di due grandi pittori", in *Il Giorno*, Milano, 22 December.
Giuseppe Raimondi, *Un'occhio sulla pittura*, Bologna, Alfa.
Silla Zamboni, "Due disegni di Morandi studente", in *Atti e Memorie dell'Accademia Clementina*, IX, Bologna.

1971

Jean Leymarie, Andrew Forge, texts in the catalogue of the anthological exhibition, Paris, Musée National d'Art Moderne, February-April; reprint of the English catalogue.
Charles Spencer, "Come Londra ha accolto Morandi", in *Bolaffi Arte*, Torino, February.
Jérôme Peygnot, "Silence, Morandi", in *Connaissaince des Art*, no. 228, Paris, February.
Michel Conil Lacoste, "Morandi, inquisiteur passionné du banal", in *Le Monde*, Paris, 10 February.
Alberico Sala, "Il quadro, la cornice e i dintorni", in *Notizie d'Arte*, Milano, March.
Domenico Cantatore, "...Sono matti; ventimila lire per un mio quadro!", in *Corriere della Sera*, Milano, 18 April.
Francesco Arcangeli, text in the catalogue of the anthological exhibition, Milano, Rotonda della Besana, May-June (texts by J. Leymarie and A. Forge).
Piero Bigongiari, "Tragicità di Morandi", in *Antichità Viva*, Firenze, May-June.
Marco Valsecchi, "Morandi nel nostro tempo", in *Il Giorno*, Milano, 9 May.
Franco Passoni, "Un doveroso omaggio all'opera di Morandi", in *Avanti!*, Milano, 11 June.
Mario De Micheli, "Un canzoniere rigoroso", in *l'Unità*, Milano, 16 June.
Curzia Ferrari, "I silenzi di Morandi", in *La Fiera Letteraria*, Roma, 27 June.
Renzo Modesti, "Morandi", in *Notizie d'Arte*, Milano, August-September.
Renzo Guasco, introduction to the catalogue of the exhibition *40 incisioni di Morandi*, Torino, Galleria Dantesca, December 1971 - January 1972.

1972

AA.VV., catalogue of the exhibi-

tion *Metamorfosi dell'oggetto*, Milano, Palazzo Reale, January-February.
J.M. (Jan Martinet), text in the catalogue of the exhibition *Morandi -Etsten*, Amsterdam, Stedelijk Museum, January-February.
Osvaldo Patani, text in the catalogue of the one-man exhibition, Milano, Galleria Eunomia, May-June.

1973

Irina Antonova, Lamberto Vitali, Franco Solmi, texts in the catalogue of the anthological exhibition, Leningrad, Ermitage Museum, April-May; Moskva, Museum Pushkin, May-June.
Maurizio Calvesi, "Tra metafisica e naturalismo", in *Corriere della Sera*, Milano, 22 April.
"Sapesse quanta voglia ho ancora di lavorare", photos by Mario De Biasi, in *Bolaffi Arte*, no. 30, Torino, May-June.
Palma Bucarelli, Cesare Brandi, texts in catalogue of the anthological exhibition, Roma, Galleria Nazionale d'Arte Moderna, May-July.
Maurizio Calvesi, "Il magico mondo di Morandi", in *Corriere della Sera*, Milano, 16 May.
Marcello Venturoli, "Pezzi anche molto rari alla grande mostra di Morandi", in *Il Globo*, Roma, 18 May.
Duilio Morosini, "Morandi, artista del dubbio", in *Paese Sera*, Roma, 19 May.
Marco Valsecchi, "Morandi fuori dalle leggende", in *Il Giorno*, Milano, 19 May.
Dario Micacchi, "Il cammino di Morandi", in *l'Unità*, Roma, 22 May.
Bruno Morini, "Morandi a Valle Giulia", in *Il Giornale d'Italia*, Roma, 22 May.
Shargia Kusumova, "Morandi all'Ermitage", in *URSS Oggi*, no. 19, 24 May.
Sandra Giannattasio, "Giorgio Morandi, un grande europeo che non lasciò mai Bologna", in *Avanti!*, Roma, 27 May.
Luigi Serravalli, "La leggenda di Giorgio Morandi", in *L'Adige*, Trento, 30 May.
Marco Valsecchi, text in the catalogue of the exhibition *Le acqueforti di Giorgio Morandi*, Urbino, Palazzo Ducale, June-July.
Antonio Del Guercio, "Morandi coscienza della borghesia", in

186

Rinascita, no. 22, Roma, 1° June.

Nello Ponente, "Ricordo di Morandi", in *Paese Sera*, Roma, 22 June.

Paul Hofmann, "Rome: Revival for 'Painter of Bottles'", in *The New York Times*, New York, 26 June.

Sandra Orienti, "Giorgio Morandi alla Galleria Nazionale d'Arte Moderna di Roma", in *Arte 2000*, no. 9, Milano, July-August.

Vittoria Marcova, "Il mondo di Giorgio Morandi", in *Il Pittore*, no. 10, Moskva, October.

Marco Valsecchi, "Dalla Metafisica al Novecento e l'anti Novecento", in *Ulisse*, Roma, November.

Roberto Longhi, *Da Cimabue a Morandi - Saggi di storia della pittura italiana*, chosen and arranged by Gianfranco Contini, Milano, Mondadori; 2nd edition, 1974.

1974

Osvaldo Licini, *Errante, erotico, eretico - Gli scritti letterari e tutte le lettere* (edited by Zeno Birolli, Francesco Bartoli, Gino Baratta), Milano, Feltrinelli.

Osvaldo Patani, *La storia del disegno italiano 1900-1974*, Torino, Fratelli Pozzo.

1975

Franco Solmi, *Opere del ventesimo secolo nelle raccolte comunali d'arte*, Bologna, Galleria Comunale d'Arte Moderna, Bologna, May.

Lamberto Vitali, text in the catalogue of the anthological exhibition, Bologna, Galleria Comunale d'Arte Moderna, May-June.

Giorgio Mascherpa, "Un museo in espansione", in *L'Avvenire*, Milano, 3 May.

Flavio Caroli, "La Nuova Galleria d'Arte Moderna di Bologna", in *Corriere della Sera*, Milano, 4 May.

Giorgio Ruggeri, "Aria nuova nei musei", in *Il Resto del Carlino*, Bologna, 5 May.

"Intenso programma di attività nella Galleria d'Arte Moderna... Morandi", in *l'Unità*, Roma, 6 May.

Luigi Lambertini, "Orgoglio di Bologna", in *Il Gazzettino*, Venezia, 7 May.

1976

Giuseppe Marchiori, text in the catalogue of the exhibition *Un confronto: due tempi - Licini/Morandi*, Bologna, Galleria Due Torri, May.

Giorgio Ruggeri, *Morandi, ultimo pittore*, in *Omaggio a Morandi*, Bologna, Galleria Marescalchi, May.

AA.VV., catalogue of the one-man exhibition (with some passages of former texts), Verona, Galleria dello Scudo, November 1976 - January 1977.

Francesco Arcangeli, *Dal romanticismo all'informale*, Bologna, Alfa; vol. I, Torino, Einaudi.

1977

Luciano Anceschi, Giuseppe Raimondi, catalogue of the exhibition *Giuseppe Raimondi fra poeti e pittori*, Bologna, Museo Civico, May-June.

AA.VV., catalogue of the exhibition *Tendenzen der Zwanziger Jahre*, Berlin, Europäische Kunstausstellung, August-October.

Janet Abramowicz, "Giorgio Morandi - A World within a Studio", in *Vanguard*, Vancouver, October.

Ted Lindenberg, catalogue of the anthological exhibition, Vancouver, The Vancouver Art Gallery, October.

Giuseppe Marchiori, text in the catalogue of the one-man exhibition, Lucca, Galleria Barsotti, October.

Giuseppe Raimondi, text in the catalogue of the one-man exhibition (with a critical anthology), Sasso Marconi, La Casa dell'Arte, October-November.

Luigi Serravalli, "Prodigioso Morandi", in *L'Adige*, Trento, 11 October.

Luigi Serravalli, "Morandi nel segno della libertà", in *L'Adige*, Trento, 9 November.

1978

Luigi Lambertini, "Il mondo in una stanza", in *Unione Sarda*, Cagliari, 18 January; the same article, with the title "Per Giorgio Morandi, pochi amici ma buoni", in *La Gazzetta Ticinese*, Lugano, 4 February.

Luigi Lambertini, "Viaggio d'artista nella propria stanza", in *Il Gazzettino*, Venezia, 5 February.

Franco Solmi, text in the catalogue of the exhibition *Metafisica del quotidiano*, Bologna, Galleria Comunale d'Arte Moderna, June-September.

Pier Giovanni Castagnoli, "Lombroso con Bonifacio VIII", in *la Repubblica*, Roma, 2 June.

Franco Solmi, text in the catalogue of the anthological exhibition, Ferrara, Palazzo dei Diamanti, July-October.

Everardo Dalla Noce, "Grande attesa per Morandi", in *Il Sole 24 Ore*, Milano, 1° July.

Marilena Pasquali, "Ferrara ripropone Giorgio Morandi", in *Paese Sera*, Roma, 16 July.

Alberico Sala, "Morandi - Autoritratto con paesaggio", in *Corriere della Sera*, Milano, 31 July.

"Morandi, polemica bolognese", in *Gazzetta del Popolo*, Torino, 0 August.

Renato Barili, "Un grattacielo in bottiglia", in *L'Espresso*, Roma, 20 August.

Giovanni Testori, "Giorgio Morandi, o la capacità di resurrezione", in *Corriere della Sera*, Milano, 20 August.

Giorgio Ruggeri, "Goditi l'arte con Morandi", in *Il Resto del Carlino*, Bologna, 21 August.

Marco Valsecchi, "Caro Morandi, caro de Pisis", in *Il Giornale Nuovo*, Milano, 1° September.

Pompilio Mandelli, "Giorgio Morandi 1907-1913", in *Analisi*, Bologna, 15 October.

Luigi Cavallo, *Disegno italiano dal futurismo al novecento*, Milano, Edizioni Galleria Il Mappamondo.

1979

Jean-Michel Folon, "Histoire d'un coup de foudre", in *Le Nouvel Observateur*, Paris, 12-18 February.

Jacques Michel, "Expositions - Gravures de Morandi", in *Le Monde*, Paris, 14 February.

Maiten Bouisset, "Morandi à la Galerie Berggruen", in *Le Matin de Paris*, Paris, 20 February.

Giuliano Briganti, Ester Coen, texts in the catalogue of the exhibition *La pittura metafisica*, Venezia, Istituto di Cultura di Palazzo Grassi, May-June; Vicenza, Neri Pozza; 2nd edition, Vicenza 1981.

Guido Ballo, text in the catalogue of the exhibition *Origini dell'astrattismo - Verso altri orizzonti del reale*, Milano, Palazzo Reale, October 1979 - January 1980.

Luigi Serravalli, "Morandi nel segno della libertà", in *L'Adige*, Trento, 9 November.

Rossana Bossaglia, *Il Novecento italiano* (with texts by Claudia Gian Ferrari e Marco Lorandi), Milano, Feltrinelli.

Maria Catelli Isola, text in the catalogue of the anthological exhibition of graphics, Bruxelles, Musée des Beaux-Arts.

Stefania Massari, text in the catalogue of the exhibition *Giorgio Morandi*, Bordeaux, Musée et Galerie des Beaux-Arts.

Zeno Birolli, text in the catalogue of the exhibition *Letteratura-arte Miti del Novecento*, Milano, Padiglione d'Arte Contemporanea.

1980

Fabrizio D'Amico, *Morandi e il "prossimo"*, text in the catalogue of the one-man exhibition, Roma, Galleria Il Gabbiano, March-April.

Renato Barilli, Franco Solmi (edited by), catalogue of the exhibition *La metafisica: gli anni Venti* (biographical entry by Marilena Pasquali), Bologna, Galleria Comunale d'Arte Moderna, May-August.

Catalogue of the one-man exhibition, Cavalese, La Casa dell'Arte, July-August.

Jean Clair, catalogue of the exhibition *Les réalismes*, Paris, Centre Georges Pompidou, December 1980 - April 1981; Berlin Staatliche Kunsthalle, May-June 1981.

Giorgio Morandi - Disegni, Bologna, Galleria Trimarchi, December.

Stefania Massari (edited by), catalogue of the exhibition *80 acqueforti di Giorgio Morandi*, Köln, Bonn, Dortmund.

Arturo Carlo Quintavalle, *Giorgio de Chirico, Severo Pozzati, Giorgio Morandi, Carlo Carrà: le ideologie e le immagini fino al 1920*, in the catalogue of the anthological exhibition at Sepo, Parma, Centro Studi e Archivio della Comunicazione.

1981

Kate Linker, "Giorgio Morandi", in *Art Forum*, New York, February.

AA.VV., catalogue of the anthological exhibition (edited by Franz A. Morat), München, Haus der Kunst, July-September.

Luigi Carluccio, text in the catalogue of the anthological exhibition, Acqui Terme, Liceo Saracco, July-September.

Alberico Sala, "Giorgio Morandi e il suo critico", in *Corriere della Sera*, Milano, 22 Luly.

Ariberto Segala, "Ecco i segreti di Morandi", in *Domenica del Corriere*, Milano, August.

Catalogue of the exhibition *Les peintres du silence*, Vevey, Musée des Beaux-Arts, August-September.

Franco Solmi, "Per Morandi gli stranieri preferiscono fare da soli", in *Il Resto del Carlino*, Bologna, 8 August.

Luigi Lambertini, "Viaggio sentimentale all'interno di una stanza", in *Il Giornale*, Milano, 12 August.

Nick Baldwin, "Morandi Show - A Big Task for Demetrion", in *Des Moines Sunday Register*, Des Moines, 23 August.

Janet Abramowicz, "Vision et Technique: The Etchings of Giorgio Morandi, 1890-1964", in *The Print Collector's Newsletter*, New York, no. 4, September-October.

James T. Demetrion, Joan M. Lukach, Kenneth Baker, Amy N Worthen, catalogue of the anthological exhibition, San Francisco, Museum of Modern Art, September-November, New York, The Solomon R. Guggenheim Museum, November 1981 - January 1982; Des Moines, Des Moines Art Center, February-March 1982.

Giulio Carlo Argan, Floriano De Santi, catalogue of the exhibition *Il linguaggio dell'incisione*, Brescia, Cellatica, October-November; Brescia, Capo di Ponte, November-December.

Allan Temko, "The Disquieting Quietude of Giorgio Morandi", in *San Francisco Chronicle*, San Francisco, 4 October.

William Wilson, "Giorgio Morandi and the Sundance Kid", in *Los Angeles Times*, Los Angeles, 18 October.

Carter Ratcliff, "A Painter of Inanimate Souls", in *Saturday Review*, San Francisco, November.

Waine Thiebaud, "A Fellow Painter's View of Giorgio Morandi", in *New York Times*, New York, 15 November.

Carlo Valentini, "La poesia di Morandi tra i grattacieli di New York", in *Il Giorno*, Milano, 19 November.

Enrico Franceschini, "La bottiglia sbarca a New York", in *L'Espresso*, Roma, 29 November.

Dede Auregli, "Giorgio Morandi trionfa a New York mentre Bologna gli prepara un museo", in *l'Unità*, Roma, 1° December.
Gianfranco Orvieto, "Retrospettiva di Morandi al Guggenheim", in *L'Osservatore Romano*, Città del Vaticano, 5 December.
Hilton Kramer, "Giorgio Morandi: A Quality of Private Meditation", in *The New York Times*, New York, 6 December.
Mark Stevens, "Morandi's Bottled Beauty", in *Newsweek*, New York, 7 December.
Theodore F. Wolff, "A Modest Jewel of Our Time - Giorgio Morandi", in *The Christian Science Monitor*, New York, 8 December.
Judith Helfer, "Meister des Italienischen Neoklassizismus", in *Aufbau*, New York, December.
Robert Hughes, "Master of Unfussed Clarity", in *Time*, New York, 21 December.
Steffan Kling, Mats Raisberg, "Morandi och historiens samtidighet - Morandi och det Metafysiska Maleriet", in *Hyärnstrom*, no.s 14-15, Gammelstad, 22 December.
Theodore F. Wolff, "The Many Masks of Modern Art", in *The Christian Science Monitor*, New York, 30 December.
Maurizio Calvesi, Giovanna Dalla Chiesa, Ester Coen, texts in the catalogue of the exhibition *La metafisica - Museo documentario*, Ferrara, Parco Massari.
Catalogue of the exhibition *Oggettività metafisica in Italia fra le due guerre*, Roma, Galleria La Medusa.
Gian Alberto Dall'Acqua, *La donazione Jesi*, Milano, Amici di Brera.
Salvatore A. Sanna, Erich Steingräber, Carla Schulz Hofmann, catalogue of the exhibition *Zur Italienischen Kunst nach 1945 - Deutsche Künstler und Italien*, Frankfurt, Frankfurter Westend Galerie.

1982
AA.VV., texts in the catalogue of the exhibition *Gli anni Trenta - Arte e cultura in Italia*, Milano, Palazzo Reale, April Mazzotta.
Nick Baldwin, "Morandi Show Much Heralded", in *Des Moines Sunday Register*, Des Moines, 10 January.

John Russel, "Realism (True and False) is Everywhere", in *The New York Times*, New York, 10 January.
Nick Baldwin, "Morandi's Genius", in *Des Moines Sunday Register*, Des Moines, February.
Franco Solmi, text in the catalogue of the exhibition *La scuola bolognese dell'acquaforte* (section dedicated to Morandi edited by Marilena Pasquali), Bologna, Galleria Comunale d'Arte Moderna, February-March 1984; Cardiff, National Museum of Wales, October-November 1984; Toulouse, Musée des Arts des Augustins, April-May 1985.
Abraham Gilam, "The Art of Quiet Revelation in an Italian Master's Hand", in *Post Dispatch*, 1° March.
Jane Bell, "Message in Bottles - The Noble Grandeur of Giorgio Morandi", in *Art News*, New York, 3 March.
Bertil Sundstedt, "Manga aktiviteter präglar Hjärnstorm", in *Norb Kuriren*, 26 April.
Marilena Pasquali, *Morandi in Galleria - Opere e documenti*, Bologna, Galleria Comunale d'Arte Moderna, May.
Franco Basile, "Morandi ai bolognesi", in *Il Resto del Carlino*, Bologna, 22 May.
Dede Auregli, "Via Fondazza l'isola sacra del solitario Morandi", in *l'Unità*, Roma, June.
Roberto Pignoni, "Per Giorgio Morandi uno spazio nella Galleria d'Arte Moderna", in *Alla Ribalta*, Bologna, 15-30 June.
Carlo L. Ragghianti, "Un eremita a Bologna", in *Il Resto del Carlino*, Bologna, 4 July.
Nico Orengo, "Andai da Morandi e gli dissi 'Mi dipinge un quadro musicale?' ", in *La Stampa*, Torino, 10 July.
Roberto Tassi, "Morandi dal vero", in *la Repubblica*, Roma, 11 August.
Roberto Bertinetti, "Morandi ammirava i sacchi di Burri", in *Il Nuovo Adige*, Verona, 14 September.
Duilio Courir, "La musica di Giorgio Morandi", in *Corriere della Sera*, Milano, 26 September.
Marilena Pasquali, "Per un centro studi dedicato a Giorgio Morandi", in *Verso l'Arte*, Cerrina Monferrato, October.
Silvano Giannelli, "Morandi - La

poesia a bassa voce", in *La Discussione*, Roma, 4 October.
Mario Pancera, "Le sorelle Morandi raccontano", in *La Domenica del Corriere*, Milano, 9 October.
Claudio Spadoni, "Morandi nel laboratorio della solitudine", in *Il Resto del Carlino*, Bologna, 23 October.
G.L. Verzellesi, "Il 'mio' Morandi era così", in *L'Arena*, Verona, 13 November.
Mauro Corradini, "Quelle emozionanti bottiglie", in *Bresciaoggi*, Brescia, 25 November.
Marilena Pasquali, "Bologna - Appello per un Museo Morandi", in *D'Ars*, Milano, December.
Maurizio Calvesi, *La metafisica schiarita - Da de Chirico a Carrà, da Morandi a Savinio*, Milano, Feltrinelli.
Walter Koschatzky, Kristian Sotriffer, *Mit Nadel und Säure - 500 Jahre Kunst der Radierung*, Wien, Tusch.
Carlo L. Ragghianti, *Bologna cruciale 1914 e saggi su Morandi, Gorni, Saetti*, Bologna, Calderini.
Federico Riccio (edited by), *La collezione Rossini d'arte contemporanea a Torino*, Torino.

1983
Rossana Bossaglia, text in the catalogue of the exhibition *Il Novecento italiano* (biographical entry by Cecilia De Carli), Milano, Palazzo della Permanente, January-March; Mazzotta, Milano.
Janet Abramowicz, "The Liberation of the Object", in *Art in America*, no. 3, New York, March.
Concetto Pozzati, "Prima inventava, poi copiava", in *L'Arena*, Verona, 23 May.
Pier Giovanni Castagnoli, Paolo Fossati, texts in the catalogue of the exhibition *Disegno italiano fra le due guerre*, Modena, Galleria Civica d'Arte Moderna, July-October.
Eugenio Riccòmini, text in catalogue of the exhibition *Da Cézanne a Morandi e oltre*, Mamiano di Parma, Fondazione Magnani-Rocca, September.
Attilio Bertolucci, "Morandi e Arcangeli - Storia di due generazioni", in *Libera Stampa*, Lugano, 24 September.
Paul Kunkel, "The Singular

Path of Giorgio Morandi", in *Architectural Digest*, New York, October.
Eugenio Riccòmini, Anna Colliva, "Un 'continuum' quasi senza fratture - Da Cézanne a Morandi sul filo della memoria", in *Leader*, no. 10, Roma, October.
Marco Marozzi, "Bologna vuol riscoprire il suo difficile Morandi e gli dedica un museo", in *la Repubblica*, Roma, 30 October.
Franco Basile, "Il museo in Galleria", in *Il Resto del Carlino*, Bologna, 4 November.
Franco Solmi, "Il Museo Morandi", in *l'Unità*, Roma, 15 November.
Franco Solmi, "Ma Morandi val ben qualche rissa", in *Il Resto del Carlino*, Bologna, 20 November.
Concetto Pozzati, " 'Investire' su Morandi significa anche arricchire culturalmente la città", in *l'Unità - Emilia Romagna*, Roma, 25 November.
Arrigo Quattrini, " 'Maestro scomodo' non omologabile, brusco ed isolato", in *l'Unità - Emilia Romagna*, Roma, 3 December.
Learco Andalò, "Grizzana, sull'Appennino, è grata (e ricorda) il pittore bolognese, in *l'Unità - Emilia Romagna*, Roma, 16 December.
Cesare Brandi, "Morandi merita un museo nel cuore di Bologna", in *Corriere della Sera*, Milano, 23 December.
Renzo Imbeni, "I doveri della città", in *Il Resto del Carlino*, Bologna, 29 December.
Francesco Berti, Arnoaldi Veli, "Come nasce un museo - Bologna e Morandi: i gesti dei singoli", *ibidem*.
AA.VV., *Handbuch Museum Ludwig - Band 2*, Köln, Museum Ludwig.
Zeno Birolli, *Sorbi, tordi & nitidezze*, Milano, Jaca Book.
Angelika Burger, *Die Stilleben des Giorgio Morandi. Eine koloritgeschichtliche Untersuchung*, Hildesheim-Zürich-New York, Georg Holms Verlag.
Luigi Carluccio, *La faccia nascosta della luna* (edited by Roberto Tassi), Torino, Allemandi.
Renato De Fusco, *Storia dell'arte contemporanea*, Bari, Laterza.
Davide Lajolo, *Conversazioni in una stanza chiusa*, Milano, Frassinelli.

Licisco Magagnato, Sandro Zanotto, texts in the catalogue of the exhibition at the Galleria d'Arte Moderna "Mario Rimoldi", Cortina D'Ampezzo; Vicenza, Neri Pozza.
Thomas M. Messer, catalogue of the exhibition *Acquisition Priorities - Aspects of Postwar Painting in Europe*, New York, The Solomon R. Guggenheim Museum.
Ilario Rossi, *Dieci personaggi che contano*, Abano Terme, Piovan.
Carlo Savoia "Giorgio Morandi" (new edition of the text published in *Il Comune di Bologna*, March-April 1939), in *Bologna anni 1930-40 - Materiali d'opere e di memorie da leggere e da vedere* (edited by Carlo Doglio and Luigi Vignali), Bologna, Atti e Memorie dell'Accademia Clementina, XVI, Bologna.
Valerio Zurlini, *Gli anni delle immagini perdute*, Reggio Emilia, Prandi.

1984
AA.VV., catalogue of the anthological exhibition of Giorgio Morandi, Sasso Marconi, La Casa dell'Arte, January-February.
Eugenio Riccòmini, "E quelle umili stanze ancora impregnate della presenza dell'artista", in *l'Unità - Emilia Romagna*, Roma, 4 January.
Franco Basile, "Ricordo di Morandi", in *Il Resto del Carlino*, Bologna, 6 January.
Andrea Emiliani, "Cari Morandi dispersi come recluti", in *Il Resto del Carlino*, Bologna, 6 January.
Luca Savonuzzi, "A Bologna un museo dedicato a Morandi", in *Il Resto del Carlino*, Bologna, 19 January.
Dede Auregli, "Bologna farà un museo per il 'suo' Morandi, in *l'Unità - Emilia Romagna*, Roma, 25 January.
Giovanna Pascoli Piccinini, "L'uomo della monocompagnia", in *Emilia-Romagna*, Bologna, February.
Luigi Lambertini, "Giorgio Morandi a vent'anni dalla morte", in *Il Giornale*, Milano, 10 February.
Mario Pancera, "Morandi 'gigante sperduto in una città di uomini piccoli' ", in *La Domenica del Corriere*, Milano, 11 February.

Franco Solmi, "Questi i Morandi che tornano a casa", in *Il Resto del Carlino*, Bologna, 14 February.

Gian Pacher, "Storia e leggenda di Morandi", in *Alto Adige*, Bolzano, 15 February.

Mauro Corradini, "Quelle epiche bottiglie", in *Bresciaoggi*, Brescia, 16 February.

Dede Auregli, "Morandi, sono questi i magnifici dieci", in *l'Unità - Emilia Romagna*, Roma, 17 February.

Renato Barilli, "Bologna: battaglia per Morandi", in *La Stampa*, Torino, 17 February.

Andrea Emiliani, Dede Auregli, Raffaolo Poggeochi, "Una leggenda che si nutre della storia quotidiana; Paesaggi, fiori e nature morte per la sua arte; I ricordi dell'amata via Fondazza, il museo nelle sale della galleria", in *l'Unità - Emilia Romagna*, Roma, 17 February.

Claudio Spadoni, "Omaggio alla lezione di Morandi", in *Il Resto del Carlino*, Bologna, 20 February.

Renzo Biasion, "Considerava inutili gli uomini", in *Oggi*, Milano, 22 February.

Claudio Cerritelli, "Filtra da tenerissima luce il colore della meditazione", in *la Repubblica - Bologna*, Roma, 22 February.

Stefano Ghiberti, "Dipingeva le bottiglie come simboli di solitudine", in *Gente*, Milano, 24 February.

Francesco Berti Arnoaldi Veli, "Morandi, troppo poco", in *Il Resto del Carlino*, Bologna, 28 February.

Franco Solmi, "Museo Morandi aperto nel 1984?", in *Emilia-Romagna*, Bologna, March.

Roberto Daolio, "Il Museo Morandi a Bologna", in *Le Arti News*, no.s 2-3, Milano, March-June.

Guido Giuffré, "Ricordare Morandi", in *La Discussione*, Roma, 5 March.

G.L. Verzellesi, "Poesia per immagini", in *L'Arena*, Verona, 5 March.

Luigi Serravalli, "Morandi e l'avanguardia a Sasso Marconi", in *La Vernice*, Venezia, May-June.

Sandra Orienti, "L'anelante sentimento della durata", in *Il Popolo*, Roma, 17 May.

Gualtieri Da Vià, "Il mondo metafisico nei disegni di Morandi", in *L'Osservatore Roma-*

no, Città del Vaticano, 20 May.

Enzo Bilardello, "L'eredità di Morandi", in *Corriere della Sera*, Milano, 21 May.

A.B., "L'arte dello spazio nelle 'nature morte' di Morandi", in *La Voce Repubblicana*, Roma, 22 May.

Andrea Rossi, Roberto Pasini, "Mio fratello Giorgio Morandi - A Bologna un museo porterà il suo nome", in *Arte*, no. 142, Milano, June.

Pietro Marino, "Il mondo sulla mensola", in *La Gazzetta del Mezzogiorno*, Bari, 17 June.

Fortunato Bellonzi, "Le contemplazioni di Morandi", in *Il Tempo*, Roma, 18 June.

Cesare Brandi, "Un amore per Morandi nato nella Selva Nera", in *Corriere della Sera*, Milano, 19 June.

T.C. (Toti Carpentieri), "Gruppo di bottiglie in un interno", in *Quotidiano di Lecce*, Lecce, 20 June.

Giuseppe La Monica, "Nature morte resuscitate", in *L'Ora*, Palermo, 20 June.

Sergio Troisi, "Morandi solitario", in *Giornale di Sicilia*, Palermo, 22 June.

Alberto Boldrini Milena Milani, Giovanna Pascoli Piccinini, "Nuova vita per le nature morte di Morandi?", in *Prospettive d'Arte*, Milano, July-August.

Aurelio Repetto, Fortunato Massucco, catalogue of the exhibition *Amate sponde - Pittura di paesaggi in Italia dal 1910 al 1984* (texts by Paolo Fossati and Giorgio Barberi Squarotti), Acqui Terme, Liceo Saracco, July-September.

Gabriella Brussich, "Tra le sospese atmosfere di Morandi", in *Messaggero Veneto*, Udine, 6 July.

Michele Dzieduszycki, "Quanti messaggi in quelle bottiglie", in *L'Europeo*, Milano, 7 July.

Lorenza Trucchi, "Con Morandi 'oltre la pittura'", in *Il Giornale*, Milano, 22 July.

Osvaldo Patani, *Le carte affascinanti*, Milano, Stanza del Borgo, September.

Silvana Sinisi, "I disegni di Morandi", in *Le Arti*, no.s 4-5, Macerata, September-December.

Eugenio Riccòmini, "Morandi e il suo tempo, e il nostro", in *Bologna*, no. 7, Bologna, October.

Luciano Bertacchini, "La critica

e Morandi: amori postumi", in *I Martedì*, Bologna, November-December.

Milena Milani, *Giorgio Morandi*, in the catalogue of the exhibition *Gli scrittori presentano i pittori*, Milano, Rotonda della Besana, November-December.

P. Lan., "I paesaggi dipinti in una stanza", in *Corriere della Sera*, Roma, 23 November.

AA.VV., catalogue of the exhibition of Giorgio Morandi (edited by Maria Corral; texts by Franco Solmi, Cesare Brandi, Carlo Bertelli, Juan Gallego, Marilena Pasquali), Madrid, Caja de Pensiones, December 1984 - January 1985, Barcelona, Caxla de Pensions, February-April 1985.

Fernando Huici, "Giorgio Morandi en la soledad de la pintura", in *Guadalimar*, no. 82, Madrid, December 1984 - January 1985.

Catalogue of the exhibition *Maestri della pittura moderna*, Firenze, Centro Tornabuoni, December 1984 - February 1985.

Dario Bonomolo, "Amore e tecnica", in *Giornale di Sicilia*, Palermo, 9 December.

Francisco Calvo Serraler, "Giorgio Morandi - La secreta belleza de lo immóvil", in *El Pais Semanal*, Madrid, 9 December.

Daniel Quintero, "La vitalidad de un clasico", in *El Pais Semanal*, Madrid, 9 December.

Cristina Gil, "Exposición antológica del artista italiano Giorgio Morandi", in *Ya*, Madrid, 10 December.

Giuliano Briganti, "Morandi alla finestra", in *la Repubblica*, Roma, 11 December.

Ana Gavín, "Giorgio Morandi: manda el espazio", in *El Alcazar*, Madrid, 11 December.

Joan Sureda, "Giorgio Morandi: pintar la pintura", in *Liberación*, Madrid, 13 December.

Miguel Logrono, "Morandi: la fortaleza de la pintura", in *Diario 16*, Madrid, 15 December.

Francisco Calvo Serraler, "Morandi, un metafisico de la pintura", in *El Pais*, Madrid, 15 December.

Renato Barilli, "Toccate quella luce", in *L'Espresso*, no. 50, Roma, 16 December.

Angel González García, "Giorgio Morandi un Robinsón de la pintura, in *Cambio 16*, Madrid, 17-24 December.

Fortunato Bellonzi, "Omaggio a

Morandi", in *Il Tempo*, Roma, 18 December.

Sebastiano Grasso, "Vivere da borghese e pensare da semidio", in *Corriere della Sera*, Milano, 19 December.

Dario Micacchi, "La vera natura di Morandi", in *l'Unità*, Milano, 19 December.

Gualtiero Da Vià, "Morandi paesaggista", in *L'Osservatore Romano*, Città del Vaticano, 20 December.

Alvaro Martinez-Novillo, "Morandi, el arte de la intimidad", in *Ya*, Madrid, 22 December.

Antonello Trombadori, Paolo Levi, Vittorio Sgarbi, "Ecco l'altro Morandi", in *L'Europeo*, Milano, 22 December.

Carlo Bertelli, "Il fascino della bottiglia", in *Il Giornale*, Milano, 23 December.

Maria Pia Farinella, "Tutti i colori del grigio", in *Giornale di Sicilia*, Palermo, 23 December.

Mariano Apa, "Morandi, tutto il mondo su un tavolo", in *Il Popolo*, Roma, 27 December.

Giorgio Mario Bergamo, "Bologna e nostalgia", in *Il Gazzettino*, Venezia, 27 December.

Marcello Passeri, "La pittura di Morandi e la musica di Petrassi", in *Gazzetta del Sud*, Messina, 28 December.

Calimero Barilli, Mario Bonetti, *20 giovani leoni*, Roma, Volpe.

Stefano Calabrese, Silvia Camerini, *L'immagine dell'Appennino bolognese*, Bologna, Nuova Alfa.

Vincenzo Cardarelli, *Il sole a picco*, Bologna, Nuova Alfa (anastatic reprint of the volume published in 1929).

Enzo Carli, *La pittura italiana - Il Novecento*, Vicenza, Banca Popolare di Vicenza.

André Chastel, *Storia dell'arte italiana*, Bari, Laterza.

Jean Clair, *Critica della modernità*, Torino, U. Allemandi & C.

Andrea Comellini, *Morandi e il suo tempo. Il periodo dagli inizi fino al 1917*, degree thesis, rapporteur Renato Barilli, Università di Bologna, academic year 1983-1984.

Il disegno italiano, Reggio Emilia, La Scaletta.

Ruggero Jacobbi, *L'avventura del Novecento*, Milano, Garzanti.

Davide Lajolo, *Gli uomini dell'arcobaleno*, Parma, Augusto Agosta Tota.

Roberto Longhi, *Scritti sul-*

l'Ottocento e Novecento, Firenze, Sansoni.

Milena Milani, *L'angelo nero*, Milano, Garzanti.

Duilio Morosini, *L'arte degli anni difficili 1928-1944*, Roma, Editori Riuniti.

Roberto Tassi, *L'opera grafica di Giorgio Morandi*, in Paolo Lagazzi, *Antologia di "Palatina"*, Parma, Edizioni La Pilotta.

Toni Toniato, catalogue of the exhibition *Opere degli artisti premiati dal 1947 al 1967*, Venezia, Fondazione Bevilacqua La Masa.

1985

"Giorgio Morandi en la Caixa", in *Antiquaria*, no. 14, Madrid, January.

Nicola Ciarletta, "Ambiguità delle divisioni", in *Questarte*, Pescara, January-March.

Anna Marzio Positani, "I colori corposi di Morandi", in *La Nuova Venezia*, Venezia, 2 January.

"Morandi - Musica de cámara del arte", in *El Alcazar*, Madrid, 2 January.

A.M. Campoy, "Giorgio Morandi, 1890-1964", in *ABC*, Madrid, 4 January.

Luis Francisco Pérez Redondo, "Giorgio Morandi, la metafisica del bodegón", in *Lapiz*, no. 22, Barcelona, February.

Marilena Pasquali, "Morandi a Madrid", in *Verso l'Arte*, III, no.s 28-29, Corrina Monforrato, February-March.

Peter Weiermair, Mercedes Garberi, catalogue of the exhibition *Italienische Kunst 1900-1980 - Hauptwerke aus dem Museo d'Arte Contemporanea, Mailand*, Frankfurt, Frankfurter Kunstverein, February-April; Berlin, Frölich & Kaufmann, Milano, Mazzotta.

Sergio Guarini, "Mito e realtà nei paesaggi di Morandi", in *Avanti!*, Roma, 14 February.

B.B., "El genio 'secreto' del arte contemporáneo: Giorgio Morandi", in *El Noticiero Universal*, Barcelona, 19 February.

"Una antologia de Morandi, en Barcelona", in *El Correo Catalán*, Barcelona, 19 February.

Enric Sales, "Morandi en Barcelona", Barcelona, 23 February.

Gloriano Paoletti, Attilio Coltorti, catalogue of the exhibition *Picasso, Miró e la grafica d'arte del Novecento*, Jesi, Palazzo dei Convegni, March-April.

AA.VV., catalogue of the exhibition *I giganti del bulino: Morandi, Bartolini, Viviani* (edited by E. Tavoni and I. Guidi; texts by L. Vitali, M. Valsecchi, G. Marchiori, C.L. Ragghianti, F. Russoli), Sasso Marconi, La Casa dell'Arte, April.

Sandra Soster, "Verso il Museo Morandi", in *Bologna*, XXV, no. 4, Bologna, April.

AA.VV., catalogue of the anthological exhibition (texts taken from the catalogue of the anthological exhibition in Madrid and Barcelona, 1984-85), Marseille, Musée Cantini, April-June.

Dede Cantini, "Il Museo Morandi può ora contare su 50 olii", in *l'Unità - Emilia Romagna*, Roma, 18 April.

Enrico Buda, "Come nasce un museo", in *La Vernice*, Venezia, May.

Marilena Pasquali, "I ventidue dipinti tornati in città" (interview to Francesco Paolo Ingrao), in *Bologna Incontri*, XVI, no. 5, Bologna, May.

Claudio Cerritelli, "Come filtrate dal segno le incisioni di Giorgio Morandi", in *la Repubblica*, Roma, 3 May.

Giorgio Soavi, "Il grigio e la rosa", in *Il Giornale*, Milano, 26 May.

Renzo Biasion, "Morandi sul rame", in *Oggi*, Milano, 29 May.

Marisa Vescovo, "Giorgio Morandi: un viandante dentro una stanza", in *Taxi*, Milano, 29 May.

Elisabeth Vedrenne, "L'atelier de Morandi vu par Folon" (photos by Jean-Michel Folon), in *Décoration Internationale*, no. 82, Paris, June.

Marisa Vescovo, "Morandi viandante in una stanza - Visitiamo la mostra di Marsiglia", in *Il Resto del Carlino*, Bologna, 5 June.

n.a.p., "Ventitré Morandi ed è già museo", in *L'Unità - Emilia Romagna*, Roma, 12 June.

Andrea Emiliani, "Morandi maestro senza tempo", in *Il Resto del Carlino*, Bologna, 18 June.

Mariella Sandrin, "L'orologio di Bologna", in *Panorama*, Milano, 30 June.

Giuseppe Mesirca, "Tris d'oro dell'incisione", in *Il Gazzettino*, Venezia, 2 July.

Patrizia Romagnoli, "Morandi in Galleria con 'Anniottanta'", in *L'Unità*, Roma, 3 July.

"The Perfect Still-life", in *International Courier*, Roma, 23 July.

Everardo Dalla Noce, "Nelle forme di Morandi c'è una sfida al tempo", in *Il Sole 24 Ore*, Milano, 28 July.

Luigi Lambertini, "Il Calvario dimenticato", in *Il Giornale*, Milano, 1° August.

"'Caro Morandi, farò esporre i tuoi quadri. Tuo Raimondi', un inedito omaggio al grande scrittore", in *L'Unità - Emilia Romagna*, Roma, 6 August.

Franco Solmi, Marilena Pasquali, texts in the catalogue of the exhibition *Morandi - Oli, disegni, acqueforti*, Firenze, Galleria Palazzo Vecchio, October-November.

Catalogue of the exhibition *Morandi e il suo tempo* (texts by Eugenio Riccòmini, Franco Solmi, Silvia Evangelisti, Marilena Pasquali, Flavio Caroli, Renato Barilli, Concetto Pozzati; entries by Marilena Pasquali and Silvia Evangelisti), Bologna, Galleria Comunale d'Arte Moderna, November 1985 - February 1986; Milano, Mazzotta.

AA.VV., *Quaderni morandiani 1. Primo Incontro Internazionale di Studi su Giorgio Morandi. Morandi e il suo tempo* (edited by Marilena Pasquali), Bologna, Galleria Comunale d'Arte Moderna; Milano, Mazzotta.

Mariano Apa, text in the catalogue of the exhibition *Licini - Opere dal 1913 al 1957*, Urbino, Palazzo Ducale, July-September; Milano, Mondadori.

Franco Solmi, *Morandi, alla Galleria Comunale d'Arte Moderna di Bologna* (documentation by Marilena Pasquali), Bologna, Grafis.

Rosalba Tardito, Franco Solmi, Marilena Pasquali, catalogue of the exhibition *Morandi. 100 opere su carta*, Milano, Pinacoteca di Brera, and Bologna, Galleria Comunale d'Arte Moderna; Milano, Mazzotta.

1986

Claudio Spadoni, catalogue of the exhibition *Il fantasma della qualità* (texts by Pietro Bonifiglioli and Franco Rella), Ravenna, Loggetta Lombardesca, March-April.

G.R., "Giorgio Morandi", in *Le Arti News*, Milano, March/April-May/June.

AA.VV., *XLII Biennale Internazionale d'Arte di Venezia. Sezione Il Colore* (edited by Attilio Marcolli), Venezia, June.

Vittorio Sgarbi, catalogue of the exhibition *Paesaggio senza territorio*, Mesola, Castello Estense; Milano, Mazzotta.

C.L. Ragghianti, "Morandi giovanissimo", in *Critica d'Arte*, Modena, October-December.

AA.VV., *Ragionamenti*, Roma, December (special issue illustrated with etching reproductions by G. Morandi).

Ettore Spalletti, *Le collezioni del Novecento 1915-1945*, Firenze, Galleria d'Arte Moderna di Palazzo Pitti, December, Firenze, Centro Di.

AA.VV., catalogue of the exhibition *Grafica italiana del Novecento. Collezione Timpanaro*, Comune di Cortona and Accademia Etrusca.

AA.VV., catalogue of the exhibition *Italics. 1925-1985. Sessant'anni di vita culturale in Italia*, Roma, Istituto dell'Enciclopedia Italiana.

Flavio Caroli, "Il nodo Longhi-Morandi", in *Bologna* (edited by Renato Zangheri), Bari, Laterza.

Pina D'Elia, *La collezione Grieco*, Bari, Pinacoteca Provinciale.

Giorgio Soavi, *Il quadro che mi manca*, Milano, Garzanti.

Rosanna Maggio Serra, *Arte moderna a Torino. 200 opere d'arte acquisite per la Galleria d'arte moderna*, Torino, U. Allemandi & C.

Francesco Messina, *Care grandi ombre*, Milano, Scheiwiller.

1987

Nino Migliori, *Paesaggi immaginati da i luoghi di Morandi* (introduction by Franco Solmi), Calendario 1987, Bologna, Confederazione Nazionale dell'Artigianato-Comitato Regionale dell'Emilia Romagna.

"Guttuso e Baj, dialogo su arte e cristianesimo", in *Alto Adige*, Bolzano, 21 January.

AA.VV., *Collezioni del XX secolo. Il primo Novecento*, Roma, Galleria Nazionale d'Arte Moderna, February; Firenze, Centro Di.

"I luoghi di Giorgio Morandi rivisti da Migliori", in *l'Unità - Emilia Romagna*, Roma, 13 February.

Franco Basile, Cesare Sughi, Gaia Giorgetti, "Museo Moran-

di, una storia infinita", in *Il Resto del Carlino*, Bologna, 22 April.

Massimo Nava, "Anche Parigi vuole i miei Morandi", in *Corriere della Sera*, Milano, 27 May.

Michele Smargiassi, "Morandi ritorna a Parigi e questa volta da trionfatore", in *l'Unità*, Milano, 29 May.

Pier Giovanni Castagnoli, Flaminio Gualdoni, texts in the catalogue of the exhibition *Disegno italiano del dopoguerra*, Frankfurt, Kunstverein, June-August; Modena, Galleria d'Arte Moderna, September-December.

Franco Solmi, Jean Clair, Lamberto Vitali, texts in the catalogue of the anthological exhibition, Paris, Hôtel de la Ville, June-August, Milano, Mazzotta.

Rossana Bossaglia, Mario Quesada, Pasqualina Spadini, texts in the catalogue of the exhibition *Secessione Romana 1913-1916*, Roma, Palazzo delle Esposizioni, June-September; Roma, Fratelli Palombi Editori.

Elena Guicciardi, "Le isole di Morandi", in *la Repubblica*, Roma, 13 June.

N.D., "Morandi tel un 'pêcheur' de la couleur perle", in *France-Soir*, Paris, 15 June.

Jean-Louis Ferrier, "Le monde tranquille de Giorgio Morandi", in *Le Point*, Paris, 29 June.

Philippe Dagen, "Images muettes", in *Le Monde*, Paris, 30 June.

"Arte e colore 'soprattutto incanto' sul lago di Garda", supplement to *Bresciaoggi*, no. 204, Brescia, July.

Flaminio Gualdoni, text in the catalogue *Soprattutto incanto*, Sirmione, ex Palazzo Comunale, July-August; Milano, Mazzotta.

Luc Vezin, "Giorgio Morandi", in *Beaux Arts Magazine*, Paris, July-August.

Johannes Gachnang, text in the catalogue of the exhibition *Italie hors d'Italie*, Nîmes, Musée d'Art Contemporain, July - September.

E.D., *Eternel éphémère*, in *7à Paris*, Paris, 1° July.

Giorgio Mascherpa, "Morandi in una preziosa mostra a Parigi. Quel filosofo della finestra", in *Avvenire*, Milano, 3 July.

Jeanine Warnod, "Le voile de Morandi", in *Le Figaro*, Paris, 7 July.

Pierre Cabanne, "L'inquiétant mutisme de Morandi", in *Le Martin de Paris*, Paris, 10 July.

Ingeborg Kuhn-Rega, "Der stille Maler", in *Luxemburger Wort*, Luxembourg, 24 July.

Lorenzo Bocchi, "Oltre mezzo secolo di paesaggi e di nature morte", in *Il Giorno*, Milano, 28 July.

Vittorio Sgarbi, text in the catalogue of the exhibition *La natura morta nell'arte italiana del Novecento*, Mesola, Castello Estense, August-October - Bari, Pinacoteca Provinciale, November-December; Milano, Mazzotta.

Walter Schönenberg, Enrico Crispolti, texts in the catalogue of the exhibition *Lucio Fontana e lo Spazialismo*, Lugano, Villa Malpensata, August-November.

Floriano De Santis, "Morandi in excelsis", in *Bergamo-oggi*, Bergamo, 4 August.

Pierre Schneider, "Les filles fragiles de Morandi", in *L'Express*, Paris, 7 August.

Francesco Poli, "L'eloquente silenzio delle cose", in *il manifesto*, Roma, 20 August.

AA.VV., texts in the catalogue of the exhibition *I Prandi librai, editori, mercanti d'Arte*, Reggio Emilia, Teatro Municipale, October-November.

Maurizio Fagiolo dell'Arco, "The world in a bottle. Morandi's variations", in *Artforum International*, no. 4, New York, December.

Marilena Pasquali, *Giorgio Morandi. La poetica, i luoghi, le opere*, text for an audio-visual programme, Bologna, Galleria Comunale d'Arte Moderna, 19 December.

Franco Basile, *Morandi. Giorni di Grizzana*, Verona, Edizioni Ghelfi.

Flavio Caroli, *La pittura contemporanea. Dal Romanticismo alla Pop Art*, Milano, Electa.

Silvia Evangelisti, *Astratto dal quotidiano. Nature morte e paesaggi di Giorgio Morandi*, in *Nove secoli d'arte a Bologna*, Torino, U. Allemandi & C.

Gilles Plazy, *Les aventures de la peinture moderne*, Paris, Liana Levy.

1988

Simonetta Lux, Ignazio Venafro, Claudio Mazzenga, texts in

Exhibitions

the catalogue of the exhibition *Renato Marino Mazzacurati e gli artisti di "Fronte"*, Roma, Università La Sapienza, Museo Laboratorio d'Arte Contemporanea, January-February.
Luigi Serravalli, "Bologna fa posto a Morandi", in *Alto Adige*, Bolzano, 2 January.
Marta Marini, "Un film-quadro per ricordare Giorgio Morandi, in *La Gazzetta di Rimini*, Rimini, 29 May.
Marc Le Bot, *Le transitoire, l'éternel*, in the catalogue of the exhibition *Les Années 50*, Paris, Musée National d'Art Moderne - Centre Georges Pompidou, June-October.
Valeria Dalle Donne, "Le silenziose stanze di Giorgio Morandi, in *la Repubblica-Bologna*, Bologna, 9 June.
Giuseppe Appella, text in the catalogue of the exhibition *Le Muse irrequiete di Leonardo Sinisgalli*, Macerata, Palazzo Ricci, July; Roma-Milano, De Luca-Mondadori.
Franco Solmi, text in the catalogue of the anthological exhibition, Massa Carrara, Palazzo Ducale, August-September; Milano, Mazzotta.
AA.VV., texts in the catalogue of the exhibition *Figure del Novecento* (section "Pittura e Incisione", edited by Silvia Evangelisti), Bologna, Accademia di Belle Arti, September-November; Bologna, Nuova Alfa.
Vittorio Fagone, Carlo Bertelli, Ewald Rathke, Ada Masoero, texts in the catalogue of the exhibition *Di Segno Italiano. Italienische Zeichnungen 1908-1988*, Frankfurt, Städtische Galerie, September-November - Zürich, Kunsthaus, March-May 1989; Milano, Mazzotta.
Marilena Pasquali, *Giorgio Morandi 1890-1990*, text in the catalogue of the one-man exhibition, Bologna, Galleria Forni, October-November.
Maurizio Fagiolo dell'Arco, catalogue of the exhibition *Realismo magico. Pittura e scultura in Italia 1919-1925*, Verona, Galleria dello Scudo, November; Milano, Mazzotta.
Walter Schönenberger, "L'arte italiana moderna e la Svizzera", in *Protagonisti dell'arte italiana*, Vaduz-Lugano, Verlag F.L.B.
AA.VV., texts in the catalogue

of the anthological exhibition (texts by Giuliano Briganti, Pier Giovanni Castagnoli, Fabrizio D'Amico, Mercedes Garberi, Flaminio Gualdoni, Marilena Pasquali and documentation by Marilena Pasquali), Tampere, Sara Hildénin taidemuseo, 4 November 1988 - 9 Januar 1989; Leningrad, Ermitage Museum, January-February 1989; Moskva, Pushkin Museum, February-March 1989; London, Accademia Italiana delle Arti, April-May 1989; Locarno, Civici Musei, Casa Rusca June-July 1989; Tubingen, Kunsthalle, October-November 1989; Milano, Electa.

1914
Bologna, Hotel Baglioni, 21-22 March (with O. Licini, M. Bacchelli, S. Pozzati, G. Vespignani).
Rome, Palazzo delle Esposizioni, Spring: *II Esposizione internazionale della Secessione*.
Rome, Galleria Sprovieri, 3 April - 15 May: *I Esposizione libera futurista*.

1917
Lugo, Scuole Comunali, November: *I Esposizione d'arte interregionale*.

1921
Berlin, Nationalgalerie für Moderne Kunst, March: *Mostra di "Valori Plastici"* (the exhibition was held in Dresden, Hannover and Munich).

1922
Florence, Palazzo Sangallo, 8 April - 31 July: *La Fiorentina primaverile*.

1926
Florence, Stanze del Selvaggio, February-March: *I Mostra d'arte del gruppo del Selvaggio*.
Milan, Palazzo della Permanente, February-March: *I Mostra del Novecento italiano*.

1927
Florence, April: *II Esposizione internazionale dell'incisione moderna*.

1928
Venice: *XVI Esposizione Biennale Internazionale d'Arte*.

1929
Milan, Palazzo della Permanente, March-April: *II Mostra del Novecento italiano*.
Pittsburgh, 19 October - 10 December: *XVIII Carnegie Prize*.
Paris, Galerie Bonaparte, 30 November - 20 December: *Exposition d'art italien moderne*.

1930
Basle, Kunsthalle, 5 January - 2 February: *Moderne Italiener*.
Bern, Kunsthalle, 16 March - 4 May: *Artisti della nuova Italia*.
Venice: *XVII Esposizione Biennale Internazionale d'Arte*.
Pittsburgh, 19 October - 10 December: *XXIX Carnegie Prize*.
Buenos Aires: *Mostra del Novecento italiano*.
Parigi, Bibliothèque Nationale, November: *Exposition de la gravure et de la médaille italienne contemporaine*.

1931
Rome, Palazzo delle Esposizioni, January-June: *I Quadriennale d'arte nazionale*.
Athens, 26 April - 3 May: *Settimana italiana in Atene*.

1932
Paris, Galerie Georges Bernheim, 4-19 March: *Artistes italiens modernes*.
Florence, IV Fiera internazionale del libro: *I Mostra dell'incisione italiana moderna*.

1933
Vienna, Künstlerhaus, 1 April - 5 June: *Moderne italienische Kunst*.
Pittsburgh, 19 October - 10 December: *XXXI Carnegie Prize*.

1934
Venice, Summer: *XIX Esposizione Biennale Internazionale d'Arte*.
United States of America: *Exhibition of Contemporary Italian Painting*.

1935
Rome, Palazzo delle Esposizioni, February-July: *II Quadriennale d'arte nazionale*.
Paris, Musée du Jeu de Paume, May-July: *L'art italien des XIXe et XXe siècles*.

1936
Pittsburgh, Carnegie Institute, 15 October - 6 December: *The 1936 International Exhibition of Paintings*.

1937
Paris, Trocadero, Italian Pavilion, May-September: *Expo '37*.
Berlin: *Mostra d'arte italiana*.
New York, Cometa Art Gallery: *Anthology of Contemporary Italian Drawing*.
Rome, Galleria di Roma: inaugural exhibition.

1938
Bern, Kunsthalle, October: *Ausstellung der Moderne Italienische Kunst*.

1939
Rome, Palazzo delle Esposizioni, February-July: *III Quadriennale d'arte nazionale*.
Pittsburgh, Carnegie Institute, 19 October - 10 December: *The 1939 International Exhibition of Paintings*.
San Francisco, Golden Gate: *Golden Gate International Exhibition of Contemporary Art*.
Kaunas: *Mostra dell'incisione*.

1940
Zurich: *Mostra d'arte italiana*.

1941
Cortina d'Ampezzo: *I Mostra delle collezioni italiane d'arte contemporanea* (1st award to the artist).

1942
Bologna, Galleria Ciangottini, April: *Collettiva di maestri italiani*.
Milan, Pinacoteca Nazionale di Brera, 7-22 November: *Mostra della collezione Pietro Feroldi*.

1943
Rome, Palazzo delle Esposizioni, May-July: *IV Quadriennale d'arte nazionale*.
Venice, Galleria del Cavallino, November: one-man exhibition of graphics.

1945
Rome, Galleria La Palma: April-May: one-man exhibition.
Florence, Galleria del Fiore, 21 April - 3 May: one-man exhibition.
Como, Galleria Borromini: *Pittura contemporanea*.

1946
Godena, Sala delle Mostre dell'Università, 24 February - 3 March: *Maestri della pittura contemporanea*.
Rome, Galleria dell'Obelisco, November: one-man exhibition.
Milano, Circolo delle Grazie: one-man exhibition.

1947
Rio de Janeiro, Ministry of Education, May: *Esposizione di pittura italiana moderna*.
Pisa, Palazzo alla Giornata, July-August: *Mostra di pittura italiana contemporanea*.

1948
Rome, Galleria Nazionale d'Arte Moderna, March-May: *Rassegna nazionale di arti figurative*.
Venice, 29 May - 30 September: *XXIV Esposizione Biennale Internazionale d'Arte*.
Venice, Galleria del Cavallino, 14 June: one-man exhibition.
Stockholm, Färg och Form, September: *Italiensk Nutdskonst* (then Göteborg, Konstmuseet, October).
Rome, Calcografia Nazionale, Autumn: anthological exhibition of graphics.

1949
Cairo, Palais Ismail Pacha, February-March: *Exposition de peinture moderne italienne depuis 1850 jusqu'à nos jours*.
Catania, February-April: *Quarant'anni d'arte italiana*.
Milan, Politecnico, 9-16 April: exhibition organized by the university students association.
Brussels, Palais des Beaux-Arts, May-June: one-man exhibition of graphics.
Salsomaggiore, Grand Hôtel des Termes, May-June: *Cinquant'anni di pittura italiana*.
New York, Museum of Modern Art, 28 June - 18 September: *Twentieth Century Italian Art*.
Milan, Galleria dell'Annunciata, December 1949 - January 1950: one-man exhibition.
Vienna, Akademie der Bildenden Künste, 10 December 1949 - 10 January 1950: *Italienische Malerei der Gegebwart*.

1950
Brussels, Palais des Beaux-Arts, 28 January - 26 February: *Art italien contemporain*.
Amsterdam, Stedelijk Museum, 3 March - 3 May: *Figuren uit de Italiaanse Schilderkunst na 1910*.
Paris, Musée National d'Art Moderne, May-June: *Exposition d'art moderne italien*.
London, Tate Gallery, 25 June - 31 July: *Exhibition of Modern Italian Art*.
Zurich, Kunsthaus, November-December: *Futurismo e pittura metafisica*.
Copenhagen: *Pittura moderna italiana*.
Lugano: *I Mostra internazionale del bianco e nero* (award for etching).

1951
Cincinnati, Cincinnati Art Museum, 2 February - 4 March: *Paintings 1900-1925*.
Göteborg, Konsthallen, February: *Esposizione d'arte italiana contemporanea* (then Helsinki, Konsthallen, March; Oslo, Kunsternes Hus, April; Copenhagen, Frie Udstilling, May).
Lordgen, 14 April: *Grafik av Giorgio Morandi* (with Carlo Carrà).
Salerno, Galleria Il Setaccio, 9 July: one-man exhibition.
Turin, Palazzo delle Belle Arti - Parco del Valentino, October:

I Mostra Italia-Francia. Pittori d'oggi.
São Paulo do Brasil, Museu de Arte Moderno, October-December: *I Bienal / Artistas italianos de hoje*.
Brussels: *Italian Art Printing*.
Hague, Gemeentemuseum: *Drie Grafici*.

1952
Paris, Musée Nationale d'Art Moderne, March: *Jeune gravure contemporaine*.
Venice, 14 June - 19 October: *XXVI Esposizione Biennale Internazionale d'Arte*.
Pittsburgh, Carnegie Institute, 16 October - 14 December: *The 1952 Pittsburgh International Exhibition of Contemporary Painting*.

1953
Stockholm, Liljevalchs Konsthall, 6 March - 12 April: *Italiensk Nutdskonst*.
Florence, Palazzo Strozzi, April-May: *Arte moderna in una raccolta italiana*.
São Paulo do Brasil, Museu de Arte Moderno, October-December: *II Bienal* (award for engraving).

1954
Hague, Gemeentemuseum, 14 April - 6 June: anthological exhibition (then Rotterdam).
Hamburg, Kunsthalle, June-July (then Cologne, Istituto Italiano di Cultura).
London, New Burlington Galleries, 25 June - 24 July: anthological exhibition.
Pallanza, Kursaal, 25 July - 30 September: *Capolavori dell'arte italiana contemporanea (1918-1930)*.
Milan, Palazzo Reale, November 1954 - February 1955: *103 dipinti del Museo d'arte di San Paolo del Brasile*.

1955
London, Institute of Contemporary Art, 9 June - 2 July: *Twentieth Century Paintings and Sculptures*.
Kassel, Museum Fridricianum, 15 July - 18 September: *Documenta I, Kunst des XX. Jahrhunderts*.
New York, Delius Gallery, 4 October - 5 November: one-man exhibition.
Rome, Galleria La Medusa, 29 October: one-man exhibition.
Rome, Palazzo delle Esposizioni, November 1955 - April 1956,

VII Quadriennale nazionale d'arte: Antologia della pittura e scultura italiane dal 1910 al 1930.

1956
New York, John Heller Gallery, January-February: *Giorgio Morandi, Massimo Campigli, Anton Music*.
New York, Columbus Gallery of Fine Arts, 9 March - 15 April: *Italian Design Today*.
Winterthur, Kunstmuseum, 24 June - 29 July: *Giorgio Morandi/Giacomo Manzù*.
Zagreb, Ljubljana, Skoplje, Belgrade, October 1956 - January 1957: *Mostra d'arte italiana contemporanea*.
Deerfield, Deerfield Academy, 20 October - 10 November: *Contemporary Italian Art*.
London, Tate Gallery, 21 November - 19 December: *Modern Italian Art from the Estorick Collection*.

1957
Plymouth, City Museum & Art Gallery, 26 January - 16 February: *Modern Italian Art from the Estorick Collection;* then Birmingham, City Museum & Art Gallery, 23 February - 16 March.
Turin, Galleria Galatea, May: one-man exhibition.
Munich, Haus der Kunst, 7 June - 15 September: *Kunstausstellung München 1957 und Ausstellung Italienischer Kunst von 1910 bis zur Genwart*.
São Paulo do Brasil, Museu de Arte Moderno, September-December: *IV Bienal* (award for the painting).
New York, World House Gallery, 5 November - 7 December: *Giorgio Morandi / Retrospective 1912-1957*.
Ivrea, Centro Culturale Canavesano, March: *L'opera grafica*.
South America, *Esposición circulante en Sur-América organizada por la Bienal de Venecia por encargo del Ministerio de Asuntos Exteriores y del Ministerio de Educación 1957: Diez años de pintura italiana*.

1958
New York, The American Federation of Art, February-June: *Manzù and Morandi*.
Lugano, 3 April - 15 June: *V Mostra internazionale di bianco e nero* (award for engraving).

Brussels, Palais des Beaux-Arts, 17 April - 21 July: *50 ans d'art moderne*.
Lincoln (Mass.), De Cordoba Museum, 27 April - 1° June: *A Decade in Review*.
Caracas, Galeria de Arte Contemporáneo, September: *Morandi, Tosi, Marino Marini, Campigli, Sironi, De Pisis*.
Turin, Galleria Galatea, October: *Disegni e incisioni di Morandi, Casorati e Spazzapan*.
Pittsburgh, Carnegie Institute, 5 December 1958 - 8 February 1959: *1896/1955 - Retrospective Exhibition of Paintings from Previous International*.
Copenhagen, Charlottenborg Palace: *Pittura italiana moderna*.

1959
Padova, Galleria Le Stagioni, January: *30 acqueforti*.
St. Etienne, Musée d'Art et d'Industrie, May: *Peintres et sculpteurs italiens du futurisme à nos jours* (then in Dijon, July; Blois, September; Lyon, October; Charleroi, December).
Rome, Palazzo Barberini, 4 June - 6 September: *Il futurismo*.
Kassel, Museum Friedricianum, 11 July - 11 October: *Documenta II, Kunst nach 1945*.
Winterthur, Kunstmuseum, 4 October - 15 November: *Mostra del futurismo*.
Turin, Galleria Civica d'Arte Moderna, 5 October - 8 December: *Capolavori d'arte moderna nelle collezioni private*.
Milan, Galleria Annunciata, December 1959 - January 1960: one-man exhibition.

1960
Milan, Palazzo Reale, April-June: *Arte italiana del XX secolo da collezioni americane*.
New York, N. Knoedler & Co., 12 April - 14 May: *The Colin Collection*.
Boston, Boston University Art Gallery, 23 April - 14 May: *Works from Private Collections*.
Ancona, Palazzo del Liceo Scientifico, 3-24 July: *Premio Marche '60*.
Lucerne, Kunstmuseum, 6 August - 18 September: *Italienische Maler der Gegenwart*.
Paris, Musée National d'Art Moderne, 4 November 1960 - 23 January 1961: *Les arts en Europe de 1884 à 1914*.

New York, World House Galleries, 6 December 1960 - 14 January 1961: one-man exhibition.

1961
New York, The Museum of Modern Art, February: *The James Thrall Soby Collection*.
Chicago, Illinois Institute of Technology, 5-30 April: *The Maremont Collection of Twentieth Century*.
Turin, *Italia '61*, Summer: *Da Boldini a Pollock* (then in Milan, Padiglione d'Arte Contemporanea).
Turin, Galleria La Bussola, June: *La figura nell'arte italiana contemporanea* (within *Italia 61*).
Amsterdam, Stedelijk Museum, 22 August - 8 September: *Polarità: il dionisiaco e l'apollineo nell'arte*.

1962
Venice, Ca' Pesaro, 16 June - 7 October: *XXXI Esposizione Biennale Internazionale d'Arte, Mostra dei grandi premi della Biennale 1948-60*.
Siegen, Haus-seel-am-Markt, 27 October - 17 November: *Giorgio Morandi Rubenspreis 1962 der Stadt Siegen*.
Turin, Galleria Galatea, December: one-man exhibition of etchings.
Milan, Galleria Lorenzelli, December 1962 - January 1963: *Mostra Magini-Morandi*.

1963
Naples, Galleria Il Centro, January-February: *40 incisioni di Giorgio Morandi*.
Paris, Grand Palais, 22 May - 3 June: *Art contemporain*.
Strasbourg, Musée des Beaux-Arts, June-September: *La grande aventure de l'art du XXe siècle*.
Viareggio, Galleria Nettuno, July: *L'opera grafica di Giorgio Morandi*.
Hamburg, Kunstverein, 28 September - 3 November: *Italien 1905-1925: Futurismus und Pittura metafisica*.
Beirut, Istituto Italiano di Cultura, October-November: *Dipinti italiani d'oggi*.
Geneva, Galerie Krugier, November: one-man exhibition.
Rome, Galleria L'Obelisco, November: one-man exhibition.
New York, Marlborough-Gerson Gallery, 2 November - 21 December: *Artist and Maece-*

nas / *A Tribute to Curt Valentin*.
Washington, National Gallery of Art, 16 December 1963 - 1° March 1964: *Paintings from the Museum of Modern Art, New York*.

1964
Zurich, Galerie Obere Zäune, March: one-man exhibition of graphics.
Bielefeld, Städtisches Kunsthaus, April-May: one-man exhibition.
Washington, Washington Gallery of Modern Art, 1° April - 3 May: *Treasures of XXth Century Art from the Maremont Collection*.
London, Tate Gallery, 22 April - 28 June: *Exhibitions 54-64 / Painting and Sculpture of a Decade*.
Venice, *XXXII Esposizione Biennale Internazionale d'Arte*, May-September: *Arte d'oggi nei musei*.
Lausanne, Palais de Beaulieu, 1° May - 24 October: *Chefs-d'œuvres des collections suisses de Manet à Picasso*.
Caracas, Fundación Eugenio Mendoza, 17-31 May: *Preferencias de los coleccionistas*.
Karlsruhe, Badischer Kunstverein, 22 June - 26 July: one-man exhibition.
Baltimore, Museum of Art, 1° August - 15 November: exhibition for the museum 50th anniversary.
Ancona, 6-29 September: *Premio Marche '64 - Omaggio a Giorgio Morandi*.
Munich, Galerie Atelier Monpti, September-October: one-man exhibition.
Milan, Galleria delle Ore, October: *Omaggio a Morandi*.
Naples, Palazzo Reale, October-November: *La natura morta italiana*.
Pittsburgh, Carnegie Institute, 30 October 1964 - 10 January 1965: *Pittsburgh International 1964. Exhibition of Contemporary Painting and Sculpture*.
Hannover, Kestner - Gesellschaft, December: *Giorgio Morandi, Alfred Kubin*.
Zurich, Kunsthaus, December 1964 - February 1965: *La natura morta italiana*.

1965
Bologna, Galleria La Loggia, January: *Giorgio Morandi e Felice Casorati*.

Wupperthal, Kunst-und Museumverein, 12 February - 14 March: one-man exhibition.
Rotterdam, Boymans-van Beuningen Museum, March-April: *La natura morta italiana*.
Milan, Galleria Annunciata, April-May: one-man exhibition.
Rome, Galleria La Medusa, May: *Marini-Morandi*.
Paris, Istituto Italiano di Cultura, June: *Morandi, De Pisis, Soffici, Donghi*.
Edinburgh, Scottish National Gallery of Modern Art, August-September: *The Collection of Works by Giorgio Morandi 1890-1964 Belonging to Professor Luigi Magnani*.
Civenna, Galleria del Ghisallo, September: *Morandi, Rosai, Sironi, Tozzi*.
Rome, Palazzo delle Esposizioni, October 1965 - March 1966: *IX Quadriennale nazionale d'arte*.
Bern, Kunsthalle, 23 October - 5 December: anthological exhibition.
Caracas, Fundación Mendoza, 1° November - 15 December: *Omaggio a Giorgio Morandi*.

1966
Milan, Galleria Annunciata, January: *Maestri del disegno*.
Rome, Galleria Nazionale d'Arte Moderna, 27 March - 25 April: *Giorgio Morandi / Opere della collezione Ingrao*.
Florence, Galleria L'Indiano, March-April: *Omaggio a Morandi*.
Rome, Calcografia Nazionale, April: *Giorgio Morandi - Mostra delle acqueforti*.
New York, Public Education Association, 26 April - 21 May: *Seven Decades 1895-1965*.
Irvine, University of California Art Gallery, 17 May - 10 June: *Five Europeans: Bacon, Balthus, Dubuffet, Giacometti, Morandi*.
Recklinghausen, Städtisches Museum, 31 May - 23 August: *Variationen über ein Thema*.
Venice, *XXXIII Esposizione Biennale Internazionale d'Arte*, 18 June - 16 October: one-man exhibition.
Grizzana, Scuole Comunali, July-August: *Omaggio a Giorgio Morandi*.
Turin, Galleria La Minima, October-November: *Omaggio a Morandi*.
Bologna, Palazzo dell'Archigin-

nasio, 30 October - 15 December: anthological exhibition.

1967
Milan, Galleria Ciranna, February-March: *Il paesaggio nell'acquaforte di Morandi*.
Florence, Palazzo Strozzi, February-May: *Arte moderna in Italia 1915-1935*.
Milan, Palazzo della Permanente, March: *I Mostra d'arte moderna e trame contemporanee*.
Ferrara, Galleria Duca d'Este, May: *Disegni di Morandi*.
New Haven, Yale University Art Gallery, 4 May - 18 June: *The Helen and Robert M. Benjamin Collection*.
Monza, Galleria Civica, 8-21 June: *Esempi di pittura italiana contemporanea*.
Guatemala, Honduras, Salvador, Nicaragua, Costarica, July-December: *Arte italiano contemporáneo - Exposición itinerante organizada por la Quadriennale di arte de Roma*.
Padova, Galleria La Chiocciola, November-December: *Manzù, Morandi, Marino*.
Turin, Galleria Civica d'Arte Moderna, November 1967 - January 1968: *Le muse inquietanti - Maestri del surrealismo*.
Washington, The Phillips Collection, 30 November 1967 - 11 January 1968: *Masters of Italian Art from the Collection of Gianni Mattioli*.

1968
Harvard, Busch-Reisinger Museum Harvard University, 12 January - 10 February: one-man exhibition.
Dallas, Dallas Museum of Fine Arts, 1° February - 3 March: *Masters of Italian Art from the Collection of Gianni Mattioli* (then San Francisco, 16 March - 21 April; Detroit, 19 June - 21 July; Kansas City, 6 October - 17 November).
Turin, Galleria Civica d'Arte Moderna, 1° February - 17 March: *I pittori italiani dell'Associazione internazionale arti plastiche UNESCO*.
Bologna, Galleria Forni, 30 March - 19 April: *Grandi Maestri Contemporanei*.
Brescia, Associazione Artisti Bresciani, April: *Incisioni di Giorgio Morandi*.
Northampton, Smith College Museum of Art, 11-28 April: *An Exhibition in Honour of Henry Russel-Hitchcock 19th

and 20th Century*.
Stuttgart, Galerie Lutz & Meyer, May: one-man exhibition.
Zagreb, Galerija Moderne Umjetnosti, 2-15 May: *Bolonjsko Slikarstvo XX Vijeka*.
Copenhagen, Kunstforeningen, September: anthological exhibition.
Bologna, Galleria de' Foscherari, October-November: *Giorgio Morandi - 75 acquarelli dal 1915 al 1963*.
Geneva, Galerie Krugier, October-November: one-man exhibition.
Oslo, Nasjonalgalleriet, 26 October - 18 November: *Giorgio Morandi. Raderinger*.
Paris, Galerie Villand & Galanis, December 1968 - January 1969: one-man exhibition.
Bologna: *Mostra della pittura bolognese nel '900*.

1969
Milan, Galleria l'Annunciata, 15 February - 21 March: *L'Annunciazione d'Oro*.
Milan, Galleria del Milione, March: *Testimonianza per Morandi*.
Boston, 23 January - 23 February: *Masters of Modern Art from the collection of Gianni Mattioli* (then New York, 5-30 March).
Brussels, Palais des Beaux-Arts, 9 September - 12 October: *Maîtres de l'art moderne en Italie 1910-1935 - Collection Gianni Mattioli*.
Haarlem, Frans Halsmuseum, 6 October - 1° December: *Modern Italian Art from Dutch Collections*.
Copenhagen, Louisiana Kunstmuseet, 8 November - 14 December: *Italiensk Kunst 1910-1935 - Gianni Mattioli Samling*.
Cortina d'Ampezzo, Centro d'Arte Dolomiti, 24 December 1969 - 10 January 1970: *Omaggio a Giorgio Morandi*.

1970
Hamburg, Hamburger Kunsthalle, 19 February - 30 March: *Italienische Kunst - Sammlung Gianni Mattioli*.
Bologna, Museo Civico, April-May: *Due decenni di acquisizioni nelle raccolte comunali d'arte*.
Strasbourg, Château de Rohan, 14 May - 15 September: *Exposition d'art moderne européen*.

Rome, Galleria Don Chisciotte, June: *33 acqueforti*.
Bologna, Palazzo dell'Archiginnasio, 12 September - 22 November: *Natura ed espressione nell'arte bolognese-emiliana*.
Madrid, Museo Español de Arte Contemporáneo, November-December: *Maestros del arte moderno en Italia 1910-1935 - Collección Gianni Mattioli* (then Barcelona, December 1970 - January 1971).
Milan, Galleria Sianesi, November-December: group exhibition.
Berkeley, University Art Museum, University of California, 6 November 1970 - 10 January 1971: *Excellence: Art from the University Community*.
Milan, Galleria del Milione, December 1970 - January 1971: *Morandi e Morlotti*.
Rome, Il Nuovo Torcoliere, December 1970 - January 1971: *L'opera grafica di Giorgio Morandi* (48 engravings)
London, Royal Academy of Art, 5 December 1970 - 17 January 1971: anthological exhibition.
Cortina d'Ampezzo, Galleria Dolomiti: one-man exhibition.

1971
Sevilla, Museo de Arte Contemporáneo, January-February: *Maestros del arte moderno en Italia 1910-1935 - Collección Gianni Mattioli*.
Milan, Galleria Sacerdoti, February-March: *Omaggio a tre grandi maestri. Magnasco, De Chirico, Morandi*.
Paris, Musée National d'Art Moderne, 9 February - 12 April: anthological exhibition.
Milan, Palazzo della Permanente, March-May: *Mostra di pittori e scultori che recitano a soggetto*.
Milan, Rotonda della Besana, May-June: anthological exhibition.
Milan, Galleria Annunciata, June-July: one-man exhibition.
Vicenza, Palazzo Chiericati, 4-26 September: *L'arte moderna nel collezionismo vicentino*.
Berlin, Nationalgalerie, 11 September - 7 November: *Metamorfosi dell'oggetto*.
Milan, Galleria Annunciata, December 1971 - January 1972: *Omaggio a Picasso*.
Turin, Galleria Dantesca, December 1971 - January 1972: one-man exhibition.

1972
Amsterdam, Stedelijk Museum, January-February: *Morandi-Etsen*.
Milan, Palazzo Reale, 17 January - 23 February: *Metamorfosi dell'oggetto*.
Milan, Galleria Eunomia, May-June: one-man exhibition.
Kyoto, National Museum of Modern Art, 15 April - 21 May: *Masters of Modern Italian Art* (then Tokio, 31 May - 2 July).
Boston, Museum of Fine Arts, 8 June - 8 October: *The Rathbone Years*.
Venice, Museo Correr, *XXXVI Esposizione Biennale Internazionale d'Arte*, 11 June - 1° October: *Capolavori della pittura del XX secolo, 1900-1945*.
Rome, Palazzo delle Esposizioni, November 1972 - May 1973: *X Quadriennale nazionale d'arte*.

1973
Leningrad, Ermitage Museum, 17 April - 10 May: anthological exhibition (then Moscow, Puṣhkin Museum, 18 May - 16 June).
Paris, Musée des Arts Décoratifs, May-June: *1928-1973 - Domus, 45 anni di architettura, design, arte*.
Rome, Galleria Nazionale d'Arte Moderna, 18 May - 22 July: anthological exhibition.
Urbino, Palazzo Ducale, June-July: *Le acqueforti di Giorgio Morandi*.
Geneva, Musée Rath, 28 June - 23 September: *Art du XX siècle - collections genevoises*.
Frankfurt, Frankfurter Westend-Galerie, October-November: one-man exhibition.

1974
Milan, Palazzo Reale, 27 May - 20 September: *50 anni di pittura italiana nella collezione Boschi-Di Stefano donata al Comune di Milano*.
Karlsruhe, Badischer Kunstverein, 22 June - 26 July: anthological exhibition.
Milan, Galleria Annunciata, December 1974 - January 1975: *Mostra di Natale*.

1975
Bologna, Galleria Comunale d'Arte Moderna, 1° May - 15 June: anthological exhibition.
Darmstadt, Kunsthalle, 24 May - 6 July: *Realismus und Realität - Ausstellung zum 11. Darmstädter Gespräch*.

Lugano, Villa Malpensata, 28 August - 9 November: *Dalle collezioni d'arte private ticinesi: maestri europei del XX secolo*.
Bologna, Galleria La Loggia, December 1975 - January 1976: *Idee per una collezione. Il disegno*.

1976
Bologna, Galleria Due Torri, May: *Un confronto: due tempi, Licini-Morandi*.
Bologna, Galleria Marescalchi, May: *Omaggio a Morandi*.
Verona, Galleria dello Scudo, November 1976 - January 1977: one-man exhibition.
Sasso Marconi, La Casa dell'Arte, 13 November 1976 - January 1977: *Idee per una collezione/1*.
Milan, Galleria Annunciata, 20 November 1976 - January 1977: *Natale con l'arte*.

1977
Milan, Centro Annunciata, 19 February: *Opere dipinte a mano*.
Bologna, Galleria La Loggia, May: *Acquerelli, disegni, gouaches*.
Berlin, Kunstausstellung, 14 August - 16 October: *Tendenzen der Zwanziger Jahre*.
Lucca, Gallleria Barsotti, October: one-man exhibition.
Vancouver, The Vancouver Art Gallery, October: anthological exhibition.
Sasso Marconi, La Casa dell'Arte, October-November: one-man exhibition.
Geneva, Musée Rath, 6 October 1977 - 15 January 1978: *Du Futurisme au Spatialisme*.
Geneva, Galerie Jeanneret, November 1977 - January 1978: one-man exhibition.
Sasso Marconi, La Casa dell'Arte, December 1977 - January 1978: *Protagonisti*.

1978
Bologna, Galleria Comunale d'Arte Moderna, 1° June - 31 August: *Metafisica del quotidiano*.
Ferrara, Palazzo dei Diamanti - Galleria Civica d'Arte Moderna, July-October: anthological exhibition.
Milano, Galleria Annunciata, 28 October-November: *Una raccolta in vendita*.

1979
Paris, Galerie Berggruen, Feb-

ruary: *Le acqueforti di Giorgio Morandi*.
Sasso Marconi, La Casa dell'Arte, 27 February - 15 June: *Protagonisti*.
Venice, Palazzo Grassi, May: *La pittura metafisica*.
Milan, Palazzo Reale, October 1979 - January 1980: *Origini dell'astrattismo - Verso nuovi orizzonti del reale*.
Bordeaux, Musée des Beaux-Arts: anthological exhibition of graphics.
Milan, Padiglione d'Arte Contemporanea: *Miti del Novecento*.

1980
Rome, Galleria Il Gabbiano, March-April: one-man exhibition.
Bologna, Galleria Comunale d'Arte Moderna, 31 May - 7 September: *La metafisica - Gli anni Venti*.
Cavalese, Casa dell'Arte, July-August: one-man exhibition.
Focette di Marina di Pietrasanta, Galleria Farsetti, July-August: one-man exhibition.
Milan, Centro Annunciata, November 1980 - January 1981: *Un bel formato*.
Bologna, Galleria Trimarchi, December: *Giorgio Morandi - Disegni*.
Paris, Centre Georges Pompidou - Musée National d'Art Moderne, December 1980 - April 1981: *Les réalismes* (then Berlin, Staatliche Kunsthalle, May-June 1981).

1981
Milan, Galleria Annunciata, 28 February - 25 March: *40 anni di mostre*.
Sasso Marconi, La Casa dell'Arte, 9 May - 11 June: one-man exhibition.
Munich, Haus der Kunst, 18 June - 6 September: anthological exhibition.
Acqui Terme, Palazzo Saracco, July-September: anthological exhibition.
Vevey, Musée des Beaux-Arts, August-October: *Les peintres du silence*.
San Francisco, Museum of Modern Art, 24 September - 1° November: anthological exhibition organized by the Des Moines Art Center (then New York, The Solomon R. Guggenheim Museum, 19 November 1981 - 17 January 1982; Des Moines, Des Moines Art Center, 1° Febru-

ary - 14 March 1981).
Cellatica, October-November: *Il linguaggio dell'incisione* (then Capo di Ponte, November-December; Trieste and Innsbruck, Spring 1982).
Florence, Galleria Santa Croce, October: one-man exhibition.
Norrbottens, Norrbottens Museum, October 1981 - April 1982: one-man exhibition.
Frankfurt, Frankfurter Westend-Galerie: *Zur italienischen Kunst nach 1945-Deutsche Künstler und Italien*.

1982
Venice-Mestre, Galleria Plus Art, January: *Disegni e acqueforti di Giorgio Morandi*.
Milan, Palazzo Reale, 27 January - 30 April: *Gli anni Trenta - Arte e cultura in Italia*.
Bologna, Galleria Comunale d'Arte Moderna, 20 February - 15 March: *La scuola bolognese dell'acquaforte*.
Bologna, Galleria Marescalchi, March: *Idee per una collezione/2*.
Piacenza, Galleria La Scaletta, April: *L'acquaforte* (then held in Rome, Galleria Il Disegno, May, and in Milan, Galleria del Milione, June).
Bologna, Galleria Comunale d'Arte Moderna, from May 1982: *Morandi in Galleria - Opere e documenti* (permanent exhibition).
Helsinki, Ateneumin taidemuseo, 19 August - 26 September: *Ars Vaticana*.
Sasso Marconi, La Casa dell'Arte, October: *Grandangolo 2*.
Milano, Galleria Philippe Daverio, 12 October - 12 November: group exhibition.
Turin, Teatro Regio, November: *Mostra della Fondazione Guido ed Ettore De Fornariis*.
Varese, Galleria Ghiggini, November: *L'acquaforte. Una tecnica, tre epoche, quindici artisti*.
Milan, Galleria Rizzardi, December: *Omaggio a Giorgio Morandi*.

1983
Zagreb, Gabinetto di Arti Grafiche dell'Accademia Jugoslava di Scienze e Belle Arti, January: *Acqueforti di Giorgio Morandi* (then Rijeka, Galerija Moderna, February).
Milan, Palazzo della Permanente, January-March: *Mostra del Novecento italiano*.

Modena, Galleria Civica, 28 July - 15 October: *Disegno italiano fra le due guerre*.
Mamiano di Parma, Fondazione Magnani-Rocca, September-October, *Da Cézanne a Morandi e oltre*.
Parma, Centro Steccata, November: *Disegni e incisioni di Giorgio Morandi*.
New York, Solomon R. Guggenheim Museum: *Aspects of Postwar Painting in Europe*.

1984
Sasso Marconi, La Casa dell'Arte, January-March: anthological exhibition.
Washington, Hirshorn Museum - Smithsonian Institution, February-April: *Contemporary Italian Art*.
Bologna, Pinacoteca Nazionale, from 26 April: *Giorgio Morandi - 10 quadri in Pinacoteca*.
Freiburg im Breisgau, Morat-Institut für Kunst und Kunstwissenschaft, May: permanent exhibition dedicated to the Morat-Institut Collection.
Rome Galleria Mara Coccia, May: *Morandi - Disegni 1915-1963*.
Sorrento, Istituto Statale d'Arte, May-June: *Omaggio a Giorgio Morandi a vent'anni dalla morte* (photographic exhibition with the collaboration of the Galleria Comunale d'Arte Moderna, Bologna).
Cardiff, National Museum of Wales, 4 October-November: *Bolognese Etching* (then Brecon, Brecknock Museum, 24 November - 22 December; Carmarthen, Carmarthen County Museum, 5 January - 2 February 1985; Llanelly, Llanelly Library, February-March 1985; Newcastle, University Art Gallery, March-April 1985), with the collaboration of the Galleria Comunale d'Arte Moderna, Bologna.
Rome, Galleria La Tartaruga, November: *Giorgio Morandi, 60 acqueforti*.
Venice, Opera Bevilacqua La Masa, November: *Opere degli artisti premiati dal 1947 al 1967*.
Milan, Rotonda della Besana, November-December: *Gli scrittori presentano i pittori*.
Rome, Galleria dell'Oca, November 1984 - 30 January 1985: *I paesaggi di Morandi*.
Madrid, Sala de Exposicciónes - Caja de Pensiones, December

1984 - January 1985: anthological exhibition (then Barcelona, Caxia de Pensions, February-March 1985).
Leningrad-Moscow-Dresden: *La natura morta nella pittura europea. XVI secolo-inizi XX secolo.*

1985
Florence, Gabinetto dei Disegni e delle Stampe degli Uffizi, February: *Dieci anni di acquisizioni. 1974 1984.*
Frankfurt, Frankfurter Kunstverein, February-April: *Italienische Kunst 1900-1980 - Hauptwerke aus dem Museo d'Arte Contemporanea, Mailana.*
Bologna, Galleria La Loggia, April: *Morandi incisore* (then Bologna, Pinacoteca Nazionale, May-September).
Sasso Marconi, La Casa dell'Arte, April: *I giganti del bulino - Morandi, Bartolini, Viviani.*
Toulouse, Musée des Augustins, April-May: *La scuola bolognese dell'acquaforte*
Marseille, Musée Cantini, 13 April - 18 June: anthological exhibition (reproposal of the exhibitions held in Madrid and Barcelona).
Florence, Galleria Palazzo Vecchio, October: one-man exhibition.
Salerno, Galleria Il Catalogo, November: one-man exhibition.
Bologna, Galleria Comunale d'Arte Moderna, 9 November 1985 - 10 February 1986: *Morandi e il suo tempo.*
Milan, Pinacoteca Nazionale di Brera, 29 November 1985 - 2 February 1986: *Morandi. 100 opere su carta* (then Bologna, Galleria Comunale d'Arte Moderna, 22 February - 14 April 1986).

1986
Ravenna, Loggetta Lombardesca, March-April: *Il fantasma della qualità.*
Reggio Emilia, Galleria La Scaletta, April: *Il disegno italiano.*
Sasso Marconi, La Casa dell'Arte, May: *Quadrangolo.*
Cortona, Accademia Etrusca, June: *La collezione Timpanaro. Grafica italiana del Novecento.*
Venice, Ca' Corner della Regina, June-September: *I premi della Biennale di Venezia.*
Venice, Giardini di Castello, June-September: *XLII Esposi-*
zione Biennale Internazionale d'Arte. Section *Il colore.*
Valdagno, Villa Marzotto, Summer: *1951-1968. I Premio Marzotto.*
Mesola, Castello Estense, July-September: *Paesaggio senza territorio.*
Turin, Società Promotrice delle Belle Arti, November 1986 - January 1987: *Arte moderna a Torino. Opere della Collezione De Fornariis.*
Bari, Pinacoteca Provinciale, December: *La collezione Grieco.*
Bologna, Galleria La Loggia, December: *Artisti bolognesi dell'incisione. Una tradizione da Morandi ad oggi.*
Cortina d'Ampezzo, Galleria Marescalchi, December 1986 - February 1987: *Opere scelte.*
Florence, Galleria Nazionale d'Arte Moderna di Palazzo Pitti, December 1986 - June 1987: *e collezioni del Novecento. 1915-1945.*
New York, Columbia University, Center for Italian Studies, December: *Italics 1925-1985. Sessant'anni di vita culturale in Italia* (organized by the Istituto dell'Enciclopedia Italiana).

1987
Rome, Galleria dell'Oca, January: *De Pisis, Morandi, Sironi.*
Rome, Galleria Nazionale d'Arte Moderna, February: opening of the new Sale del Novecento.
Genoa, Galleria Devoto, March: *Itinerario intorno alla natura morta di ieri e di oggi.*
Rome, Galleria F. Russo, April: group exhibition.
Rome, Studio d'Arte Grafica, April: *Grafica dei Maestri Contemporanei.*
Bologna, Galleria Marescalchi, May: group exhibition.
Milan, Studio Diomede, May: *Grafica dei Maestri Contemporanei.*
Turin, Studio d'Arte Scuola Romana, May-June: *Scuola Romana. Natura morta.*
Frankfurt, Kunstverein, June-August: *Disegno italiano del dopoguerra* (then Modena, Galleria Comunale d'Arte Moderna, September-December).
Rome, Palazzo delle Esposizioni, June-September: *Le "Secessioni" romane.*
Paris, Hôtel de la Ville, 12 June - 20 August: anthological exhibition (with the collaboration of
the Galleria Comunale d'Arte Moderna, Bologna).
Cremona, Galleria Il Triangolo, July: *Il quadro che mi manca.*
Sirmione, ex Palazzo Comunale, July-August: *Soprattutto incanto.*
Turin, Galleria Civica d'Arte Moderna, July-August: *1945-1965. Arte italiana e straniera.*
Nîmes, Musée d'Art Contemporain, July-September: *Italie hors d'Italie* (organized by the Museo d'Arte Contemporanea, Rivoli).
Como, Galleria Solenghi, August-September: group exhibition.
Mesola, Castello Estense, August-October: *La natura morta nell'arte italiana del '900* (then Bari, Pinacoteca Provinciale, November-December).
Lugano, Villa Malpensata, August-November: *Lucio Fontana e lo Spazialismo.*
Orzinuovi, Castello San Giorgio, August-November: *Inediti da una collezione d'arte moderna* (then Lignano Sabbiadoro, Centro Civico, April-September 1988).
Lugano, Museo Cantonale d'Arte, September: opening of the museum and presentation of the permanent collections.
Como, Fondazione Antonio Ratti, September-October: *Arte svelata. Collezionismo privato a Como tra l'800 e il 900.*
Brescia, Galleria Il Segno Contemporaneo, November: *Paesaggio come metafora.*
Seregno, Sala Mariani, November: *Opere di grafica internazionale.*
Tolentino, Galleria Giraldi, November: group exhibition.
Ivrea, Servizi Culturali Olivetti, November-December: *Morandi e Montale.*
Bologna, Galleria Comunale d'Arte Moderna "Giorgio Morandi", December: new arrangement of the Raccolta Morandi.
Biella, Galeria Mercurio, December 1987 - January 1988: *Maestri del Novecento.*
Brescia, Galleria Schreiber, December 1987 - January 1988: *Fogli del Novecento.*

1988
Rome, Università La Sapienza, Museo Laboratorio di Arte Contemporanea, January-February: *Renato Marino Mazzacurati e gli artisti di "Fronte".*
Verona, Società Letteraria, January: *Arcana Scheiwiller.*
Rome, Studio d'Arte Grafica, March: *Grafica di maestri contemporanei.*
Munich, Haus der Kunst, March-May: *Mythos Italien. Wintermärchen Deutschland.*
Reggio Emilia, Galleria 13, April, group exhibition.
Busto Arsizio, Galleria Italiana Arte, May: *Opere in carta.*
Lecco, Galleria Altair Nuova, May: *Opere grafiche.*
Brescia, Associazione "Arte e Spiritualità", May-June: opening of the Raccolta d'arte moderna.
Pavullo, Galleria Comunale d'Arte Moderna, May-June: *Amici pittori.*
London, Hayward Gallery, May-August: *Impressionism and modern vision* (works from the Phillips Collection of Washington).
Sarnano, Galleria Il Loggiato, June: *Anni Venti-Quaranta. Maestri della pittura del Novecento.*
Monza, Galleria Studio Aperto, June-July: group exhibition.
Rome, Galleria Il Narciso, June-July: *Grafica italiana dal dopoguerra ad oggi.*
Paris, Centre Georges Pompidou - Musée National d'Art Moderne, June-October: *Années 50.*
Macerata, Palazzo Ricci, July-October: *Le Muse irrequiete di Leonardo Sinisgalli.*
Massa Carrara, Palazzo Ducale, 4 August - 25 September: anthological exhibition.
Bologna, Accademia di Belle Arti, 5 September - 10 November: *Figure del Novecento.*
Frankfurt, Stadtische Galerie, 22 September - 6 November: *Di Segno Italiano. Italienische Zeichnungen 1908-1988* (then Zurich, Kunsthaus, 3 March - 7 May 1989).
Bologna, Galleria Forni, 8 October-November: one-man exhibition.
Verona, Galleria dello Scudo, 27 November 1988 - January 1989: *Realismo magico - Pittura e scultura in Italia 1919-1925.*
Tampere, Sara Hildénin taidemuseo, 4 November 1988 - 9 January 1989: anthological exhibition (organized by the Galleria Comunale d'Arte Moderna, Bologna).

Catalogue of the works

Paintings

1. *Landscape*, 1910
oil on cardboard on canvas,
37.7 × 48 cm
signed lower right:
Morandi
Bologna, private collection
Exhibitions: Rome, 1973, no. 1,
repr.; Bologna, 1975, no. 1, repr.;
Munich, 1981, no. 1, repr.; San
Francisco-New York-Des Moines, 1981-82, no. 1, repr.; Madrid-Barcelona-Marseille, 1984-
85, no. 1, repr.; Bologna, 1985,
no. 6, repr.
Bibliography: Vitali, 1977, no.
1.

2. *Landscape*, 1913
oil on cardboard, 41 × 55 cm
signed and dated on the back:
Morandi / luglio 1913
Bologna, Galleria Comunale
d'Arte Moderna "Giorgio
Morandi"
(donated by Morandi's sisters)
Exhibitions: Bologna, 1914;
Rome, 1973, no. 3, repr.; Sasso
Marconi, 1983; Madrid-Barcelona-Marseille, 1984-85, no. 2,
repr.; Bologna, 1985, no. 10,
repr.; Rome, 1987, no. 141, repr.
Bibliography: Vitali, 1977, no.
7; Pasquali, 1982, p. 4; Solmi,
1985, p. 25.

3. *Landscape*, 1913
oil on canvas, 62 × 43 cm
signed and dated lower right:
Morandi / 913
Bologna, Pinacoteca Nazionale
Exhibitions: Bologna, 1914; Paris, 1968-69, no. 1, repr.; Bologna, 1984, repr.; Bologna, 1985,
no. 2, repr.; Bologna, 1988, no.
2, repr.
Bibliography: Vitali, 1964[1],
1965[2], 1970[3], pl. 5; Vitali, 1977,
no. 6.

4. *Still life*, 1918
oil on canvas, 71.5 × 61.5 cm
signed and dated lower centre:
Morandi 918
Leningrad, Ermitage Museum
Exhibitions: Bologna, 1966, no.
17, repr.; London, 1970-71, no.
30, repr.; Paris, 1971, no. 30,
repr.; Leningrad-Moscow, 1973,
no. 1, repr.; Leningrad-Moscow-
Dresden, 1984, no. 60, repr.
Bibliography: "La Raccolta",
Bologna, 1919, no. 11/12, p. 133,
repr.; catalogue Ermitage Museum, I, 1958, p. 216, repr.;

Vitali, 1964[1], 1965[2], 1970[3], no.
37, repr.; Arcangeli, 1964, no.
12, repr.; Carrà, 1968, no. 187,
repr.; Giuffré, 1970, no. 9, repr.;
catalogue Ermitage Museum,
1976, p. 156, repr.; B.N. Terno-
vietz, *Lettere, memorie, documenti*, Moskva 1977, pp. 135-
136; Vitali, 1977, no. 37; Solmi,
1978, p. 41, repr.; catalogue *Morandi e il suo tempo*, Bologna,
1985, p. 41, repr.

5. *Still life*, 1920
oil on wood, 30.5 × 44.5 cm
signed and dated lower right:
Morandi 920
Bologna, Galleria Comunale
d'Arte Moderna "Giorgio
Morandi"
(donated by Morandi's sisters)
Exhibitions: Rome, 1939, no. 9;
Rome, 1973, no. 25; Bologna, p.
103, repr., 1980; Sasso Marconi,
1983; Madrid-Barcelona-Marseille, 1984-85, no. 6; Bologna,
1985, no. 27.
Bibliography: Beccaria, 1939,
pl. XVI; Barbaroux, Giani, 1940,
pl. 105; Brandi, 1942[1], pl. XVI;
1952[2], pl. XVIII; Giani, 1942, pl.
89; Vitali, 1964[1], 1965[2], 1970[3], no.
46; Brandi, 1976, pl. 6; Vitali,
1977, no. 57; Pasquali, 1982, p.
4; Solmi, 1985, p. 26; Evangelisti,
1987, p. 149; Fagiolo dell'Arco,
1987, p. 106.

6. *Still life*, 1921
oil on canvas, 38.2 × 55 cm
signed and dated lower right:
Morandi 921
Bologna, private collection
Exhibitions: Edinburgh, 1965,
no. 1; Bologna, 1968; Zagreb,
1968, no. 56; Milan, 1970-71, no.
1, repr.; Bologna, 1980, p. 104,
repr.; Sasso Marconi, 1983; Bologna, 1985, no. 30, repr.; Paris,
1987, no. 13, repr.
Bibliography: Vitali, 1977, n. 59.

7. *Landscape*, 1921
oil on canvas, 33 × 29 cm
signed bottom centre: Morandi
Bologna, private collection
Exhibitions: Rome, 1939, no. 11;
Florence, 1967, f.c.; Bologna,
1968; Zagreb, 1968, no. 55;
Rome, 1973, no. 28, repr.; Sasso
Marconi, 1983; Bologna, 1985,
no. 28, repr.
Bibliography: Bardi, 1957, pl. 6;
Vitali, 1964[1], 1965[2], 1970[3], pl. 50;
Vitali, 1977, no. 66; Evangelisti,
1987, p. 148.

8. *Flowers*, 1923-1924
oil on canvas, 40 × 29 cm
signed top centre: Morandi
Bologna, Pinacoteca Nazionale
Exhibitions: Bologna, 1984,
repr.; Bologna, 1985, no. 32,
repr.
Bibliography: Vitali, 1964[1],
1965[2], 1970[3], p. 61; Vitali, 1977,
no. 86.

9. *Flowers*, 1924
oil on canvas, 58 × 48 cm
Bologna, Galleria Comunale
d'Arte Moderna "Giorgio
Morandi"
(donated by Morandi's sisters)
Exhibitions: Edinburgh, 1965,
no. 2, repr.; Venice, 1966, no. 21;
Bologna, 1966, no. 24, repr.;
London, 1970-71, no. 20, repr.;
Paris, 1971, no. 20, repr.; Milan,
1971, no. 23, repr.; Leningrad,
1973, no. 3, repr.; Moscow, 1973,
no. 3, repr.; Ferrara, 1978, no. 8,
repr.; San Francisco-New York-
Des Moines, 1981-82, no. 10,
repr.; Sasso Marconi, 1983; Madrid-Barcelona-Marseille, 1984-
85, no. 9, repr.; Bologna, 1985,
no. 33, repr.; Paris, 1987, no. 15,
repr.
Bibliography: Giuffré, 1970,
no. 2; Vitali, 1977, no. 88; Pasquali, 1982, p. 4; Folon, 1985,
XXIII; Solmi, 1985, p. 27.

10. *Still life*, 1924
oil on canvas, 52.5 × 66 cm
signed and dated lower right:
Morandi 1924
Milan, Civico Museo
d'Arte Contemporanea
(donated by Boschi-Di Stefano)
Exhibitions: Milan, 1974, p. 102,
repr.; Munich, 1981, no. 12,
repr.; Madrid-Barcelona-Marseille, 1984-85, no. 14, repr.
Bibliography: Vitali, 1977, no.
100.

11. *Self-Portrait*, 1925
oil on canvas, 63 × 48.5 cm
Mamiano di Parma,
Fondazione Magnani-Rocca
Exhibitions: Cortina d'Ampezzo, 1941; Turin, Galleria La Bussola, 1961; Florence, 1967, no.
1208, repr.; Paris, 1968-69, no. 4;
Bologna, 1975, no. 10, repr.;
Mamiano di Parma, 1983, p. 30,
repr.
Bibliography: Mazzariol, 1958,
p. 60, repr.; Siblik, 1965, pl. 24;

Brandi, 1976, pl. 8; Vitali, 1977,
no. 113; Magnani, 1982, no. 2,
repr.

12. *Still life*, 1925
oil on canvas, 51 × 57.5 cm
signed upper centre: Morandi
Leningrad, Ermitage Museum
Bibliography: Soffici, 1932,
repr. f.t.; Brandi, 1942[1], pl. XXV,
1952[2], pl. XXVI; Valsecchi, 1964,
p. 16, repr.; Vitali, 1964[1], 1965[2],
1970[3], pl. 70; Vitali, 1977, no.
107.

13. *Still life*, 1929
oil on canvas, 52 × 47 cm
signed on the back: Morandi
Modena, private collection
Exhibition: Rome, 1965-66, no.
13, repr.; Cortina d'Ampezzo,
1969-70, pl. I; Geneva, 1977-78;
Ferrara, 1978, no. 29, repr.; Munich, 1981, no. 13, repr.; San
Francisco-New York-Des Moines, 1981-82, no. 11, repr.; Madrid-Barcelona-Marseille, 1984-
85, no. 15, repr.; Bologna, 1985,
no. 39, repr.; Paris, 1987, no. 19,
repr.; Bologna, 1988, no. 13,
repr.
Bibliography: Siblik, 1965, pl.
28; Vitali, 1977, no. 140.

14. *Still life*, 1929
oil on canvas, 54 × 64 cm
signed lower left: Morandi
Milan, Civico Museo
d'Arte Contemporanea
Exhibitions: Venice, 1930, no.
15c; Ancona, 1964, no. 11 (?);
Ferrara, 1978, no. 13, repr.; Munich, 1981, no. 16, repr.; San
Francisco-New York-Des Moines, 1981-82, no. 13, repr.;
Frankfurt, 1985, p. 93, repr.
Bibliography: Nicodemi, Bezzo-
la, 1935, no. 1627; Caramel, Piro-
vano, 1973, vol. V, no. 260, pl.
175; Vitali, 1977, no. 146.

15. *Still life*, 1932
oil on canvas, 62.2 × 72 cm
signed and dated upper left:
Morandi / 1932
Rome, Galleria Nazionale
d'Arte Moderna (deposited
by Galleria Comunale d'Arte
Moderna, Rome)
Exhibitions: Rome, 1935, no. 9
(?); Winterthur, 1956, no. 17;
Munich, 1981, no. 17, repr.; Ma-
drid-Barcelona-Marseille, 1984-
85, no. 17, repr.; Rome, 1987.
Bibliography: Vitali, 1977, no.

170; catalogue *Morandi e il suo
tempo*, Bologna 1985, p. 65,
repr.

16. *Still life*, 1935
oil on canvas, 63.7 × 55 cm
signed and dated lower left:
Morandi 1935
Bologna, Pinacoteca Nazionale
Exhibitions: Pittsburgh, 1936;
New York, 1957, no. 3, repr.;
New York, 1960-61, no. 2; Paris,
1968-69, no. 8; London, 1970-71,
no. 37; Paris, 1971, no. 37; Milan,
1971, no. 41, repr.; Bologna,
1984, repr.; Bologna, 1985, no.
46, repr.; Bologna, 1988, no. 19,
repr.
Bibliography: Cairola, 1946, pl.
CCIII; Vitali, 1977, no. 193.

17. *Landscape*, 1935
oil on canvas, 50 × 70 cm
signed and dated lower right:
Morandi 1935
Milan, Civico Museo
d'Arte Contemporanea
(donated by Boschi-Di Stefano)
Exhibitions: London, 1970-71,
no. 35, repr.; Paris, 1971, no. 35,
repr.; Milan, 1971, no. 40, repr.;
Milan, 1974, repr. p. 99; Ferrara,
1978, no. 15, repr.; Munich, 1981,
no. 19, repr.; Bologna, 1985, no.
47, repr.; Paris, 1987, no. 21,
repr.
Bibliography: Vitali, 1977, no.
195.

18. *Landscape*, 1935
oil on canvas, 54 × 60 cm
signed lower right: Morandi
signed and dated on the back:
Morandi 1935
Modena, private collection
Exhibitions: New York, 1957,
no. 5; Florence, 1967, no. 1225;
Cortina d'Ampezzo, 1969-70, pl.
VI; Bologna, 1988, no. 18, repr.
Bibliography: Vitali, 1977, no.
202.

19. *Landscape*, 1935-1936
oil on canvas, 60.3 × 71 cm
Bologna, private collection
Exhibitions: Ferrara, 1978; no.
17, repr.; Munich, 1981, no. 21,
repr.; San Francisco-New York-
Des Moines, 1981-82, no. 16,
repr.
Bibliography: Vitali, 1977, no.
211.

20. *Landscape*, 1936
oil on canvas, 46 × 61.5 cm
Bologna, private collection

Exhibitions: Edinburgh, 1965, no. 5, repr.; Venice, 1966, no. 39, repr.; Bologna, 1966, no. 51, repr.; Copenhagen, 1968, no. 6, repr.; Milan, 1970-71, no. 5, repr.; London, 1970-71,no. 38, repr.; Paris, 1971, no. 38, repr.; Milan, 1971, no. 42, repr.; Leningrad, 1973, no. 8, repr.; Moscow, 1973, no. 8, repr.; Bologna, 1975, no. 19, repr.; Ferrara, 1978, no. 20, repr.; Munich, 1981, no. 24, repr.; San Francisco-New York-Des Moines, 1981-82, no. 18, repr.; Sasso Marconi, 1983; Bologna, 1985, n. 50, repr.
Bibliography: Giuffré, 1970, pl. 25; Vitali, 1977, no. 215.

21. *Landscape*, 1936
oil on canvas, 45.5 × 71 cm
signed lower left: Morandi
dated on the back: 1936
Bologna, Pinacoteca Nazionale

Exhibitions: New York, 1957, no. 2; Bern, 1965, no. 50; London, 1970-71, no. 30, repr.; Paris, 1971, no. 30, repr.; Milan, 1971, no. 43, repr.; Bologna, 1984, repr.; Bologna, 1985, no. 51, repr.
Bibliography: Vitali, 1964[1], 1965[2], 1970[3], pl. 97; Vitali, 1977, no. 217.

22. *Still life*, 1936
oil on canvas, 47.5 × 60 cm
Bologna, Galleria Comunale
d'Arte Moderna "Giorgio Morandi"
(donated by Morandi's sisters)

Exhibitions: Ferrara, 1978, no. 19, repr.; Madrid-Barcelona-Marseille, 1984-85, no. 22, repr.; Bologna, 1985, no. 49, repr.; Paris, 1987, no. 22, repr.
Bibliography: Vitali, 1977, no. 209; Pasquali, 1982, p. 4; Solmi, 1985, p. 29.

23. *Still life*, 1940
oil on canvas, 42 × 53 cm
signed upper centre: Morandi
Milan, Civico Museo
d'Arte Contemporanea
(donated by Boschi-Di Stefano)

Exhibitions: Milan, 1974, repr. pp. 110-111; Geneva, 1977-78; Munich, 1981, no. 27, repr.; Madrid-Barcelona-Marseille, 1984-85, no. 24; Bologna, 1985, no. 56, repr.
Bibliography: Vitali, 1977, no. 262.

24. *Landscape*, 1940
oil on canvas, 35 × 50 cm
signed and dated lower left:
Morandi 1940
Milan, Civico Museo
d'Arte Contemporanea
(donated by Boschi-Di Stefano)

Exhibitions: Milan, 1974, repr. p. 109; Munich, 1981, no. 29, repr.; Madrid-Barcelona-Marseille, 1984-85, no. 21, repr.
Bibliography: Vitali, 1964[1], 1965[2], 1970[3], pl. 108; Vitali, 1977, no. 273.

25. *Still life*, 1941
oil on canvas, 41 × 49.5 cm
signed and dated lower right:
Morandi / 1941
Campione d'Italia,
S. Lodi collection

Exhibitions: Bologna, 1985, no. 62, repr.
Bibliography: Cairola, 1946, pl. CCVII; Mazzariol, 1958, repr.; Vitali, 1977, no. 290.

26. *Still life*, 1941
oil on canvas, 27 × 52.5 cm
signed and dated lower centre:
Morandi 1941
Mamiano di Parma,
Fondazione Magnani-Rocca

Exhibitions: Edinburgh, 1965, no. 6, repr.; Paris, 1968-69, no. 12, repr.; Milan, 1971, no. 50, repr.; Rome, 1973, no. 69, repr.; Bologna, 1975, no. 24, repr.; Ferrara, 1978, no. 24, repr.; Mamiano di Parma, 1983, p. 32, repr.
Bibliography: Vitali, 1977, no. 313; Magnani, 1982, no. 4, repr.

27. *Still life*, 1942
oil on canvas, 47 × 40.5 cm
signed and dated lower centre:
Morandi 1942
Mamiano di Parma,
Fondazione Magnani-Rocca

Exhibitions: Hague, 1954, no. 30; London, 1954, no. 27; Edinburgh, 1965, no. 8, repr.; Bologna, 1966, no. 69, repr.; Paris, 1968-69, no. 16, repr.; Milan, 1971, no. 56, repr.; Rome, 1973, no. 70, repr.; Ferrara, 1978, no. 30, repr.; San Francisco-New York-Des Moines, 1981-82, no. 25, repr.; Mamiano di Parma, 1983, p. 25, repr.
Bibliography: Vitali, 1964[1], 1965[2], 1970[3], no. 128, repr.; Arcangeli, 1964, no. 38, repr.; Valsecchi, 1964, p. 28, repr.; Vitali,

1977, no. 384; Solmi, 1978, no. 97, repr.; Magnani, 1982, no. 7, repr.

28. *Flowers*, 1942
oil on canvas, 25 × 30 cm
signed and dated lower left:
Morandi / 1942
Modena, private collection

Exhibitions: Paris, 1987, no. 28, repr.
Bibliography: Vitali, 1977, no. 347.

29. *Flowers*, 1942
oil on canvas, 30 × 26 cm
signed and dated lower right:
Morandi / 1942
Modena, private collection

Exhibitions: Ferrara, 1978, no. 32, repr.; Madrid-Barcelona-Marseille, 1984-85, no. 33, repr.; Paris, 1987, no. 29, repr.
Bibliography: Vitali, 1977, no. 352.

30. *Landscape*, 1942
oil on canvas, 27.5 × 52 cm
signed on the back: Morandi
signed and dated on the
frame: Morandi 1942
Modena, G. Salvaterra
collection

Exhibitions: Bern, 1965, no. 65; Venice, 1966, no. 53; Bologna, 1966, no. 68, repr.; Munich, 1981, no. 40, repr.; San Francisco-New York-Des Moines, 1981-82, no. 27, repr.; Madrid-Barcelona-Marseille, 1984-85, no. 35, repr.; Paris, 1987, no. 27, repr.
Bibliography: Vitali, 1964[1], 1965[2], 1970[3], pl. 136; Giuffré, 1970, pl. 29; Vitali, 1977, no. 395.

31. *Landscape*, 1943
oil on canvas, 41.5 × 53 cm
Florence, Banca Toscana

Exhibitions: Rome, 1973, no. 75, repr.
Bibliography: Vitali, 1977, no. 454.

32. *Still life*, 1943
oil on canvas, 28 × 38 cm
signed lower right: Morandi
Campione d'Italia,
S. Lodi collection

Bibliography: Vitali, 1977, no. 437, repr.

33. *Still life*, 1943
oil on canvas, 30 × 45 cm
signed lower right: Morandi
Modena, private collection

Exhibitions: Geneva, 1977-78; Ferrara, 1978, no. 33, repr.; Munich, 1981, no. 41, repr.; San Francisco-New York-Des Moines, 1981-82, n. 28, repr.; Madrid-Barcelona-Marseille, 1984-85, no. 40, repr.; Bologna, 1985, no. 69, repr.; Paris, 1987, no. 31, repr.; Bolgona, 1988, no. 22, repr.
Bibliography: Vitali, 1977, no. 420.

34. *Courtyard of via Fondazza*, 1945-1947
oil on canvas, 56 × 58 cm
signed and dated on the back:
Morandi 1945/47
Bologna, private collection

Bibliography: Vitali, 1977, no. 589.

35. *Flowers*, 1946
oil on canvas, 18 × 17 cm
signed lower right: Morandi
Tolentino, private collection

Bibliography: Vitali, 1977, no. 500; catalogue Brerarte, Milan, Spring, 1974, repr. on the cover.

36. *Flowers*, 1948
oil on canvas, 45 × 35 cm
signed lower right: Morandi
dated on the back: 1948
Bologna, Conti collection

Bibliography: Vitali, 1977, no. 595.

37. *Still life*, 1948
oil on canvas, 44 × 47.5 cm
signed on the back: Morandi
Mamiano di Parma,
Fondazione Magnani-Rocca

Exhibitions: Hague, 1954, no. 53; London, 1954, no. 50; Edinburgh, 1965, no. 13, repr.; Mamiano di Parma, 1983.
Bibliography: Vitali, 1977, no. 640.

38. *Still life*, 1948
oil on canvas, 35.9 × 50 cm
signed lower right: Morandi
Bologna, private collection

Exhibitions: Bologna, 1966, no. 82, repr.; Leningrad, 1973, no. 18, repr.; Moscow, 1973, no. 18, repr.; Bologna, 1975, no. 29, repr.; Ferrara, 1978, no. 46, repr.; Sasso Marconi, 1983; Bologna, 1985, no. 79, repr.; Paris, 1987, no. 34, repr.
Bibliography: Vitali, 1977, no. 649.

39. *Still life*, 1949
oil on canvas, 25 × 35 cm
Bologna, Galleria Comunale
d'Arte Moderna "Giorgio Morandi"
(donated by Morandi's sisters)

Exhibitions: Milan, 1970-71, no. 10, repr.; Ferrara, 1978, no. 50, repr.; Munich, 1981, no. 49, repr.; Madrid-Barcelona-Marseille, 1984-85, no. 44, repr.; Bologna, 1985, no. 82, repr.; Paris, 1987, no. 35, repr.
Bibliography: Vitali, 1977, no. 674; Pasquali, 1982, p. 5; Solmi, 1985, p. 34; Evangelisti, 1987, p. 155.

40. *Still life*, 1949
oil on canvas, 36 × 45.2 cm
Bologna, Galleria Comunale
d'Arte Moderna "Giorgio Morandi"
(donated by Morandi's sisters)

Exhibitions: Ferrara, 1978, no. 49, repr.; Munich, 1981, no. 51, repr.; Madrid-Barcelona-Marseille, 1984-85, no. 41, repr.; Bologna, 1985, no. 81, repr.
Bibliography: Vitali, 1977, no. 691; Pasquali, 1982, p. 5; Solmi, 1985, p. 35; Evangelisti, 1987, p. 152-153.

41. *Still life*, 1949
oil on canvas, 32 × 50 cm
signed on the back: Morandi
Mamiano di Parma,
Fondazione Magnani-Rocca

Exhibitions: Hague, 1954, no. 53; London, 1954, no. 50; Edinburgh, 1965, no. 14, pl. 13; Mamiano di Parma, 1983, p. 56, repr.
Bibliography: Vitali, 1977, no. 687.

42. *Still life* (1951)
oil on canvas, 28 × 52 cm
signed lower left: Morandi
Milan, private collection

43. *Still life* (1952)
oil on canvas, 35 × 40 cm
signed lower left: Morandi
Bologna, Conti collection

Bibliography: Vitali, 1977, no. 833.

44. *Still life*, 1953
oil on canvas, 33 × 45.5 cm
signed lower centre: Morandi
Tampere, Sara Hildénin taidemuseo

Exhibitions: New York, 1960-

61, no. 25; Karlsruhe, 1964, no. 9.
Bibliography: Vitali, 1964[1], 1965[2], 1970[3], pl. 202; Vitali, 1977, no. 890.

45. *Courtyard of via Fondazza*, 1954
oil on canvas, 49 × 54 cm
signed lower left: Morandi
Mamiano di Parma,
Fondazione Magnani-Rocca

Exhibitions: Edinburgh, 1965, no. 18, repr.; Rome, 1973, no. 87, repr.; Mamiano di Parma, 1983, p. 59, repr.
Bibliography: Vitali, 1977, no. 927; Magnani, 1982, no. 12, repr.

46. *Still life*, 1955
oil on canvas, 25.5 × 30.5 cm
signed lower left: Morandi
Winterthur, Kunstmuseum
(donated by Heinz Keller)

Exhibitions: Winterthur, 1956, no. 56; Hannover, G.M. Kestner Gesellschaft, 1964, no. 7; Geneva, Galerie Krugier, 1962; Recklinghausen, 1966, repr.; London, 1970-71, no. 65, repr.; Paris, 1971, no. 76, repr.; Milan, 1971, no. 76, repr.; Nîmes, 1987, no. 51, repr.
Bibliography: Vitali, 1977, no. 952.

47. *Still life*, 1956
oil on canvas, 33 × 38 cm
signed and dated lower centre: Morandi 56
Mamiano di Parma,
Fondazione Magnani-Rocca

The work, dated 1936 in the *Catalogo generale dei dipinti* edited by Lamberto Vitali, after an exhaustive analysis of the sign lower centre and of the composition stylistic characters, proves to be dated 1956.

Exhibitions: Edinburgh, 1965, no. 6, repr.; Ferrara, 1978, no. 18, repr.; Mamiano di Parma, 1983, p. 31, repr.
Bibliography: Vitali, 1977, no. 210; Magnani, 1982, repr.; cover.

48. *Still life*, 1957
oil on canvas, 27 × 40 cm
signed lower left: Morandi
Hamburg, Hamburger
Kunsthalle

Exhibitions: Siegen, 1962, no. 13; Munich, 1981, no. 73, repr.
Bibliography: Arcangeli, 1964, pl. 52; A. Hentzen, *Erwerbungen 1951-1957, Gemälde,* in

Jahrbuch der Hamburger Kunstsammlungen, vol. III, Hamburg 1958, no. 54; H. Hofman, J. Müller-Hauck, *Katalog der Meister des 20. Jahrhunderts der hamburger Kunsthalle,* Hamburg 1969, p. 87; Vitali, 1977, no. 1032.

49. *Courtyard of via Fondazza*, 1959
oil on canvas, 40.5 × 45.5 cm
Bologna, private collection

Exhibitions: Cortina d'Ampezzo, 1969-70, pl. XXI; Sasso Marconi, 1981, repr.; Sasso Marconi, 1983; Madrid-Barcelona-Marseille, 1984-85, no. 55, repr.; Bologna, 1985, no. 103, repr.; Mesola, 1986, p. 25, repr.; Paris, 1987, no. 47, repr.; Bologna, 1988, no. 26, repr.
Bibliography: Vitali, 1964[1], 1965[2], 1970[3], pl. 244; Vitali, 1977, no. 1167.

50. *Still life*, 1959
oil on canvas, 25 × 35 cm
signed lower left: Morandi
Modena, private collection

Exhibitions: Paris, 1968-69, no. 31, repr.; Ferrara, 1978, no. 69, repr.; Madrid-Barcelona-Marseille, 1984-85, no. 57, repr.; Paris, 1987, no. 46, repr.
Bibliography: Vitali, 1977, no. 1138.

51. *Still life*, 1960
oil on canvas, 30 × 40 cm
signed lower left: Morandi
Modena, private collection

Exhibitions: Munich, 1981, no. 86, repr.; Madrid-Barcelona-Marseille, 1984-85, no. 58, repr.; Paris, 1987, no. 49, repr.
Bibliography: Vitali, 1977, no. 1171.

52. *Still life*, 1960
oil on canvas, 30.5 × 40.5 cm
dated on the back: 1960
Bologna, Galleria Comunale d'Arte Moderna "Giorgio Morandi"
(donated by the artist)

Exhibitions: Bologna, 1975, no. 37, repr.; Ferrara, 1978, no. 70, repr.; Munich, 1981, no. 90, repr.; Madrid-Barcelona-Marseille, 1984-85, no. 60, repr.; Bologna, 1985, no. 104, repr.
Bibliography: Vitali, 1977, no. 1197; Pasquali, 1982, p. 6; Solmi, 1985, p. 38.

53. *Still life*, 1961
oil on canvas, 25 × 30 cm
signed lower left: Morandi
Winterthur, Kunstmuseum

Bibliography: Vitali, 1977, no. 1232.

54. *Landscape*, 1961
oil on canvas, 50.5 × 30.5 cm
Bologna, private collection

Exhibitions: Zagreb, 1968, no. 69; Munich, 1981, no. 93, repr.
Bibliography: Vitali, 1977, no. 1251.

55. *Landscape*, 1962
oil on canvas, 30 × 35 cm
Bologna, private collection

Exhibitions: Milan, 1970-71, no. 16, repr.; Munich, 1981, no. 99, repr.; San Francisco-New York-Des Moines, 1981-82, no. 62, repr.
Bibliography: Vitali, 1977, n. 1290.

56. *Landscape*, 1962
oil on canvas, 25.5 × 31 cm
signed lower right: Morandi
Bologna, Galleria Comunale d'Arte Moderna "Giorgio Morandi" (deposited by the Banca del Monte di Bologna e Ravenna)

Bibliography: Vitali, 1977, no. 1292.

57. *Still life*, 1963
oil on canvas, 20.5 × 35.5 cm
signed lower right: Morandi
Bologna, private collection

Exhibitions: Zagreb, 1968, no. 71; Bologna, 1968; Bologna, 1985, no. 114, repr.
Bibliography: Vitali, 1977, no. 1300.

58. *Still life*, 1963
oil on canvas, 19.5 × 24.5 cm
signed lower right: Morandi
Mamiano di Parma,
Fondazione Magnani-Rocca

Exhibitions: Edinburgh, 1965; no. 20, repr.; Paris, 1968-69, no. 40, repr.; Mamiano di Parma, 1983, p. 40, repr.
Bibliography: Vitali, 1977, no. 1304.

59. *Still life*, 1963
oil on canvas, 30 × 35 cm
signed lower left: Morandi
Bologna, private collection

Exhibitions: Bern, 1965, no.

102; Venice, 1966, no. 83; Bologna, 1966, no. 107, repr.; Copenhagen, 1968, no. 17, repr.; London, 1970-71, no. 78, repr.; Paris, 1971, no. 78, repr.; Leningrad, 1973, no. 24, repr.; Moscow, 1973, no. 24, repr.; Bologna, 1975, no. 39, repr.; Ferrara, 1978, no. 78, repr.; Munich, 1981, no. 102, repr.; San Francisco-New York-Des Moines, 1981-82, no. 63, repr.; Sasso Marconi, 1983; Madrid-Barcelona-Marseille, 1984-85, no. 66, repr.; Bologna, 1985, no. 115; Paris, 1987, no. 53, repr.
Bibliography: Vitali, 1965[2], 1970[3], pl. 260; Giuffré, 1970, pl. 44; Vitali, 1977, no. 1323.

60. *Landscape*, 1963
oil on canvas, 40 × 45 cm
signed lower centre: Morandi
Bologna, Galleria Comunale d'Arte Moderna "Giorgio Morandi"
(donated by Morandi's sisters)

Exhibitions: Pittsburgh, 1964-65, no. 155; Bern, 1965, no. 103; Milan, 1970-71, no. 19, repr.; Ferrara, 1978, no. 77, repr.; Munich, 1981, no. 103, repr.; Madrid-Barcelona-Marseille, 1984-85, no. 63, repr.; Bologna, 1985, no. 112, repr.; Paris, 1987, no. 52, repr.
Bibliography: Vitali, 1977, no. 1332; Pasquali, 1982, p. 6; Solmi, 1985, p. 40.

61. *Still life*, 1964
oil on canvas, 25.5 × 30.5 cm
signed lower left: Morandi
Bologna, private collection

Exhibitions: Bern, 1965, no. 104; Bologna, 1966, no. 108, repr.; Copenhagen, 1968, no. 18; Milan, 1971, no. 93, repr.; Rome, 1973, no. 122, repr.; Ferrara, 1978, no. 79, repr.; Munchen 1981, no. 104, repr.; Sasso Marconi, 1983; Madrid-Barcelona-Marseille, 1984-85, no. 67, repr.; Bologna, 1985, no. 116, repr.
Bibliography: Vitali, 1965[2], 1970[3], pl. 264; Vitali, 1977, no. 1342.

Watercolours

62. *Brown still life*, 1920
watercolours on paper,
17.5 × 23 cm
signed and dated lower right:
Morandi ottobre 920
Tolentino, private collection

Exhibitions: Venice, 1966; Bologna, 1966, no. 2; Madrid-Barcelona-Marseille, 1984-85, no. 69; Milan-Bologna, 1985-86, no. 2.
Bibliography: Leymarie, 1968, no. 1.

63. *Landscape* (1956)
watercolours on paper,
16.1 × 20.6 cm
signed lower centre: Morandi
Bologna, private collection

Exhibitions: Bologna, 1966, no. 9; London-Paris, 1970-71, no. 80; Milan, 1971, no. 95; Leningrad-Moscow, 1973, no. 2; Munich, 1981, no. 106; Madrid-Barcelona-Marseille, 1984-85, no. 71; Milan-Bologna 1985-86, no. 3, repr.; Paris, 1987, no. 55, repr.
Bibliography: Leymarie, 1968, no. 9; Giuffré, 1970, p. 35; Zurlini, 1973, no. 8.

64. *Landscape* (*Inside of via Fondazza*), c. 1956
watercolours on paper,
21.2 × 22.6 cm
signed lower centre: Morandi
Verona, private collection

Exhibitions: Milan-Bologna, 1985-86, no. 4, repr.; Paris, 1987, no. 56, repr.

65. *Landscape* (1957)
watercolours on paper,
16.5 × 23 cm
signed lower centre: Morandi
Bologna, private collection

Exhibitions: Bologna, 1968, repr.; Sasso Marconi, 1977, repr.; Milan-Bologna, 1985-86, no. 5, repr.; Sirmione, 1987, p. 26, repr.
Bibliography: Leymarie, 1968, no. 15.

66. *Landscape*, 1957
watercolours on paper,
21 × 31 cm
signed and dated lower centre: Morandi 1957
Modena, private collection

Exhibitions: Ferrara, 1978, no. 2; Madrid-Barcelona-Marseille, 1984-85, no. 73; Milan-Bologna, 1985-86, no. 6, repr.; Massa Carrara, 1988, no. 23, repr.

67. *Landscape*, 1957
watercolours on paper,
34 × 25 cm
signed and dated lower centre: Morandi / 1957
Venice, private collection

Exhibition: Bologna, 1968.
Bibliography: Leymarie, 1968, p. 19, repr.

68. *Landscape,* 1957
watercolours on paper,
16 × 21 cm
signed and dated lower centre: Morandi 1957
Biella, private collection

Exhibitions: Bologna, 1968, repr.; Rome, 1981, Galleria Arco D'Alibert; Milan, 1983, Galleria Blu; Portofino, 1983; Madrid-Barcelona-Marseille, 1984-85, no. 70; Milan-Bologna, 1985-86, no. 7, repr.
Bibliography: Leymarie, 1968, no. 11.

69. *Landscape* (1957-1958)
watercolours on paper,
29 × 24.5 cm
signed lower centre: Morandi
Bologna, private collection

Exhibitions: Sasso Marconi, 1977, repr.; Milan-Bologna, 1985-86, no. 9, repr.; Sirmione, 1987, p. 27, repr.

70. *Landscape* (1958)
watercolours on paper,
15.5 × 23.5 cm
signed lower left: Morandi
Tolentino, private collection
Previously in Rome, Galleria dell'Oca

71. *Landscape,* 1958
watercolours on paper,
31 × 21 cm
signed and dated lower centre: Morandi / 1958
Modena, G. Salvaterra collection

Exhibitions: Milan-Bologna, 1985-86, no. 11, repr.; Paris, 1987, no. 57, repr.; Massa Carrara, 1988, no. 24, repr.

72. *Landscape* (1959)
watercolours on paper,
16 × 21 cm
Milan, private collection

Exhibitions: Bologna, 1968, no. 37; Milan-Bologna, 1985-86, no. 21, repr.
Bibliography: Leymarie, 1968, no. 37.

73. *Landscape* (1958)
watercolours on paper,
33 × 25 cm
signed lower left: Morandi
Milan, private collection

Exhibitions: Bologna, 1968; Milan-Bologna, 1985-86, no. 15, repr.
Bibliography: Leymarie, 1968, no. 32.

74. *Still life* (1958)
watercolours on paper,
23.5 × 32 cm
signed lower centre: Morandi
Turin, A. and M. Forchino collection

Exhibitions: Madrid-Barcelona-Marseille, 1984-85, no. 75, repr.; Milan-Bologna, 1985-86, no. 10, repr.
Bibliography: Leymarie, 1968, no. 29.

75. *Flowers* (1959)
watercolours on paper,
21.8 × 21.2 cm
signed lower centre: Morandi
Modena, private collection

76. *Landscape* (1959)
watercolours on paper,
21 × 26 cm
signed lower centre: Morandi
Bologna, private collection

Exhibitions: London-Paris, 1970-71, no. 6; Milan, 1971, no. 101; Leningrad-Moscow, 1973, no. 3; Ferrara, 1978, no. 8; Munich, 1981, no. 115; Madrid-Barcelona-Marseille, 1984-85,, no. 80; Milan-Bologna, 1985-86, no. 18, repr.; Paris, 1987, no. 58, repr.
Bibliography: Leymarie, 1968, no. 34; Zurlini, 1973, p. 27, repr.

77. *Landscape* (*House in ruins*) (1959)
watercolours on paper,
21 × 16 cm
signed lower centre: Morandi
Venice, private collection

Exhibitions: Bologna, 1968.
Bibliography: Leymarie, 1968, p. 44 b, repr.

78. *Still life* (1959)
watercolours on paper,
16 × 23.6 cm
signed lower centre: Morandi
on the back: A Ettore Gian Ferrari, 8.4.1959
Milan, private collection

Exhibitions: Acqui Terme, 1981, repr.; Milan-Bologna, 1985-86, no. 20, repr.

79. *Still life* (1959)
watercolours on paper,
22.5 × 30.5 cm
signed lower centre: Morandi
Biella, private collection
(certification by Maria Teresa Morandi, 16.10.1986)

80. *Still life* (1959)
watercolours on paper,
27 × 37 cm
signed lower centre: Morandi
Bologna, private collection

Exhibitions: Bologna, 1966, no. 11; Ferrara, 1978, no. 11; Munich, 1981, no. 118; San Francisco-New York-Des Moines, 1981-82, no. 73; Madrid-Barcelona-Marseille, 1984-85, no. 78; Milan-Bologna, 1985-86, no. 19, repr.
Bibliography: Leymarie, 1968, no. 43, repr.; Zurlini, 1973, no. 73.

81. *Still life* (1959-1960)
watercolours on paper,
27.7 × 15.8 cm
signed right: Morandi
Modena, private collection

82. *Still life,* 1960 ca.
watercolours on paper,
21 × 27 cm
Verona, private collection

Exhibitions: Milan-Bologna, 1985-86, no. 22, repr.; Paris, 1987, no. 60, repr.

83. *Still life* (1962)
watercolours on paper,
21 × 30 cm
signed lower centre: Morandi
Venice, private collection

Exhibitions: Bologna, 1968.
Bibliography: Leymarie, 1968, p. 56, repr.

84. *Still life* (1962)
watercolours on paper,
15.8 × 20.9 cm
Bologna, private collection

Exhibitions: Bologna, 1966, no. 3; London-Paris, 1970-71, no. 91; Milan, 1971, no. 106; Ferrara, 1978, no. 13; Munich, 1981, no. 121; San Francisco-New York-Des Moines, 1981-82, no. 80; Madrid-Barcelona-Marseille, no. 83; Milan-Bologna, 1985-86, no. 23, repr.; Paris, 1987, no. 61, repr.
Bibliography: Leymarie, 1968, no. 51, repr.; Giuffré, 1970, p. 6; Zurlini, 1973, no. 45.

85. *Still life* (1962)
watercolours on paper,
16 × 21 cm
signed lower left: Morandi
Bologna, private collection

Exhibitions: Rome, 1973, no. 115; Ferrara, 1978, no. 12; Munich, 1981, no. 123; San Francisco-New York-Des Moines, 1981-82, no. 79; Madrid-Barcelona-Marseille, 1984-85, no. 82; Milan-Bologna, 1985-86, no. 24, repr.; Paris, 1987, no. 62, repr.
Bibliography: Leymarie, 1968, no. 58; Zurlini, 1973, no. 43.

86. *Still life* (1962)
watercolours on paper,
14 × 21 cm
signed lower centre: Morandi
Bologna, private collection

Exhibitions: Bologna, 1968, p. 61; Sasso Marconi, 1977, repr. (dated 1959); Milan-Bologna, 1985-86, no. 25, repr.; Sirmione, 1987, p. 25, repr.
Bibliography: Leymarie, 1968, p. 61, repr.

Drawings

87. *Still life,* 1928
pencil on paper, 27 × 38 cm
signed and dated lower centre: Morandi 1928
Bologna, private collection

Exhibition: Bologna, 1966, no. 4; Ferrara, 1978, no. 3; Munich, 1981, no. 131; San Francisco-New York-Des Moines, 1981-82, no. 85; Modena, 1983, p. 94; Madrid-Barcelona-Marseille, 1984-85, no. 87; Milan-Bologna, 1985-86, no. 27, repr.; Paris, 1987, no. 64, repr.
Bibliography: Neri Pozza, 1976, no. 29; Tavoni, I, 1981, no. 26.

88. *Still life,* 1930
thick pencil on paper,
29 × 23.2 cm
(irregularly shaped
and shredded on lower part)
signed and dated lower left: Morandi / 930
Bologna, private collection

Exhibitions: Bologna, 1966, no. 6, repr.
Bibliography: Neri Pozza, 1976, repr.; Tavoni, II, 1984, no. 337, repr.

89. *Shells,* 1932
pencil on paper,
18.4 × 25.8 cm

signed and dated lower right: Morandi 1932
Modena, G. Salvaterra collection

Exhibition: Reggio Emilia, 1966; Lugano, 1977; Madrid-Barcelona-Marseille, 1984-85, no. 89; Milan-Bologna, 1985-86, no. 28, repr.; Paris, 1987, no. 66.
Bibliography: Patani, 1974, pl. 232; Tavoni, II, 1984, no. 341.

90. *Bottles,* 1932
pencil on paper, 17 × 24.5 cm
signed and dated lower centre: Morandi 1932
Modena, G. Salvaterra collection

Exhibitions: Madrid-Barcelona-Marseille, 1984-85, no. 88; Milan-Bologna, 1985-86, no. 29, repr.; Paris, 1987, no. 65, repr.
Bibliography: Patani, 1974, no. 231; Tavoni, I, 1981, no. 36.

91. *Still life,* 1932
pencil on paper,
19.5 × 29.5 cm
signed and dated lower right: Morandi 1932
Bologna, private collection
previously in Florence, Vallecchi collection

92. *Still life,* 1941
pencil on paper, 28.5 × 35 cm
signed and dated lower centre: Morandi 1941
Bergamo, private collection

Exhibitions: Milan-Bologna, 1985-86, no. 31, repr.

93. *Flowers,* 1946
pencil on paper, 31 × 22.5 cm
signed and dated lower centre: Morandi 1946
Bologna, private collection

Exhibitions: Bologna, 1966, no. 13, repr.; Ferrara, 1978, no. 7, repr.; San Francisco-New York-Des Moines, 1981-82, no. 86, repr.
Bibliography: Neri Pozza, 1976, repr.; Tavoni, II, 1984, no. 372, repr.

94. *Still life,* 1948
pencil on paper, 24 × 33 cm
Bologna, Galleria Comunale d'Arte Moderna "Giorgio Morandi"
(donated by Morandi's sisters)

Exhibitions: Bologna, 1966, no. 16; Ferrara, 1978, no. 8; Munich, 1981, no. 137; San Francisco-

New York-Des Moines, 1981-82, no. 88; Milan-Bologna, 1985-86, no. 35, repr.; Frankfurt-Modena, 1987, repr.
Bibliography: Tavoni, I, 1981, no. 98.

95. *Still life*, 1948
pencil on paper, 21 × 29 cm
signed and dated lower centre: Morandi 1948
Biella, private collection

Exhibitions: Milan-Bologna, 1985-86, no. 36, repr.

96. *Still life*, 1949
pencil on paper, 23 × 32 cm
signed and dated lower centre: Morandi 1949
Bergamo, C. Traglio collection

Exhibitions: Milan-Bologna, 1985-86, no. 40, repr.

97. *Still life*, 1949
pencil on paper, 34 × 25 cm
signed and dated lower centre: Morandi 1949
Bologna, private collection

Exhibitions: Bologna, 1966, no. 19; London-Paris, 1970-71, no. 102; Milan, 1971, no. 118; Leningrad-Moscow, 1973, no. 6; Ferrara, 1978, no. 10; Munich, 1981, no. 142; San Francisco-New York-Des Moines, 1981-82, no. 92; Madrid-Barcelona-Marseille, 1984-85, no. 95; Milan-Bologna, 1985-86, no. 41; Paris, 1987, no. 69, repr.
Bibliography: Tavoni, I, 1981, no. 114, repr.

98. *Still life*, 1951
pencil on paper, 15.6 × 22.5 cm
initialed and dated lower centre: M. 1951
Bologna, private collection

Exhibitions: Bologna, 1966, no. 20; Ferrara, 1978, no. 12.
Bibliography: Tavoni, I, 1981, no. 130, repr.

99. *Still life*, 1952
pencil on paper, 23.6 × 32.5 cm
signed and dated lower centre: Morandi / 1952
Bologna, private collection

Exhibitions: Bologna, 1966, no. 22, repr.; London-Paris, 1970-71, no. 102; Milan, 1971, no. 119, repr.; Ferrara, 1978, no. 13.
Bibliography: Neri Pozza, 1976; Tavoni, I, 1981, no. 134, repr.

100. *Still life*, 1953
pencil on paper, 16.5 × 24.5 cm
signed and dated lower centre: Morandi 53
Bologna, private collection

Exhibition: Bologna, 1966, no. 25; Munich, 1981, no. 144; Madrid-Barcelona-Marseille, 1984-85, no. 99; Milan-Bologna, 1985-86, no. 43, repr.; Paris, 1987, no. 70, repr.
Bibliography: Neri Pozza, 1976, pl. 61; Tavoni, I, 1981, no. 140.

101. *Still life*, 1958
pencil on paper, 16.5 × 24 cm
signed and dated lower left: Morandi 1958
Bologna, private collection

Exhibitions: Bologna, 1966, no. 27; Rome, 1973, no. 14; Munich, 1981, no. 147; San Francisco-New York-Des Moines, 1981-82, no. 96; Madrid-Barcelona-Marseille, 1984-85, f.c.; Milan-Bologna, 1985-86, no. 44, repr.; Paris, 1987, no. 71, repr.
Bibliography: Tavoni, II, 1984, no. 419.

102. *Still life*, 1958
pencil on paper, 16.5 × 23.5 cm
signed and dated lower right: Morandi / 1958
Bologna, private collection

On the back is a *Still life* signed and dated 1957, erased by Morandi himself.

Exhibitions: Sasso Marconi, 1977; Ferrara, 1978, no. 17; Madrid-Barcelona-Marseille, 1984-85, no. 96; Milan-Bologna, 1985-86, no. 45, repr.
Bibliography: Tavoni, I, 1981, no. 181.

103. *Still life*, 1959
pencil on paper, 24 × 32.9 cm
signed and dated lower centre: Morandi / 1959
dedicated lower left: a Leone Pancaldi / Morandi
Bologna, private collection

On the back is a *Landscape*, signed but not dated, cancelled by Morandi himself.

Exhibitions: Sasso Marconi, 1984, no. 69; Madrid-Barcelona-Marseille, 1984-85, no. 101; Milan-Bologna, 1985-86, no. 48, repr.

Bibliography: Tavoni, II, 1984, no. 440.

104. *Landscape* (1960)
pencil on paper, 21.3 × 27.6 cm
signed lower centre: Morandi
Bologna, private collection

Exhibitions: Sasso Marconi, 1977; Ferrara, 1978, no. 19; Madrid-Barcelona-Marseille, 1984-85, no. 103; Milan-Bologna, 1985-86, no. 51, repr.
Bibliography: Neri Pozza, 1976, repr.; Tavoni, I, 1981, no. 228.

105. *Landscape* (1961)
pencil on paper, 16.5 × 24 cm
signed lower centre: Morandi
Bologna, private collection

Exhibitions: Milan-Bologna, 1985-86, no. 56, repr.; Paris, 1987, no. 74, repr.
Bibliography: Tavoni, I, 1981, no. 236, repr.

106. *Still life*, 1962
pencil on paper, 24 × 32.7 cm
signed and dated lower centre: Morandi / 1962
Bologna, private collection

Exhibitions: Bologna, 1966, no. 32; London-Paris, 1970-71, no. 106; Milan, 1971, no. 122.
Bibliography: Tavoni, I, 1981, no. 286, repr.

107. *Still life* (1962)
pencil on paper, 16.5 × 24 cm
signed lower left: Morandi
Bologna, private collection

Exhibitions: Sasso Marconi, 1984, p. 85; Madrid-Barcelona-Marseille, 1984-85, no. 110; Milan-Bologna, 1985-86, no. 58, repr.
Bibliography: Tavoni, II, 1984, no. 488.

108. *The clock*, 1962
pencil on paper, 16 × 23 cm
signed and dated lower right: Morandi 1962
Bologna, private collection

Exhibitions: Ferrara, 1978, no. 21; Sasso Marconi, 1984, p. 88; Madrid-Barcelona-Marseille, 1984-1985, no. 106; Milan-Bologna, 1985-86, no. 62, repr.
Bibliography: Tavoni, I, 1981, no. 285.

Bibliography: Tavoni, II, 1984, no. 440.

109. *Landscape* (1962-1963)
pencil on paper, 32.5 × 23.5 cm
signed lower left: Morandi
Bologna, S. Conti collection

Exhibitions: Milan-Bologna, 1985-86, no. 64, repr.

110. *Still life* (1963)
pencil on paper, 18.2 × 27.4 cm
signed lower right: Morandi
Bologna, private collection

Exhibitions: Sasso Marconi, 1977; Milan-Bologna, 1985-86, no. 66, repr.
Bibliography: Tavoni, I, 1981, no. 297.

111. *Still life*, 1963
pencil on paper, 13.9 × 22 cm
signed and dated lower right: Morandi 1963
Bologna, private collection

Exhibitions: Milan-Bologna, 1985-86, no. 68, repr.
Bibliography: Tavoni, II, 1984, no. 502.

Engravings

112. *Grizzana landscape*, 1913
engraving on zinc, 16.2 × 23.4 cm
the plate is in Rome, Calcografia Nazionale
not signed or dated
Bologna, Galleria Comunale d'Arte Moderna "Giorgio Morandi"

Bibliography: Vitali, 1957[1], 1964[3], no. 2.

113. *Still life with bottle and jug*, 1915
engraving on copper, 15.4 × 12.5 cm
the plate is in Rome, Calcografia Nazionale
signed and dated lower right: Morandi 1915
Modena, private collection

Bibliography: Vitali, 1957[1], 1964[3], no. 3.

114. *Still life with sugar pot, lemon and bread*, 1921 or 1922
engraving on copper, 8.4 × 10.1 cm
another ruined engraving is on the back of the plate, which is in Rome, Calcografia Nazionale
not signed or dated

Bologna, Galleria Comunale d'Arte Moderna "Giorgio Morandi"

Bibliography: Vitali, 1957[1], 1964[3], no. 9.

115. *Still life with bread basket* (small plate), 1921
engraving on copper, 11.8 × 15.4 cm
the plate is in Rome, Calcografia Nazionale
signed lower centre: Morandi
Medolla, E. Ferri collection

Bibliography: Vitali, 1957[1], 1964[3], no. 14.

116. *Bouquet of wild flowers*, 1924
engraving on zinc, 20.5 × 16.3 cm
the plate is the reverse of no. 20 (Vitali), and is in Rome, Calcografia Nazionale; the composition is the counterpart of painting no. 71 (Vitali)
not signed or dated
Bologna, Galleria Comunale d'Arte Moderna "Giorgio Morandi"

Bibliography: Vitali, 1957[1], 1964[3], no. 22.

117. *Striped vase with flowers*, 1924
engraving on zinc, 23.5 × 20.1 cm
the plate is the reverse of no. 21 (Vitali), and is in Rome, Calcografia Nazionale
not signed or dated
Bologna, Galleria Comunale d'Arte Moderna "Giorgio Morandi"

Bibliography: Vitali, 1957[1], 1964[3], no. 23.

118. *Landscape (Chiesanuova)*, 1924
engraving on copper, 15.8 × 15.5 cm
the plate has on the back an head not graved by Morandi, and is in Rome, Calcografia Nazionale; the composition is the counterpart of painting no. 110 (Vitali)
not signed or dated
Bologna, Galleria Comunale d'Arte Moderna "Giorgio Morandi"

Bibliography: Vitali, 1957[1], 1964[3], no. 24.

119. *The garden in via Fondazza*, 1924
engraving on zinc,
10.9×15.1 cm
the plate has on the back
a stroked out landscape, and
is in Rome, Calcografia
Nazionale; the composition
is the counterpart of painting
no. 102 (Vitali)
not signed or dated
Bologna, Galleria Comunale
d'Arte Moderna "Giorgio
Morandi"

Bibliography: Vitali, 1957[1],
1964[3], no. 25.

120. *The road*, 1927
engraving on zinc,
19.5×26.1 cm
the plate is in Rome,
Calcografia Nazionale
signed and dated lower
right: Morandi 1927
Bologna, private collection

Bibliography: Vitali, 1957[1],
1964[3], no. 30.

121. *Poggio landscape*, 1927
engraving on copper,
23.4×29 cm
the plate has on the back a
figure not graved by Morandi,
and is in Rome, Calcografia
Nazionale
not signed or dated
Bologna, Galleria Comunale
d'Arte Moderna "Giorgio
Morandi"

Bibliography: Vitali, 1957[1],
1964[3], no. 33.

122. *Poggio in the morning*,
1928
engraving on zinc,
24.8×24.8 cm
the plate is in Rome,
Calcografia Nazionale
signed and dated lower left:
Morandi / 1928
Modena, private collection

Bibliography: Vitali, 1957[1],
1964[3], no. 44.

123. *Large still life with
a lamp on the right*, 1928
engraving on copper,
25.2×34.9 cm
the plate, stroked out,
is in Milan, owned by
Lamberto Vitali
not signed or dated
Bologna, private collection

Bibliography: Vitali, 1957[1],
1964[3], no. 46.

124. *Still life with fruit
bowl, long bottle and twisted
bottle*, 1928
engraving on zinc,
23.4×18.2 cm
the plate is in Rome,
Calcografia Nazionale; the
composition is the counterpart
of painting no. 28 (Vitali)
signed and dated lower
centre: 1917. Morandi
Bologna, private collection

Bibliography: Vitali, 1957[1],
1964[3], no. 50.

125. *Still life*, 1930
engraving on copper, left side
23 cm, right side 22.7×29 cm
the plate is in Rome, Calcografia Nazionale; the composition
is the counterpart of painting
no. 152 (Vitali)
signed and dated lower
centre: Morandi 1930
Medolla, E. Ferri collection

Bibliography: Vitali, 1957[1],
1964[3], no. 73.

126. *Still life with six
objects*, 1930
engraving on copper,
19.8×23.7 cm
the plate, stroked out, is in
Bologna, owned by Morandi
sisters signed and dated lower
centre (in reverse): Morandi
1930 Bologna, private
collection

Bibliography: Vitali, 1957[1],
1964[3], no. 124.

127. *Grizzana landscape*,
1932
engraving on copper,
29.9×23.9 cm
the plate is in Rome,
Calcografia Nazionale
not signed or dated
Medolla, E. Ferri collection

Bibliography: Vitali, 1957[1],
1964[3], no. 96.

128. *Large dark still life*, 1934
engraving on copper,
29.6×38.4 cm
the plate, which is the
counter part of painting
no. 99 (Vitali), is in Rome,
Calcografia Nazionale
not signed or dated
Bologna, Galleria Comunale
d'Arte Moderna "Giorgio
Morandi"

Bibliography: Vitali, 1957[1],
1964[3], no. 107.

129. *Roffeno landscape*, 1936
engraving on copper,
15.8×19.9 cm
the plate is in Rome,
Calcografia Nazionale
not signed or dated
Bologna, private collection

Bibliography: Vitali, 1957[1],
1964[3], no. 108.

130. *Still life with seven
objects in a roundel*, 1945
engraving on copper
26.7×29.9 cm
the plate is in Rome,
Calcografia Nazionale; the
composition is the counterpart
of painting no. 425 (Vitali)
signed and dated lower
centre: Morandi 1945
Bologna, Galleria Comunale
d'Arte Moderna "Giorgio
Morandi"

Bibliography: Vitali, 1957[1],
1964[3], no. 111.

131. *Large circular still life
with a bottle and three
objects*, 1946
engraving on copper,
25.8×32.5 cm
the plate, which has on the
back a first version of *While
road*, is in Rome, Calcografia
Nazionale; the composition is
the counterpart of painting
no. 515 (Vitali)
signed and dated lower
left: Morandi 1946
Bologna, Galleria Comunale
d'Arte Moderna "Giorgio
Morandi"

Bibliography: Vitali, 1957[1],
1964[3], no. 113.

132. *Still life with four
objects*, 1947
engraving on copper,
17.1×12.8 cm
the plate, once owned by
Cesare Brandi, is in Bologna,
owned by Morandi sisters
signed lower centre: Morandi
Medolla, E. Ferri collection

Bibliography: Vitali, 1957[1],
1964[3], no. 114.

133. *Still life with four
objects and three bottles*, 1956
engraving on copper,
20.3×19.9 cm
the stroked out plate, which
has on the back part of no.
129 (Vitali), is in Rome,
Calcografia Nazionale; the
composition is the counterpart

of painting no. 989 (Vitali)
signed lower right: Morandi
Bologna, private collection

Bibliography: Vitali, 1957[1],
1964[3], no. 117.